This monograph focuses on the strategic concepts, planning and the limited success of the Polish milita... le ... the Brit... ... of March 1939 and then throughout th

The ... ... the Polish Military to its two Western a... France and the ... Kingdom leading up to the war, and the respite they received due to Poland's spirited defense that degraded German offensive capability by at least half a year. Recreated in France, the Polish Military conceptualized a liberation policy of encouraging both France and the United Kingdom to undertake a Balkan Strategy to Poland's freedom. Polish relations, with Hungary in particular, and Romania, while British relations with Greece and Turkey, made this a promising policy option. In early 1941, Britain did send troops to aid Greece and the Poles were also about to send their Middle East-based force to Greece.

This Balkan strategy was strongly shared and espoused by Churchill and on the British planning table till late Summer 1944 when the Americans prevailed in landing forces in the south of France, rather than pushing north in Italy and possibly putting forces across the Adriatic into friendly Croatia and Slovenia. This American policy was undoubtedly due to the pressures of finalizing the European war as soon as possible to get on with the war against Japan, and possibly also influenced by the American foreign policy of accommodating Stalin, who did not want Western Allies in his bailiwick.

One of the minor successes was an air supply link to the Polish Underground Forces but its capacity did not meet the needs or expectations.

Attempts to reconcile with the Soviets failed to materialize any benefits to the Polish cause, but Polish forces extracted from the Soviets by agreements between Churchill and Stalin, were prized by the British and strengthened British capability in the Middle East.

Following the Tehran Conference Polish strategic planning became irrelevant as at the same time the actual strength of the Polish Armed Forces and their professionalism increased.

When in early 1945 Churchill asked his staffs for a possible military operation to push the Soviets back out of Poland - Operation Unthinkable, the Polish military in the West and potential clandestine forces in Poland became a major asset. This plan was not supported by the Americans or the important segment of the British coalition Government, the Labour Party, and further events in 1945 led to the decline in influence once enjoyed by the Polish military in the West.

Michael Peszke was born in 1932 in Dęblin Garrison, Polish Air Force Academy, where his father was on the faculty. He left Poland on September 17 1939 following the German and Soviet Invasions. In July 1941, after an Atlantic crossing at the height of the Battle of the Atlantic, he joined up with his father who was Polish liaison officer in RAF Training Command, and then in the Air Force planning Section of the Polish Commander in Chief in London. These experiences and many talks with his father led to a lifelong interest in and research into Polish military history and numerous publications. On arriving in the UK he enrolled in Saint Joseph's College, Dumfries, followed by two years at John Fisher School in Purley, Surrey, and in 1950 was accepted to Trinity College, Dublin University and its School of Medicine, qualifying in 1956. Postgraduate studies followed in the United States. The author retired from academic life in 1999 and is Emeritus Professor of Psychiatry, University of Connecticut Health Center, Farmington, Connecticut, USA; Emeritus Member of the American College of Psychiatrists; Distinguished Life Member of the American Psychiatric Association; Member of the Polish Institute of Arts and Sciences of America; Member, Royal United Service Institute, London.

THE ARMED FORCES OF POLAND IN THE WEST 1939–46

Strategic Concepts, Planning, Limited Success But No Victory!

HELION STUDIES IN MILITARY HISTORY NO 13

MICHAEL ALFRED PESZKE

HELION & COMPANY LTD

Helion & Company Limited
26 Willow Road
Solihull
West Midlands
B91 1UE
England
Tel. 0121 705 3393
Fax 0121 711 4075
Email: info@helion.co.uk
Website: www.helion.co.uk
Twitter @helionbooks
Blog http://blog.helion.co.uk

Published by Helion & Company 2013

Designed and typeset by Bookcraft Ltd, Stroud, Gloucestershire
Cover designed by Bookcraft Ltd, Stroud, Gloucestershire
Printed by Lightning Source Ltd, Milton Keynes, Buckinghamshire

Text and maps © Michael Alfred Peszke 2013
Photographs © as indicated

Front cover: Scotland, 1943. A group photo of the men of the Polish Parachute Brigade.
"The Polish Parachute Brigade is now composed of the best material and is reserved in the
hands of the Polish Commander-in-chief for operations in Poland".
(British War Office Allied Quarterly Report, TNA WO 193/42 80751)

Rear cover: Scotland, 1941. General Sikorski hosted the Royal couple on a visit to the
Polish First Army Corps. Scotland, early 1941. (PISM)

ISBN 978–1–908916–54–9

British Library Cataloguing-in-Publication Data.
A catalogue record for this book is available from the British Library.

For details of other military history titles published by Helion & Company Limited
contact the above address, or visit our website: http://www.helion.co.uk.

We always welcome receiving book proposals from prospective authors.

Whatever happens,
With or without ammunition,
Fight we must
And fight we shall.
Marshal Edward Smigły-Rydz addressing his staff, 1938.

All we could do for the present was to get on with it and see what happened.
Churchill, in November 1940, addressing an army conference.

I personally had no illusions and few hopes. But I believed that the game should be played through to the end, to the last political card and to the last shot.

Count Edward Raczyński, Polish Ambassador to the British Government. 1943.
I have fought a good fight
I have finished my course
I have kept the Faith.
Words engraved on the Polish Air Force Monument, Northolt, London.

DEDICATION

To my Family,

To those dead who have inspired us and cherished us with their love,

To those alive, whom I love and who have supported me;

Alice Margaret,

      Michele Halina,

      Michael Alexander,

      Michael William Sherman,

      Sophie Irena Maria,

      Nicholas Edward,

      Olivia Eugenia.

      And to future generations, who will build on our successes, learn from our mistakes, be inspired to keep the faith, and perhaps, I hope, be proud of their roots.

The author

      No man, may love the beauty of his race,
      Unless he knows the path by which he came,
      Unless, he knows that blood washed hallowed place ,
      Where histories of the ages call his name.
      Victoria Janda, *The Heritage*

CONTENTS

LIST OF ILLUSTRATIONS

LIST OF MAPS

ACKNOWLEDGEMENTS

I am grateful to the staff of the British National Archives (Kew) for their assistance, and to Dr. Andrzej Suchcitz, Keeper of the Archives at the Polish Institute in London. I have profited from the collection of the Polish Heritage Collection at Central Connecticut State University, New Britain, Connecticut and the two University archivists and librarians, Mgr. Ewa Wolynska and Mgr. Renata Vickery.

Also the Director, Ms. Ulla M. Virks BA, MA, MLIS and librarian, Ms. Melanie S. Makin, BA, MLIS. of the Cross Mills Library, in Charlestown, Rhode Island, who have been able to locate the most exotic books in the most out of the way libraries and obtained them on inter library loans, and have been of great help with modern and arcane methods of electronic communication.

The author wishes to acknowledge the generous support received from the Polish Army Veterans Association of America Foundation, Inc. in the United States, which facilitated archival research in London.

Finally to Duncan Rogers of Helion and Company.

FOREWORD

George Sanford

Emeritus Professor of East European Politics, University of Bristol

Poland's existence as a state and nation was endangered by Nazi Germany during the Second World War while its independence and interwar frontiers were threatened by the Soviet Union. The aggressive neighbours united on the basis of the Nazi-Soviet Pact to partition and occupy Poland in September 1939. Marshal Piłsudski and his Foreign Minister, Józef Beck, motivated by unreliable support from their 1921 French ally and the UK had attempted to 'balance' between their totalitarian neighbours in the 1930s. Poland's already serious security dilemma became acute with defeat and subsequent inhuman occupation by their 'two enemies'. The Poles who escaped abroad and their Government-in-Exile, first in Paris, and then, in London, therefore, faced enormous problems with limited resources in attempting to safeguard the Polish cause.

Although the *emigré* Poles became historical losers and victims with the loss of Poland's eastern frontier (counter-balanced by the gain of the western Oder-Neisse territories) as well as by the establishment of Soviet communist rule at the end of the Second World War there is now growing debate about this outcome. Michael Peszke performs a signal service in this book, crowning a lifetime study of the subject, by demonstrating the extent and continuing nature of the contribution made by Polish soldiers, airmen and sailors to the Allied cause throughout the war. He deals authoritatively with the major military episodes – Narvik, France 1940, the North African and Italian campaigns, with the highlights of Tobruk and Monte Cassino, the 1944 Warsaw Uprising and Arnhem - as well as the issues of intelligence, de-cyphering (Enigma) and air-corridor support to the Home Army resistance in Poland.

But just as importantly, Michael Peszke makes a spirited and balanced defence of the rationality of wartime Polish policy and military strategy facing near impossible conditions. Harold Macmillan noted that the Poles in the West 'lost their country but kept their honour' by fighting on even, after, what they felt was betrayal over their eastern frontier was arranged at Teheran and announced at Yalta. What Churchill called keeping 'alive the soul of Poland' - the nineteenth century tradition of political emigration - was manifested again when thousands of Poles were given the choice of settling in Britain postwar, rather than returning to their Soviet dominated country. The Polish Government-in-Exile pursued a Balkan policy throughout the war as strategically the quickest and most direct way back to their homeland. Its diplomatic and military efforts, outside Poland, attempted the maximum leverage on their Western, especially, British, allies to follow this direction. However, the American favoured western orientation eventually prevailed with the invasions of Italy and Northern France. This strategic decision left Stalin with a clear run to achieving overwhelming Soviet military, and thus political, control of Poland and the remainder of Eastern Europe and the Balkans except for Greece and Yugoslavia. The key factor for the London Poles was always insufficient Western support due to the overwhelming weight of the Soviet Union's military contribution from Stalingrad onwards and Roosevelt's optimistic hope that Soviet-American understanding would ensure world peace through the United Nations at the end of the war. One cannot blame the western leaders for giving priority to their *realpolitik* national interests but Sikorski's once glowing reputation has, therefore, now had to be re-appraised in the light of such indicative episodes as Churchill's and Roosevelt's 'lies' over Katyn. By 1945 the stark choice was between keeping the flame of Polish alive in exile represented by Sosnkowski and Anders or trying to save whatever was possible as demonstrated by Mikołajczyk's participation in the Provisional Government. The relative viability of the latter policy was shown by communist Poland's turn away from full-blown Soviet totalitarianism after 1956 while the former camp had to wait till 1989 to secure its historical justification.

Polish responses to Poland's post partition security dilemma were characterised by Adam Bromke as recurring idealist versus realist orientations dividing Poles over strategies for national survival. After the fall of communism democratisation, marketisation, inclusion in the global capitalist economy and above all, EU and NATO membership, have now transcended Poland's historical security dilemma and replaced it with modernisation issues. While Polish perceptions of national victim-hood have been challenged Michael Peszke's study clears away the debris of past polemics and hostile propaganda and helps the reader to understand a major aspect of the history of the Second World War and its role in shaping the modern world.

INTRODUCTION

To appreciate the situation faced by the Poles in September 1939 it is important to understand the preceding twenty years of Polish independence and how its geo-political situation slowly eroded following the euphoric days of victory over the Soviets in 1920. The monograph presents this period, one of attempts to navigate a non-alignment policy between its two neighbours, and of building up mutual assistance treaties with Western democracies.

The German invasion of Poland on September 1, 1939 resulted in two Western Powers, France and the United Kingdom, allied with Poland in mutual assistance pacts, declaring war on Germany. The German attack on Poland was shortly followed by the Soviet invasion of Eastern Poland. This culminated in Poland's partitioning and resulted in the Polish Government seeking refuge in Allied France.

The first step of the Polish Government was to negotiate financial and jurisdictional agreements with its two allies, France and the United Kingdom, pertaining to the recreation of the Polish Armed Forces on their territory. This was the official beginning of the Polish Armed Forces in the West. The establishment of the Polish Forces was a top down process. The Polish Government formed the Polish Forces headquarters and staff, and these in turn began the prolonged process of recruitment and training.

The very first element of this land, air and sea force, that amounted to well over 200,000 men and women at war's end in May 1945, was in fact the Polish Destroyer Division that arrived in British waters on September 1 1939. But the numbers swelled by a process of recruitment of Polish immigrants living in France, and the evacuation of thousands of Polish military who had escaped from the German-Soviet tap into Romania and Hungary.

As an allied country, the Polish Government sought to play its part in the coalition war against Germany, but also planned the liberation of the Home Land. Both tasks were the function of the Polish Military Headquarters but the two challenges were diametrically different. In the first instance, Polish contributions were most welcome but Polish forces did not construct their own unique policies or strategies, merely followed allied strategies. In the second instance, Polish Staffs planned strategic policies, which occasionally were consistent with allied interests but also often appeared exotic and as the war went on, at odds with allied policies.

There was a continuity in the Polish military and the Polish Government between from the earliest days of Poland's recreation in November, 1918 and the Second World War. The officers corps of the recreated Polish Army in the West was a direct continuation of the pre-war cadre and shared similar traditions. The senior cadre, from colonel above, all had fought in the Polish-Soviet war of 1919–1920 and all were imbued with a tradition of resistance and insurrection. There was a consensus in the officer cadre that the humiliating years of appeasement to foreign potentates at the end of the 18th Century, would not be repeated.

The strategic plans for liberating the Home Land were based on hopes as well as experiences gleaned from the First World War. If one accepts the general premise that the Second World War was a continuation of the First Great War, and the inter-war period merely a twenty year armistice, the other hypothesis pointed to the end of the Great War, and a strategy that was partially implemented, the Balkan strategy.

Thus the while the Poles always planned, and hoped and fought to the best of their ability for a total German defeat, the matter of how to deal with the Soviets underwent many planning vacillations. But the Balkan route always seemed to offer the best prospect since Poland had pre-war relationships with both Hungary and Romania.

There was another element in the Polish struggle for independence during the years of the Great War, the Polish clandestine organization, the Polska Organizacja Wojskowa, commanded by Edward Smigły-Rydz and owing allegiance to Józef Piłsudski. This was the other factor in Polish planning – nourish the clandestine forces in occupied Poland and plan for the best case scenario. Polish strategy for a Balkan route to defeating Germany was also shared by Churchill who was, as was his wont, intrigued by any permutation of an offensive that would minimize the trench warfare and direct bloodshed. A great exponent of the blockade, he wanted to grasp the nettle of capturing Norway and blocking German steel imports passing through Norwegian ports. But he also became involved in the Balkans, with Greece and then the Aegean Campaign in 1944 since his strategic fantasy was to seduce the Turks to the Western Alliance. But while Churchill saw the Balkan strategy as leading to the capture of Vienna, there is no evidence that he believed that this route would lead all the way to Poland. If implemented it would have kept the Balkan States free from Soviet Communism and accomplished one of the major Churchillian goals, a free Mediterranean. As it was Churchill managed, in spite of strenuous and acrimonious objections from the Americans, to safeguard Greece in 1944. This Balkan policy was subtly opposed by Stalin and dismissed by the Americans as of little importance to winning the war in Europe.

This monograph is not a history of the many battles in which Poles participated during the five-year war. It is an account of the attempts, political, diplomatic and military by the Polish Staffs to implement the Balkan Strategy, how it failed and the many aspects which worked against the Poles.

1

RESURRECTION OF THE POLISH STATE

Resurrection of the Polish State – Polish Military preserves Polish Independence – Strategic alliances with France and Romania – Locarno Treaty weakens French alliance – Piłsudski's *coup d'état* – Non-aggression treaties and declarations signed with Russia and Germany – The emerging and imminent threat from Germany – Polish-French talks in Rambouillet and France grants Poland credit for re-armament – Munich appeasement – Germans occupy Prague – Great Britain offers Poland a guarantee – British and French Staff talks with Poles in Warsaw – Poles share the enigma secret with Western allies – London talks regarding a military credit for Poland – Great Britain and Poland sign a Mutual Assistance Treaty – British and French pressure on the Polish Government to allow the Soviet armies to move into Poland ostensibly to protect the Poles from the Germans.

The period between the end of Great War (1914–1918) and the onset of the Second World War in 1939 has often and correctly been called an armistice. After the end of the Great War, France and the United Kingdom were exhausted, the United States retired into its protective isolationism, two of the losers were biding their time for revenge. The third power, Austria-Hungary, had disintegrated into its constituent ethnic nations. Italy and Turkey remained on the sidelines, the latter shedding huge tracts of land in the Middle East. All became active or passive players in the Second World War.

Accepting this thesis it is reasonable to begin the history of the Polish Military in the Second World War, with the events which unfolded in that so called peace-time era and how they inexorably led to the invasions of Poland by the Germans on September 1st, 1939 followed by the Soviet invasion of September 17th.

Poland's independence, after a hundred years of partitions, was born in a crucible of war, blood and destruction.[1] From 1914 to 1917 it was the stage for protracted fighting between the Russian Empire on one side and the Germans and Austrians on the other. All three partitioning powers conscripted Poles, who were coerced to fight for their oppressive enemies, undoubtedly on many an occasion against each other, shedding fraternal blood.[2]

As on so many occasions, Poles once again attempted to control their own destiny. A small group of patriotic Poles, led by Józef Piłsudski, organized paramilitary units, named legions, which were armed by, and fought alongside, the Austrians against the Russians. With the defeat of the Russians by the Germans in 1917, Piłsudski refused to ally himself with the Germans, who were actively fighting the Western Coalition, and refused to take an oath of allegiance to the Kaiser. He was arrested with his immediate chief of staff, Kazimierz Sosnkowski, and both imprisoned in Magdeburg.[3] His First Brigade was dissolved by the Germans, and soldiers forcibly inducted into German or Austrian armies, while the officers were interned.

In the West two great patriotic Poles, Ignacy Paderewski and Roman Dmowski, networked the Western Allies in Paris, London and even Washington and were able to get President Wilson of the United States to state that a free Poland with access to the Baltic was one of the war aims of the United States. These two Polish patriots also represented the Polish State at the Paris Conference.[4]

As Germany finally accepted defeat in the West, and was in the process of negotiations for an armistice, Piłsudski and his close ideological companion, Kazimierz Sosnkowski, were released by the Germans and arrived back in Warsaw to a most enthusiastic reception. The German-sponsored Polish Regency Council that had been governing the German occupied part of Poland then nominated Piłsudski to be the temporary Head of State pending elections and duly dissolved itself.

It has been a major polemical point whether Polish Independence in 1918 was the result of the Western Coalition conditions pressure on the Germans, or had already occurred. The British Prime Minister Lloyd-George supported Weimar Germany against France and Poland, and also opposed Polish aspirations for historic Polish boundaries in the East. He also prevailed in denying Poland the City of Gdansk and opposed Polish desiderata for East Prussia being a demilitarized area, analogous to German territory west of the Rhine.

---

1   Piotr s. Wandycz, *Lands of Partitioned Poland*, 1795–1921, Harvard U. Press, 1969.
2   Martin Gilbert, *The First World War. A Complete History*, Henry Holt and Company, NY 1994. p.79. Gilbert states that two million Poles fought in the armies of the partitioning powers, and that 450,000 were killed. Antony Polonsky, *Politics in Independent Poland. 1921–1939*, Oxford University Press, 1972.
3   Wacław Jedrzejewicz, *Piłsudski. A Life for Poland*, N.Y. Hippocrene Books, 1982.
4   Margaret MacMillan, *Paris 1919. Six Months that Changed the World*, Random House, NY., 2001.

The head of the British military mission in Poland in 1919–1920, [as well as in 1939] General Sir Adrian Carton De Wart wrote:

> I cannot remember our government [i.e. the UK] agreeing with the Poles over any question, and there were many: Danzig, that first nail in Poland's coffin; Vilna, Eastern Galicia, Teschen; the demarcation of the Russian-Polish frontier; and Upper Silesia.

Also,

> Britain with her usual anti-Polish policy was definitively opposed to giving it (i.e. Eastern Galicia) to the Poles. I went to Paris to see Mr. Lloyd George on the matter and to try to persuade him either to give Eastern Galicia outright to the Poles, or at any rate to use his influence to that end. He refused point-blank and he never spoke to me again.[5]

On November 11th 1918 there was a Polish Head of State, and a free capital city, but the country lacked a uniform currency or legal system and most importantly lacked defined boundaries, which were being contested by all neighbours, except for Romania and Latvia. A major attribute of any sovereign state is its armed force, and in that respect, thanks to the Piłsudski Legions and the more numerous Polska Organizacjia Wojskowa, now coming out of its clandestine activity, Poland was well served. Military equipment came primarily from captured German and Austrian arsenals and, in time, from French surplus supplies.

But for the next two years there was no peace. National uprisings by Poles against the German in Poznania were successful, in Silesia only partially. Conflicting claims for territory, inevitably made of a mixture of historical, economic and alleged self-determination of the ethnic preferences of the indigenous populations were settled by Western coalition supervised plebiscites. The Czechs grabbed Cieszyn, while Polish forces were engaged in the East. The Poles, in turn, annexed Wilno, enraging the Lithuanians.

Neither the Germans nor the Poles were satisfied since millions of Poles were left on the German side, and similar numbers of Germans in Poland. In addition there were other ethnic minorities in Poland of questionable loyalty to the new State. Poland did get access to the Baltic but lacked a port since Gdansk had been denied to Poland and became a Free City under the League of Nations. It also became a flash point for future Polish-German relations. Less well-known but of significant

---

5   Adrian Carton De Wart, Happy Odyssey. *The Memoirs of Lt. General Sir Adrian Carton de Wiart,* Jonathan Cape, London, 1950. p. 119. Lloyd George continued to be inimical to Poland and was the center of a small group that blamed Poland for its failures in September 1939, and was critical of the Chamberlain Government for entering into a treaty with Warsaw in 1939. Edward Raczyński, *In Allied London,* Weidendeld and Nicolson, London, 1962, pp.37–38.

importance was Poland's failure to persuade the Western Coalition to demilitarize East Prussia.

Ukrainian incursions against Lwów were repelled but eventually a war was fought against the Red Russian armies. Piłsudski, who was the Head of State and commanded the Polish Armies, hoped for a federation of the three nations – Poles, Ukrainians and Lithuanians.[6] This did not generate unanimous support in the Polish nation, which was exhausted by "collateral damage" of the Great War and not convinced of the merits of Piłsudski's foreign policy. The citizens of Lithuania were now more interested in their own national identity rather than looking back to the old Commonwealth of two nations. The Ukrainians were mostly negative to Poland though one prominent Ukrainian leader, Petlura, joined with the Poles in the attempt to liberate his country from the Soviets.[7]

This allegedly Polish war of aggression was condemned by Lloyd-George but tacitly supported by the French with surplus military material. The British attempted to arbitrate between the Poles and Soviets, and depending on which side seemed in the ascendancy, such overtures were either welcomed or ignored. But it led to the proposed Curzon Line, in reality two Curzon lines, name after the British Foreign Minister, Lord Curzon. In the final conclusion of the war, at the Riga Treaty of 1921, the line was not mentioned but got a new life in during the Second World War.[8]

The overwhelming Polish victory over the Soviets in 1920, in the outskirts Warsaw, followed by the annihilation of the Soviet armies at a more strategic, but less well-known campaign of the Niemen, led to an armistice with the Soviets and finalized by the Riga Treaty. This military success, albeit much less than what Piłsudski hoped for, and the finalization of the plebiscites in the West, seemed to put Poland on a peaceful track. A stamp from that period shows a symbolic scene, a peasant plowing and a sword buried in earth, but available just in case. The Polish Army which had appeared seemingly out of nowhere had prevailed.[9]

Many have argued in retrospect that the success of the Polish Army, great as it was in fact, was ephemeral. But this analysis, which has its proponents, misses a number of vital political aspects, both of international strategic and diplomatic importance. The Polish Army was now a major determinant of Polish foreign policy and of the attitudes of other states to Poland.

Poland lacked colonies, though it aspired to them even during the early years of the Second World War. Poland lacked financial resources, and, except for coal, natural

6   M.K. Dziewanowski, Joseph Piłsudski. *A European Federalist, 1918–1922*, Hoover Institute, 1969.

7   Piotr S. Wandycz, *Soviet-Polish Relations 1917–1921*, Harvard U., 1969.

8   Jerzy Borzecki, *The Soviet-Polish Peace of 1921 and the Creation of Interwar Europe*, Yale University Press, New Haven, 2008.

9   Adam Zamoyski, *Warsaw 1920. Lenin's Failed Conquest of Europe*, Harper Press, 2007 and Lord Edgar D'Abernon, *The Eighteenth Decisive Battle of the World, Warsaw, 1920*, Hodder and Stoughton, London, 1931.

wealth. Because of the Polish Army and its success it became an attractive partner to France and to Romania. France feared Germany and Romania feared the Soviets, while Poland feared both. As a consequence a military and political agreement was signed by Piłsudski in Paris in February 1921 in which both sides agreed to give active military support to each other in event of German attack. The French stopped short of such a guarantee in event of a Polish war with the Soviets, but they promised a positive posture. Poland in turn undertook to permanently field thirty infantry divisions.[10]

Shortly after, in March 1921, Romania and Poland signed a mutual assistance treaty in event of an attack by the Soviets on either partner. The Polish military was a national institution which had proved its mettle in a country that had been devastated and was poverty stricken.

Following the war the first Polish Parliament made Piłsudski Marshal of Poland, and in a very moving ceremony the marshal's baton was presented to him by the youngest soldier who was a holder of the Virtuti Militari.

For a while Piłsudski attempted to stay at the command structure of the Polish Forces. He was unable to adjust to the political infighting which only barely passed for democracy and retired to his country estate.

The Germans refused to agree or psychologically accept the loss of their eastern territories. On April 22 1922 the Soviets and Germany signed a treaty of collaboration at Rapallo. Since the Germans were theoretically precluded from having an air force or an army exceeding 100,000 men, they co-operated with the Soviets in developing new weapons.[11]

In October 1925 Poland felt that her French partner had weakened its contractual obligation to Poland by the signing of the Locarno Treaty. In this treaty the Weimar Republic accepted the finality of its Western borders with France, but not in the East, with Poland and Czechoslovakia only agreeing to pursue revindication by peaceful means.[12] That element of the Treaty was disappointing but what was of great concern was that the French modified their military agreement with Poland – their support would be conditional on whether the League of Nations determined that aggression had occurred.

The German foreign minister, Stresemann, who negotiated the Locarno Treaty, received the Nobel Peace Prize, and the Germans undertook a customs war with Poland, with which they expected to break the Polish economy and force Poland

---

10   League of Nations treaty Series, Geneva 1923, XVIII, pp.12–13. Piotr S. Wandycz, *France and Her Eastern Allies, 1919–1925*, Minnesota University Press, Minneapolis, 1961.

11   Harald von Riekhoff, *German-Polish Relations 1918–1933*, Johns Hopkins Press, 1971. Mueller, "Rapallo Reexamined: A New Look at Germany's Secret Military Collaboration with Russia in 1922", *Military Affairs*, 40, 1976. pp.109–117.

12   Anna M. Cienciala and Titius Komarnicki, *From Versailles to Locarno. Keys to Polish Foreign Policy, 1919–1925*, University Press of Kansas, 1984.

to a negotiating position. At the same time both Germany and the Soviets worked to undo the results of the Paris Treaty and the Polish victory over the Soviets by a military co-operation which defied the Versailles Treaty. The Germans and Soviets signed a "Neutrality Pact" on April 24, 1926, and received a Soviet guarantee that Polish-German boundaries would not be recognized by the Soviets. However, as the Germans were conspiring to wreck Poland's economy, they were also concerned that Poland might entertain a preventive war.[13]

A weakening alliance with France, a German customs war, frequent changes in the Polish Government due to multiple parties with divergent agenda as well as an economic crisis, slowly eroded the international status of Poland. This led to the *coup d'état* of Piłsudski on May 12, 1926.[14]. By any legal definition Piłsudski was a dictator, but, it can be argued, an unwilling one. He never became president but while he did hold variously named offices, his main interest was the Polish Armed Forces and foreign policy. He also curtailed the influence and penetration of Polish economy and military by French interests.

But even under Piłsudski the Polish Government attempted to sail between the Scylla and Charybdis of the Soviet potential threat and the acute German customs war. The first required constant vigilance on the Eastern border, the second had a negative impact on Polish economy but did not lead to the economic collapse which the Germans intended. Poland wanted to have good relations with both neighbors, to be beholden to neither and to preserve its boundaries, particularly access to the rich coal fields of Silesia and to the Baltic.[15] This charted the Polish foreign policy of non-involvement.

With this as the guiding light, Poland negotiated a non-aggression treaty with the Soviets in 1932. When Adolf Hitler became the Chancellor of Germany Poland is alleged to have sought a joint French preventive war.[16] Since France was not receptive but Hitler was possibly concerned that it might be, a declaration of non-aggression with Germany was signed in 1934. As a prelude to this Piłsudski dismissed the relatively pro-French foreign minister, August Zaleski, and appointed one of his very close confidantes, allegedly for many years an officer in the intelligence service, Colonel Józef Beck, to the post. It is worth emphasizing that Poland had been urged to negotiate a settlement with Germany, but once Poland did it was in turn criticized for becoming, allegedly, an ally of Hitler.

---

13   Robert M. Citino, *The Evolution of Blitzkrieg Tactics. Germany Defends Itself against Poland, 1918–1933*, Greenwood Press, Westport CT, 1987.

14   Joseph Rothschlid, *Joseph, Piłsudski's Coup d'Etat*, Columbia University Press, NY, 1966; Antony Polonsky, *Politics in Independent Poland, 1921–1939*, Oxford University Press, 1972.

15   Roman Debicki, *Foreign Policy of Poland, 1919–1939. From the Rebirth of the Polish Republic to World War II*, Praeger, NY, 1962. Jozef Korbel. *Poland Between East and West: Soviet and German Diplomacy toward Poland, 1918–1933*, Princeton University Press, Princeton, 1963.

16   See Gordon A. Craig and Felix Gilbert, eds. *The Diplomats, 1919–1939*, Princeton University Press, Princeton, 1981, pp.612–614.

Piłsudski died in 1935 and was succeeded as Inspector of the Armed Forces by General Edward Śmigły-Rydz, one of Piłsudski's closest collaborators and part of the inner core – the legionaries. Since Piłsudski had held a crucial, but not an elected post, there was a certain amount of internal competition for assuming his mantle. The compromise achieved seemed to be seamless, a leadership of three; President Ignacy Mościski; the Foreign Minister, Józef Beck; and the Inspector of the Army, Edward Śmigły-Rydz. Shortly, Śmigły-Rydz received the marshal's baton.

But events outside of Polish control continued to impinge on this policy of good relations with the two neighbors. Poland refused Hitler's proposal that it join the anti-Comintern pact. When Hitler ordered his troops into the demilitarized area, west of the Rhine, in defiance of the Treaty of Paris, the Poles offered military support to the French but the proposal was turned down since the French were now intent on coordinating their German policy with the United Kingdom. But the Polish overture to France warmed the nearly moribund alliance and France gave substantial military credits to the Polish Army. Also, German defiance of the Versailles Treaty by moving into the Rhineland, reverted the original meaning of the Polish- French military alliance. It was no longer dependent on a League of Nations definition of aggression.[17]

The situation deteriorated to a crisis point in March 1939 when the Germans occupied Prague. Till that date the British Government had been loath to get involved in affairs of East-Central Europe. This policy was well expressed by Sir Alexander Cadogan, who wrote "we must cut our losses in Central and Eastern Europe – let Germany, if she can, find her 'lebensraum', and establish herself, if she can, as a powerful economic unit."[18]

The main pillar of Poland's foreign policy was the 1921 political and military agreement signed with France, which went through many vicissitudes. For France the only attraction of a Polish alliance was the Polish Army. But Beck had a great vision for Poland and its place in East-Central Europe. Poland's overtures to the Czechoslovak Government had foundered on a mutual distrust. Prague was happy to enter into economic negotiations with Poland but used the excuse of Poland's unresolved border disputes with Germany as an excuse for avoiding any military ties. Prague's cosy relationship with the Soviets further negatively affected the general feeling in Poland already poisoned by the problem of Cieszyn (Teschen). Beck conceptualized a counterweight to both Germany and the Soviets which would include Hungary, Romania, and even Italy. This required a common border with Hungary and the possibility of Slovakia becoming independent and thus a potential partner in this *inter mare* (i.e.

---

17 For an excellent account of the intricacies of Polish-French relations and French complete dependence on Britain for a lead in confronting Germany, see George Sakwa, "The Franco-Polish Alliance and the Remilitarization of the Rhineland", *The Historical Journal*, XVI, (1973) pp.125–146. For a discussion of the manner in which Poland utilized the French military credits, see Michael Alfred Peszke, "Poland's Preparation for World War Two", *Military Affairs* 43 (1979), pp.18–24.

18 Dilks, David, ed., *The Diaries of Sir Alexander Cadogan*, London, G.P. Putnam's Sons, 1972, p.119.

between the Baltic and the Black Sea) coalition. This was a grand vision but Poland had insufficient economic strength and a very undesirable geo-political position to effect this foreign policy concept. The political ground in those countries was not unsympathetic to the idea, but it failed to mature prior to 1939. What is important for the theses underlying this monograph was that the concept of an independent South-Eastern Europe in some form of alliance with Poland continued throughout the war and was integral to the Polish Balkan strategy.

The German move into the remnant territories of the Czech-Slovak Republic crystallized British policy, since Neville Chamberlain felt that Hitler had reneged on his 1938 Munich agreements. Chamberlain, the British Prime Minister of Britain, had desperately wanted to avoid the bloodshed of the Great War. He had brought back a letter from Munich in which Hitler foreswore any further territorial expansions. He was disheartened and decided that Hitler could no longer be trusted. In a major speech at the end of March 1939 he gave a British guarantee of Polish sovereignty, albeit not its boundaries.

The German move into Prague gave Poland and Hungary a common border, and it also freed Slovakia from the Czech yoke. However, rather than looking to Poland, the Slovak government became a German satellite. The fate of Slovakia was one that Hitler undoubtedly had in mind for Poland.[19]

The British guarantee gave Józef Beck, the Polish foreign minister, an opening he had worked and hoped for all along, namely active British involvement in East-Central European affairs. The British guarantee to Poland was controversial in the United Kingdom it was also seen by many as a great success of the Polish foreign minister.[20] Following the September Campaign of 1939 Józef Beck, ignominiously interned by the allied Romanians, and forgotten by his own countrymen, wrote his own reflections in the *Final Report*.[21]

The crux of the matter which decided the British Government in changing its East European foreign policy was the British Chief of Staff's memorandum regarding the Polish Armed Forces. Simon Newman cites the comments of the British staff.

---

19 After the liberation of all of East-Central Europe from Soviet communist control in 1989, Slovakia once again broke away from Prague and has pursued a successful independent course as part of the European Union and NATO.

20 Roberts, chapter "On the diplomacy of Colonel Beck" in *The Diplomats, 1919–1939*, Princeton University Press, Princeton, 1981.

21 Józef Beck, *The Last Report*, Speller, New York 1957. Also, Antony Polonsky, *Politics in Independent Poland, 1921–1939*. Oxford University Press, London, 1972, pp.470–483. His own epitaph was the he had ensured that a German aggression against Poland became a World War - in retrospect a hollow statement given what happened to Poland. See, Halik Kochanski, *The Eagle Unbowed, Poland and the Poles in World War Two*, Allen Lane, London, 2012, and Timothy Snyder, *Bloodlands: Europe between Hitler and Stalin*, Basic Books, NY, 2010.

The value of Poland lay not in the capacity of her army to launch an offensive against Germany, which was virtually non-existent, but in her capacity to absorb German divisions. Above all she must not be allowed to supplement them by subordinating her foreign policy to Hitler's, or to allow them free reign in the West by maintaining an attitude of benevolent neutrality.

Furthermore, the British staff stated that "it was better to fight with Poland as an ally than without her".[22]

Hitler responded to the British guarantee by cancelling the non-aggression declaration with Poland and also the very recently concluded London Treaty on tonnage limitations. The Poles in turn instituted a partial mobilization of their western garrisons.

This was a controversial change of British policy but most political commentators believe that Chamberlain still hoped that Poland with such a guarantee would be more amenable to negotiating with Germany regarding its very tenuous, and one can say ambiguous rights, in the Free City of Danzig.

The Polish Government in turn worked at making the Chamberlain Guarantee of March into a treaty. In April 1939 the Polish Foreign Minister, Józef Beck, made a highly successful visit to Britain and was entertained by the Royal Family in Windsor Castle. The continued sticking point for the British as well as the French was whether German aggression in Danzig would constitute a cause for war. The Poles demanded this as a definitive *casus belli*.

Poland, 1939. Marshal Edward Smigły-Rydz reviewing a tank battalion of the Polish Pomeranian Army in the Summer of 1939. This army was to support the 'Intervention' Corps in event of a localised German putsch in the Free City of Danzig. The tanks are Polish-built 7TPs.
(Photo from the collection of George Bradford and Steven Zaloga)

22 Simon Newman, *March 1939: The British Guarantee Poland*, Oxford University Press, 1976.

Beck probably correctly assumed that were the Germans to make a limited *putsch*, internal or external on the Free City of Danzig, and made no further seeming demands on Polish sovereignty, the Western Powers would accept this as a very happy resolution. Beck was determined to make this a Rubicon and he succeeded, although at a cataclysmic cost to the Polish State.

Beck's pre-occupation with Polish rights in the Free City of Danzig led to a major disagreement with Marshal Smigły-Rydz, the Polish Inspector General and wartime designee for Commander-in-Chief. Beck prevailed in having an improvised corps of two infantry divisions pushed into the vicinity of Danzig, to immediately respond to any German act. Then, to firm up the Intervention Corps, the Pomorze Army was tasked with moving north of Torun into the so-called Polish Corridor to give it support. This was moving a significant Polish force into a potential trap, which in reality turned out to be a catastrophic one. Smigły-Rydz called it a strategic absurdity. The divisions were lost for no cause while the strategic reserve which was being formed in the region of Lódź (Armia *Prusy*) was depleted.

Critics of Beck's policy abound. But these critics come at Beck from right and left. The most prevalent criticism, then and even now, was Beck's unwillingness to accede to the proposed Western initiative to have the Soviet Union join in the anti-German coalition. Critics forget that the Soviet condition was to have Soviet troops move into Poland, not just in one area, but along the whole boundary. There was significant conviction in Poland that if the Soviets moved in, they would never leave Polish territory once established in an ostensible defensive posture. That had been the Polish experience in the late 18th Century when Russian armies roamed free in the dysfunctional Polish Kingdom – another painful historical memory that influenced Polish policies throughout the war.

Much more rational is the criticism of Beck for his adamant stance on the Free City of Danzig. The thriving port of Gdynia, constructed in the twenties, connected to the Polish hinterland by a major new rail system, was sufficient for Poland's commercial needs. Beck was adamant in seeing the status of the Free City as a litmus test of Polish-German relations though he was always willing to discuss the status of the Free City with Germany, but not willing to accede to its outright annexation by Germany.

Beck's attitude on Danzig enjoyed overwhelming popular support in Poland as, in fact, did his policy of standing up to Hitler.

The summer of 1939 saw military staff discussions in Warsaw, as well as labored negotiations in London for British economic aid to upgrade the Polish Armed Forces. In this regard the French were more forthcoming. The British Government was reluctant to grant Poland the amount requested and Sir John Simon, the British Chancellor of the Exchequer, demanded that Poland devalue its currency and scale down its competitive coal exports.[23]

---

23   Kaiser, David E., *Economic Diplomacy and the Origins of the Second World War. Germany, Britain France and Eastern Europe, 1930–1939.* Princeton U. Press, Princeton, 1980.

In July 1939 General Sir Edmund Ironside, British General Inspector of Overseas Forces, visited Poland. His mission was to ensure that the Poles did not act precipitously in Danzig, but also to give moral support to the Poles. His report to the British Government was a very important and correct in hindsight analysis, and can be summarized that the "The military effort they [i.e. Poles] have made is little short of prodigious". He added "we ought not to make so many conditions to our financial aid. Time is short". In one of the most pertinent and possibly the most important point, he stated "one of the ways of convincing Hitler that we are serious is by granting this monetary aid to Poland". His advice was not heeded.[24] During the summer of 1939 Polish-British and Polish-French staff held discussions in Warsaw on a number of issues. The French agreed to undertake shuttle bombing of Germany in event of war.[25] It was also agreed that the Polish surface warships would sail for the United Kingdom when war was imminent. It was during one of these meetings that the Poles shared their success in breaking the German codes – Enigma – with their Western Allies. Lewin concludes "they had made Ultra possible".[26] This Allied debt to the Poles is acknowledged by Sir F. Harry Hinsley and Alan Stripp, who wrote, "I should stress the original and vital contribution made by the Poles. The Poles had always been brilliant cryptographers … "[27] The diaries and London despatches of the British military attaché in Warsaw, Edward Roland Sword, are important in understanding the Polish process and difficulties in preparing for the inevitable conflict.

Both Britain and France, the latter always mindful of its historical and traditional alliance with Russia, made attempts to inveigle the Soviets in the anti-German camp. Soviet conditions were to have unrestricted access for entering Polish territory, a condition which the Poles refused to consider.[28] As war became ever more imminent, the British and French exerted ever-increasing pressure on the Poles to formally agree to have Soviet armies move into Poland, allegedly to support the Poles against the Germans. The Polish Government, with bitter memories of the Prussians and Russian Tsarist armies rampaging through the Polish Kingdom, leading to its partitions, adamantly refused.[29]

---

24 McLeod, R. and Denis Kelly, *Time Unguarded, The Ironside Diaries 1937–1940*, David McKay Company, New York, 1962, pp.76–82. See also, Elizabeth Turnbull and Andrzej Suchcitz, eds. *Edward Roland Sword. The Diary and Despatches of a Military Attaché in Warsaw, 1938–1939*, Polish Cultural Foundation, London, 2001, pp.135–140. This monograph is regrettably not sufficiently well-known.
25 PISM Archives Lot A. I. 2/11
26 Ronald Lewin, *Ultra Goes to War. First Account of World's World II's Greatest Secret Based on Official Documents*, Hutchinson & Co., London, 1978.
27 Sir F. Harry Hinsley and Aalan Stripp , *The Inside Story of Bletchley Park. Code Breakers*, Oxford University Press, Oxford, 1994.
28 Anita Prażmowska, *Britain, Poland and the Eastern Front, 1939*, Cambridge University Press, 1987.
29 TNA CAB 104/44.

On August 23rd Poland's two neighbors, seemingly until that day ideological enemies, signed the Molotov–Ribbentrop pact.[30]

The Polish Government had worked strenuously at making the Chamberlain Guarantee into a binding treaty. Finally on the eve of the war, 25th August 1939, the British and Polish governments signed a Treaty of Mutual Assistance. The Polish ambassador in London, Count Edward Raczyński, described the process in his post-war memoirs. [31]

One does not need to be a cynical observer of the events of the day to appreciate that the British Government became concerned that faced with a German–Soviet Treaty, Poland's foreign policy might be swayed to a compromise with Germany. Did Beck consider such an alternative option at the last moment? Were the British worried that he might? Currently available archives do not answer that question but intuitive and cynical opinions abound. After all, at the time of the March 1939 guarantee the British military were concerned lest the Polish forces "supplement them [i.e. the German armed forces] by subordinating her foreign policy to Hitler's, or allow them free rein in the West by maintaining an attitude of benevolent neutrality".

The Treaty of Mutual assistance certainly decided Poland's fate. Initially it stunned Hitler, who had been convinced that the "worms" in London and Paris would not go to war on Poland's behalf. He postponed his attack, which had been scheduled for August 26th. Incidentally that was day that all ground components of the Polish Military Aviation (Air Force) were dispersed to secret bases on the basis of the Polish intelligence reports.[32]

Hitler was also advised by Mussolini that Italy would sit the war out. However, the German leader quickly recovered his nerve and the German military machine crossed the Polish border on September 1. To attempt to persuade the neutrals or faint of heart, Alfred Helmut Naujocks, a member of the SS, arranged an alleged Polish provocation by staging an attack on a German radio station at Gleiwitz in Silesia. Foreign observers were shown bodies of dead men dressed in Polish army uniforms. The reality was that these were tragic concentration camp victims killed and their bodies arranged in a staged fashion. Hitler was determined to have his war.[33]

---

30 Geoffrey Roberts, *The Unholy Alliance: Stalin's pact with Hitler*, Indiana U. Press, Bloomington, 1989.

31 Edward Raczyński , *In Allied London*, Weidenfeld and Nicolson, London, 1962. The British account of this process is to be found in *The British War Blue Book. Documents Concerning German-Polish Relations and the Outbreak of Hostilities between Great Britain and Germany on September 3, 1939.*

32 Mieczysław Cieplewicz and Marian Zgórnik, *Przygotowanie Niemieckie do agresji na Polske w 1939 roku w świetle sprawozdań odziału II sztabu głównego Wojska Polskiego. Dokumenty*. Polska Akademia Nauk, Cracow, 1969.

33 Gerhard L. Weinberg, *The Foreign Policy of Hitler's Germany. Starting World War II, 1937–1939*, Chicago, University of Chicago Press, 1980.

2

WAR

Last minute Polish military dispositions – Germany and the Soviets invade Poland -Consequences of the September Campaign – Evacuation of Polish military through Hungary and Romania to France – A clandestine secret military organization is planned to function behind German lines in event of war.

The less than peaceful interwar armistice came to an end on September 1st 1939 when the German Forces carried out their Fuhrer's directive – *Case White*. In general the war in Germany was at the very best accepted as a reasonable response to alleged Polish arrogance and public anger and humiliation at the loss of Eastern Lands. Some Germans were opposed but many were enthusiastic.[1]

The Second Polish Republic had enjoyed less than 21 years of freedom, and its birth and survival during this period of armistice was very much a function of the Polish Army. It had saved Poland from Russia in 1920, its presence and success had led to alliances with France and Romania which preserved Polish integrity during that period and led to seemingly meaningful alliances with Western Powers. The French alliance (1921) turned out to be a broken reed but Poland did receive significant French loans for re-armament. The actual presence of the Polish Army had also brought the British into the alliance in 1939. It is of course a legitimate historical debate whether what actually ensued was a success of Polish policy, but the armed forces of the Republic did give the government options. In political memoirs written after the September Campaign while interned in Romania, Beck insisted that he had been able to make the German attack on Poland into a grand anti-German coalition. But at what cost, it has to be asked?

---

1   Richard Hargreaves, *Blitzkrieg Unleashed. The German Invasion of Poland, 1939*. Pen and Sword, Barnsley, 2008; Alexander B. Rossino, *Hitler Strikes Poland. Bliztkrieg, Ideology and Atrocity*, University Press of Kansas, Lawrence KS, 2003; Steven J. Zaloga, *Poland 1939. The birth of Blitzkrieg*, Osprey, Oxford, 2002.

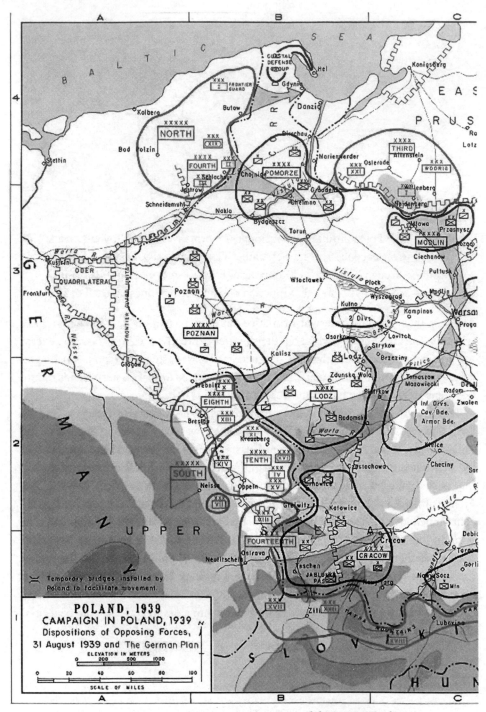

*Situation in Poland 1939 – dispositions of the opposing forces
and the German plan.*

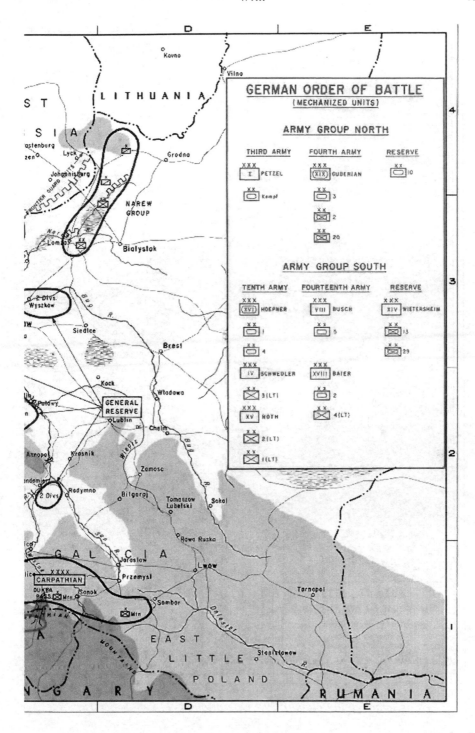

GERMAN ORDER OF BATTLE
(MECHANIZED UNITS)

ARMY GROUP NORTH

THIRD ARMY	FOURTH ARMY	RESERVE
I PETZEL	XIX GUDERIAN	10
Kampf	3	
	2	
	20	

ARMY GROUP SOUTH

TENTH ARMY	FOURTEENTH ARMY	RESERVE
XVI HOEPNER	VIII BUSCH	XIV WIETERSHEIM
1	5	13
4		29
IV SCHWEDLER	XVIII BAIER	
5(LT)	2	
XV HOTH	4(LT)	
2(LT)		
1(LT)		

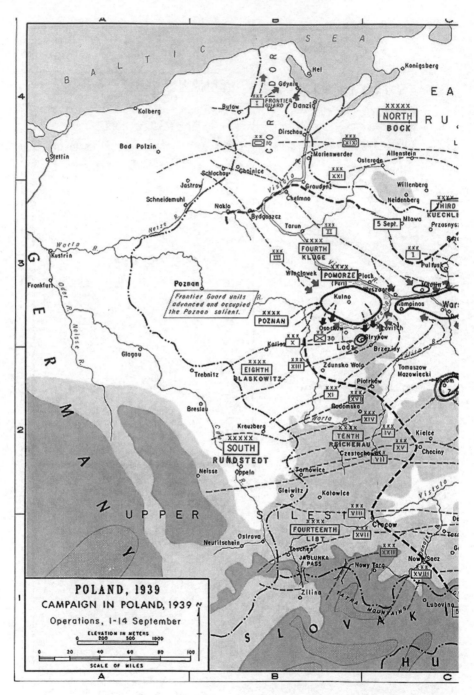

Campaign in Poland 1939 – Operations 1–14 September.

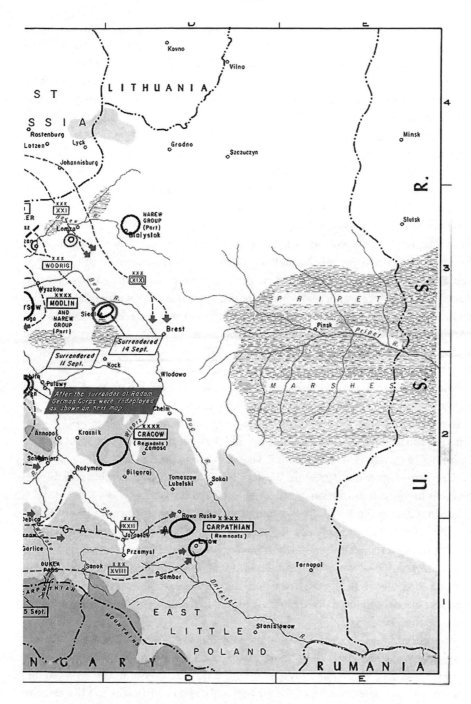

There are many narratives about the September 1939 Campaign. One can agree that it was a cataclysmic event which led to partition, genocide, and devastation of the country. But there are also many myths and distortions. The initial German success in breaking the Polish defence line seemed to suggest that the Poles were caught by surprise. Actually, the Polish intelligence services correctly estimated the day and hour of the German attack. As early as May 1939 all Polish ship-owners were given instructions that returning vessels have a minimum of ten days' supply of bunker oil at all times in a case of emergency departure. In late August 1939 all Polish merchant ships were kept out of the Baltic and Polish ships in Gdynia were ordered to sail, with or without cargoes. The Polish Destroyer Division, by agreements with the British in the summer of 1939, sailed for the United Kingdom on August 30 1939 and were in Leith on September 1st. This was, in fact, the first element of the Polish Forces in the West.

On August 30 1939 Poland ordered general mobilization. The ambassadors of France and Britain in Warsaw strongly urged that this be rescinded since it might be seen as a provocation to Hitler and make the last minute negotiations for preserving peace difficult. More importantly it was pointed out that the Western democracies might find such a Polish action as incompatible with the principles of mutual assistance in case of German attack. Very valuable time was lost, and much confusion ensued, as the Poles rescinded their general mobilization and then once again issued orders for its implementation. There was no such confusion in the Polish Military Aviation [Air Force], already mobilized, which moved its flying units on the eve of the war to join up with their ground crews that had already been dispersed.

Two historians gave the best summary of what confronted the Poles in 1939. "The Poles were in a simply impossible position, and their most valuable industrial regions lay immediately adjacent to Germany." They further comment that "as they had with the Czechs in September 1938 [the Western allies] applied considerable pressure on the Poles to delay mobilization in order not to offend the Germans".[2]

The task facing the Polish Commander-in-Chief, Marshal Edward Smigły-Rydz, was impossible. The only chance for success was to hold out for the projected six to eight weeks and await the French offensive promised on the fifteenth day of the French declaration of war. The plan devised was to force the Germans to develop their forces as soon as they crossed the border. The other strategic task was to attempt to protect the most industrialised regions, which, in the case of Silesia, were adjacent to the German border.

Smigły-Rydz had another political problem on his agenda. The Poles did not completely trust the British, let alone the French, to honor their obligations to Poland. They were aware that only a year before the Czechoslovak Government had been abandoned. The position of the British ambassador in Berlin and his close to

---

2   Murray, Williamson and Allan R Millett, *A War to be Won. Fighting the Second World War*, Cambridge, MA., Belknap Press of Harvard University, 2000, pp.47–51.

desperate attempts to get Hitler to be reasonable at Poland's expense, did not inspire confidence in Warsaw.[3] The Poles were concerned lest a military move into the Free City of Danzig and some Polish western territories, specifically Silesia, be condoned by the West and in turn led to Hitler being reasonable.

Polish skepticism about Allied commitment to Polish territorial integrity was proven correct, when in October 1939 the British Secretary of State (Foreign Office) Lord Halifax refused any British involvement in confronting Soviet aggression.[4]

This concern about British and French intentions led to Polish army dispositions which further exposed the Poles to a German encirclement. Polish divisions were moved into the exposed corridor between Germany and East Prussia and a whole army was lost. The Polish Commander-in-Chief had hoped to make a last stand on the so-called Romanian beachhead, where he expected military supplies from the West via Romanian ports and also hoped for an energetic offensive on the part of Poland's Western allies.

In pre-war staff exercises General Tadeusz Kutrzeba, the Director of Poland's Staff Academy, assessed Polish military potential as being able to hold out for six weeks against Germany unless the French implemented their offensive. Were it not for the Soviet invasion this judgment would undoubtedly have been correct.

In spite of the at times tenacious defence by many units, and short brilliant tactical success of the Poznan Army west of Warsaw, in the Battle of Bzura, the Poles were inexorably pushed back.

One of the tactical successes which for a time raised Polish spirits was the battle of the *ad hoc* Southern Army Group formed on September 10 1939 and commanded by General Kazimierz Sosnkowski. By itself this battle was nearly irrelevant to the campaign, but it did elevate Sosnkowski above many other senior generals for his skill, tenacious spirit and bravery. He took over the command of the group by flying to the isolated divisions in a small communication plane. When all was lost due to Soviet and German pressure, his small and diminishing force was disbanded and everybody was on their own. Sosnkowski avoided capture and in civilian clothing made his escape over the Carpathians to Hungary and hence to France, arriving in mid-October 1939.

The Soviet invasion of September 17th was the *coup de grace* to Poland's defenses. The Polish armed forces were caught in a vice from which there was no escape except by a small number of units already moved to the very south-east part of Poland on the border of Romania.[5]

---

3   Henderson, Neville, *Failure of a Mission. Berlin, 1937–1939*, G.P. Putnam's, NY, 1940.

4   At a meeting of the British Cabinet on September 18, 1939 Lord Halifax pointed out that the Anglo-Polish Agreement did not apply to Soviet aggression. See Anita Prażmowska, *Britain, Poland and the Eastern Front 1939*, Cambridge University Press, Cambridge, 1987, p.191.

5   Geoffrey Roberts, *The Unholy Alliance: Stalin's pact with Hitler*, Indiana University Press, 1989. David G. Williamson succinctly analyses a situation, too often ignored or glossed over, in his monograph *Poland Betrayed. The Nazi-Soviet Invasions of Poland of 1939*, Pen and Sword, Barnsley, 2009.

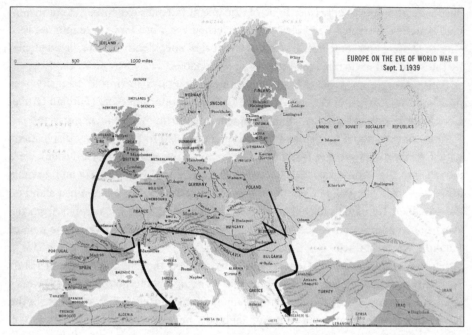

Europe in 1939. Shown are the evacuation routes of Polish military personnel to France after the September 1939 Campaign.

While the Poles were being destroyed the French army made limited, and, it should be stated, successful incursions into the German lines. The Royal Air Force, after one bloody attack on Heligoland, limited its operations to leaflet dropping. Warsaw held out to September 27th and Hitler took his victory parade on the lovely Ujazdowski Avenue. Hitler basked in his success and the German populace rejoiced and accepted the triumph.[6] But Beck's analysis was also prescient – the Germans had opened the pandora's box which led to a World War.[7]

The Polish Government did not surrender, and neither did the Polish Army at its command level. Many units, surrounded decimated armies, and eventually the capital city – Warsaw – did surrender. This was followed by the capitulations of the Modlin fortress and the Hel peninsula. The Poles were going to continue at the side of their Western Allies – in the West.

The last symbolic resistance of the Poles in the September Campaign was the patrol of the Polish submarine, O.R.P. *Orzeł*.[8] Five of Poland's submarines, including the *Orzeł*, attempted to interdict German shipping between the main German ports

---

6   Nicholas Bethell, *The War Hitler Won. The Fall of Poland, September, 1939*, Holt, Rinehart and Winston, NY, 1972

7   Sidney Aster, *1939. The Making of the Second World War*, Simon and Schuster, NY, 1973.

8   The prefix O.R.P. stands for Okręt Rzeczyspospolitej Polskiej, which translates as 'Warship of the Polish Republic'.

and East Prussia. The five submarines that composed the Submarine Division were the *Wilk*, *Ryś*, *Żbik*, *Sęp* and *Orzeł* and all were tasked with laying mines between German and East German ports and attempting to interdict German shipping in the Baltic. The Germans, in turn, aware of the Polish submarines, minimized their sea traffic. After entering a neutral Estonian port to disembark a sick captain, *Orzeł* was interned, and partially disarmed. Its escape was described by Churchill as an "epic".[9] But even after escaping, *Orzeł* patrolled the Baltic till a decision was made to sail for the United Kingdom, which was reached on October 14 1939. The Germans were well aware of the Polish submarines, but having established ground connections between their territories halted all shipping and made an effort to hunt down the Poles. *Wilk* also broke out from the Baltic to the United Kingdom while three others entered Swedish ports and were interned.[10]

The Poles were painted by their critics as politically delusional and militarily suicidal. For citizens and historians of Western countries, it is difficult to appreciate how much late 18th Century Polish history and the ensuing partitions influenced the thinking of the Polish leadership, and how much it was going to continue to pervade the attitude of the Polish Government in Exile. But it should also be kept in mind that the Poles knew that their chance of surviving was dependent on their allies – the French and British – keeping their pledges made in Warsaw staff meetings.

The Poles kept their bargain and at the end of the September Campaign the Germans were, by their own admission, unable to continue without significant pause. Over 200 German tanks were lost and over 400 aircraft destroyed or beyond repair. The bulk of the German forces had been committed to defeating the Poles and the expenditures of ammunition, gasoline and material preclude concurrent operations in the West. According to German archives, 75% of all German losses were in the last two weeks of the September Campaign. The French had had their chance and missed it.[11]

The best short commentary on the Polish effort was penned by German historians – "the inadequacy of Polish political judgment was reflected in the belief of effective support from Britain and France". The German historians also acknowledge that the "decisive factor was the political and military starting position which it has to be admitted could not have been greatly improved. The gallantry in action shown by the overwhelming mass of Polish troops and acknowledged by the *Wehrmacht* could do no more than mitigate the weakness just listed."[12]

Sir John Keegan commented that "the Polish Army sustained resistance from September 1 until October 5, five weeks, which compares favourably with six and

9   Winston S. Churchill, *The Gathering Storm*, Cassell, London, 1948, p.435.

10   TNA ADM 1/1/9971. Also, Michael Alfred Peszke, *Poland's Navy*, 1918–1945, Hippocrene Books, New York, 1999.

11   Kennedy, Robert M., *The German Campaign in Poland (1939)*, Dept. of the Army (USA) Pamphlet No. 20–255, Washington DC, 1956, pp.120–131.

12   *Germany and the Second World War*, Vol. 2, Oxford U. Press, 1991.

half weeks during which France, Britain, Belgium and Holland kept up the fight in the West the following year".[13]

But the disastrous campaign had one other seminal result, namely a psychological loss of faith by the Polish public in the Polish pre-war government and even more in the officer corps of the Polish Armed Forces. This sentiment only abated in June 1940 when the Poles saw their French and British allies defeated by the Germans, without Soviet assistance, in only a few more weeks than the Polish Campaign. But in 1939 and early 1940 there was bitter soul searching and semi-legal witch hunts against pre-war politicians and mid to senior level officers.

Poland and its citizens were now exposed to a brutal, fanatical racial persecution by both occupiers. In the West the Germans are notorious for the tragic fate of the Jewish citizens but the persecution of the Polish intelligentsia and priests is not generally known or acknowledged. All Polish universities were closed and the professors of Cracow's Jagiellonian University were arrested and sent to a German concentration camp. Western territories were incorporated into the German Reich.

As the war went on Poles, young men living in those incorporated territories, were involuntarily conscripted for the German Army.[14]

In the East the Soviet occupation was insidious and Poles by the hundreds of thousands were arrested and sent to various Soviet gulags. Within months the Soviets also organized elections in which the majority of the local population in overwhelming numbers professed enthusiasm and voted for joining the Soviet republics. However, all Poles who were considered to be community leaders, such as police officers, firemen, teachers and judges, were arrested and sent to various Soviet work camps.[15]

Polish soldiers captured by the Germans were by and large treated correctly. One has to at least speculate that the Germans, and particularly the officer corps of the *Wehrmacht*, were not quite sure as to the final political outcome and many in the German Army undoubtedly still hoped for a rump Polish state with a Polish army, under German control, as a fire wall against the predictably short-lived alliance with the Soviets.

The Soviets saw all Polish officers and reserve officers as enemies of the state, to be treated as criminals. This led to the horrible murder of thousands of Polish military at places like Katyn. (More about this later.)

All of that part of Europe that fell to these two tyrannies now endured the unimaginable.[16]

---

13   Sir John Keegan, *The Battle for History. Re-fighting World War II*, Vintage Books, NY, 1996, pp.67–68.
14   Jan T. Gross, *Polish Society Under German Occupation: The Generalgouvernement, 1939–1944*, Princeton University Press, Princeton, 1979.
15   Jan T. Gross, *Revolution from Abroad: The Soviet Conquest of Poland's Western Ukraine and Western Belorussia*, Princeton University Press, Princeton, 1988; Keith R. Sword, *Deportation and Exile. Poles in the Soviet Union, 1939–1948*, Macmillan, London, 1996.
16   Timothy Snyder, *Bloodlands. Europe Between Hitler and Stalin*, Basic Books, NY, 2010.

EVACUATION OF THE POLISH GOVERNMENT AND MILITARY

The Soviet invasion, more than the inexorable German pressure and their motorized breakthroughs, foiled Polish attempts to anchor a defensive line on the Romanian boundary. The plan and hope was that Western supplies would come through the Romanian ports and then be moved to south-east Poland.

The British Staff analyzed the rail capability in Romania from ports to the Polish border, and a British freighter with some supplies, escorted by the Polish destroyer *Błyskawica*, left the United Kingdom on September 18 heading for the Mediterranean and ultimately Romanian Black Sea ports.[17] But the south-eastern flank was just too exposed and only a few platoon-strength border guard units faced the invading Soviet forces. The Polish Government decided to accept the invitation of the French Government to relocate to France, as had been the case for the Belgians in the Great War. Since the Polish Government and High Command had already retreated under German pressure to the south-east corner of Poland the only possible route to France was through Romania. It appears that no thought was given to using any of the Polish Lot Airline Lockheeds or the PZL–37 Łoś bombers, to at least airlift the President.

Polish sources aver that the Romanians had a treaty of mutual military assistance signed in 1921 in event of a Soviet attack on either country. The Soviet invasion of Poland obligated them to a military response on behalf of Poland. But Beck realized the cold facts and given the hopeless Polish situation, the Polish Foreign Minister formally released the Romanians from their legal treaty obligation in exchange for a guaranteed passage of the Government to France.[18] Once in Romania the Polish Government were interned. This attempted transit to France became one of the most controversial events in the Polish experience of the Second World War and has been portrayed by Polish Communists as the Polish leadership fleeing and abandoning their country.

Polonsky believes that the pressure for this internment came from the Germans and cites German documents which record such negotiations. Undoubtedly the Germans did put pressure on the Romanians but there is some indirect evidence that the French were not displeased to have to deal with a different Polish leadership, particularly one led by people from the very pro-French *Front Morges*, whose main leader was Sikorski.[19] Sikorski had crossed the Romanian border in his car and very

---

17   TNA WO 193/764.

18   Polonsky questions whether the Romanians had actually agreed to such a *droit de passage*. But he also omits any reference to the fact of the military assistance treaty was waived by the Poles. His doubt may be justified, but it is still a question. *Politics in Independent Poland*, p.501.

19   Ibid., p.501. *Front Morges* was the name given to a group of Polish statesmen who were led by Ignacy Paderewski. They were very pro-French, and also strongly anti-Piłsudski, as well as being opposed to his successors.

shortly afterwards contacted the French ambassador to Poland, also in Romania, and the two travelled by train to Paris. He was welcomed by the French.

Thousands of Polish soldiers were also ordered to cross into neutral countries with the expectation, that was realized, that they would be able to continue travel to the Western allies. But with some exceptions these were primarily training, staff and rear echelons. However the exception, and the most significant group to be saved, were nearly 7,000 personnel or nearly 70% of the Polish Military Aviation, the precursor of the recreated Polish Air Force in the West.

The aviation service had been slowly squeezed into south-east Poland by the German advance, but with the Soviet invasion the bases were threatened and by that time also lacking logistical support. About 200 military aircraft flew to Romania and many were subsequently used by the Royal Romanian Air Force in the war against the Soviets – one of the most obvious refutations to the aspersion the Polish Air Force was destroyed on the ground on the first day of the war.[20]

Hungary, with which the Poles also shared a border, was the destination of many ground forces, the foremost being the 10th Motorized Cavalry Brigade, the famous Black Brigade.

It was called the "Black" Brigade because of the black leather jackets worn by the cadre. This brigade later evolved in Scotland into the Polish Armoured Division and was part of the Allied force in North-West Europe, 1944–1945.[21]

Most Polish military interned in Hungary and Romania were treated in a very correct manner and both countries were accommodating to the Polish exodus as long as it was discreetly managed. The Romanians, and even the Hungarians, were as motivated to see the Poles escape as the Poles wished to leave. Thousands of supposedly interned Polish soldiers were transported in a more or less secret manner to France or its French mandate – Syria.[22]

---

20   See also Cajus Bekker, *Luftwaffe War Diaries*, Doubleday, NY, 1968, who contradicts these widely held beliefs (pp.38–59). Alexander Statiev describe the use of these Polish planes by the Royal Romanian Air Force - "Antonescu's Eagles Against Stalin's Falcons: The Romanian Air Force, 1920–1941", *The Journal of Military History*, Vol. 66, No. 4, October 2002, p.1087.

21   Evan McGilvray, *The Black Devils' March. A Doomed Odyssey. The 1st Polish Armoured Division, 1939–1945*, Helion, Solihull, UK, 2005.

22   My father's experience was typical and generic and I was old enough to have been a witness. He escaped in the trunk of taxi from a barely guarded hotel in Calimanesti where many Polish officers were interned. On reaching the functioning Polish embassy in Bucharest he was part of a milling crowd of Polish military all attempting to pretend to be civilians wearing military uniforms that had been dyed with buttons cut off, but even there, some still had their silver buttons. The Polish embassy was funded by some of the Polish gold evacuated from Poland. It supported the evacuees, bought tickets to France and assisted in obtaining transit visas for people like my father. The embassy also provided false papers on which thousands of military, like my father, traveled through Yugoslavia and Italy to France, which in his case was reached in early November 1939. He also obtained a British visa in Bucharest, but only arrived in the United Kingdom after the French capitulation in June 1940.

British archives document that London instructed their Bucharest embassy to issue visas and assistance to Poles crossing into Romania who were in category B, defined as "persons who might be of service to the Polish Government abroad".[23]

Some Polish troops, including neatly 1,500 aviation personnel, also sought refuge in Lithuania and were interned, however, it proved difficult to arrange the escape of Poles from Lithuania, since the Germans controlled the sea and the Soviets the major boundary. Some were flown out to Sweden but most were eventually captured by the Soviets when that unfortunate country, attempting to stay neutral, was taken over by the Soviets in 1940.

A CLANDESTINE SECRET MILITARY ORGANIZATION IS FORMED IN OCCUPIED POLAND

Even as the evacuation was being organized the Poles were planning a clandestine force in occupied Poland, and already thinking of the manner in which their forces in the West would return to liberate their Homeland.

Prior to the war the Polish Staff had conceptualized that sabotage and intelligence gathering groups composed of dedicated and patriotic citizens would be formed to act behind German lines. The man behind the Polish plans was Lt. Colonel Edmund Charaszkiewicz.[24] Polish plans for such irregular warfare had been discussed with the British and certain sabotage and communication devices shared. The British were primarily and unashamedly interested in ensuring that Polish oil fields, refineries, bridges and rail lines were sabotaged.[25]

The rapid advance of the German mobile columns, aided by the reverse of Polish plans, namely German "fifth columnists", did not allow the Poles to fully develop their plans, though bridges were blown all over the country, tragically, at times, before evacuating Polish columns could utilize them.[26]

On September 26th a Polish plane, a PZL- 46 Sum, interned by the Romanians, was surreptitiously taken over by Stanisław Riess, a test pilot for the P.Z.L. (Polskie Zakłady Lotnicze). On the pretense of flying within Romania, he flew a passenger, Major Edmund Galinat, the personal emissary of the interned Marshal Smigły-Rydz, to the G.O.C. Warsaw.

Józef Jaklicz, an officer in the Polish staff, wrote that on September 16, before the Soviet invasion, Marshal Edward Smigły- Rydz met with Major Galinat to instruct

---

23   TNA FO 371/23158. Category A were civilians who, according to the British consular staff in Romania, wished to head for Palestine.
24   Andrzej, Kwiecien, Marcin and Grzegorz Mazur, *Zbió Dokumentów pplk. Edmunda Charaszkiewicza*, Kśięgarnia Akademicka, Cracow, 2000.
25   TNA HS 4/195. British-Polish discussions from May 1939 throughout July 1939.
26   TNA HS 4/193. British report of Polish accounts of German sabotage behind Polish lines.

him to infiltrate into territories already abandoned by the Poles but barely controlled by the Germans and to organize a clandestine movement.[27] The Soviet invasion of September 17 and the Ukrainian irredentist movement made this venture impossible.

Riess landed on the grounds of a race track, an old air base, Mokotów, in Warsaw, which was a piece of no-man's land between Polish and German positions. The emissary was disembarked and after three and half hours, when an artillery cannonade masked the noise of the engine, Riess took off and landed in neutral Lithuania, since he clearly was not prepared to face the irate Romanians. Riess eventually made it to the United Kingdom through Sweden and with his background became a test pilot, losing his life in an accident in 1942 testing a Halifax bomber at the Royal Air Force Testing base, Boscombe Down.[28]

Major Edmund Galinat, the emissary, carried two orders, the first to the Commanding General of the Warsaw garrison to surrender and the second to the most senior officer of the legionary core to form a clandestine secret army, akin to the 1917 Polska Organizacja Wojskowa. By a coincidence General Michael Karasiewicz-Tokarzewski, in beleaguered Warsaw and a legionary, had already been planning to form a clandestine military once Warsaw's capitulation had taken place, an inevitable development. He became the first G.O.C. of Poland's Underground Movement. K.A. Merrick, wrote, "Poland had a fully operative underground network in place before the Germans had finished shooting."[29]

It is perhaps odd that a seemingly minor event as this deserves such mention and emphasis but it was a first step in the formation of a very extensive clandestine force that continued for close to six years.

September 26th is celebrated as Poland's Home Army Day.

This was Marshal Edward Smigły- Rydz's last executive order, and also his attempt to ensure that the torch of Polish leadership was carried on by the officers of the Piłsudski tradition. Smigły-Rydz also escaped from Romanian internment in late 1939 to Hungary where there were strong pre-war connections between various Polish and Hungarian intelligence services. The Hungarian Regent, Admiral Horthy, had good relations with the Poles, and undoubtedly did his part in shielding the Polish Marshal from the Germans. Smigły-Rydz then arranged a clandestine Carpathian crossing into occupied Poland, hoping to be able to take part or even possibly be in command of the Polish Underground. He died of a heart attack shortly after arriving in occupied Warsaw.

His arrival in occupied Poland in 1941, after the German attack on the Soviets, and more importantly after the controversial Sikorski–Maisky agreement, was seen by

---

27   *Zeszyty Historyczne*, Vol. 12, 1967, pp.14–162.
28   PISM A. I 3/1.
29   K.A. Merrick, *Flights of the Forgotten*, Arms and Armour Press, London, 1989.

Sikorski, already in London, as a potential challenge to not merely his leadership, but also to the course of his foreign policy.[30]

One day after Warsaw capitulated, the fortress of Modlin surrendered, while the peninsula of Hel and naval port of Hel fought on until October 1. On October 4 General Kleberg and his decimated divisions fought the last symbolic battle at Kock in Eastern Poland.

---

30   PISM. A. XII. 1/12.

3

RECREATION OF THE POLISH REPUBLIC IN EXILE IN FRANCE

Polish Government and Military Recreated in France and Great Britain – The Phoney War on Land in the West – General Sikorski proposes the Balkan Route to liberating Poland – British Blockade of Germany – Poland's navy part of the blockade – Finnish interlude and French plans for Polish assistance to the Finns – Sikorski begins tentative staff plans for opening up air link to occupied Poland – Polish attempts to base part of the Air Force in the United Kingdom – discreet reaching out to the Soviet Union through Britain to form a Polish Army – End of Phoney War – Germans invade Norway – Polish troops in Narvik – French Capitulation – evacuation of Polish Forces from France to the United Kingdom.

For a number of weeks the Poles faced a constitutional crisis. The Polish President, Mościski, and all members of the government were interned in Romania. There ensued complicated behind-the-scenes diplomatic and political maneuvering. During this time, short in days but having a major impact, Poland's foreign policy was in the hands of two skilled and sophisticated ambassadors who led it through the interregnum. Edward Raczyński in London and Julian Łukasiewicz in Paris were able to finalize the process in which the interned President appointed Władysław Raczkiewicz, already in Paris, as his successor. Raczkiewicz was loath to accept this post, and stated that he would resign it immediately when and if Sosnkowski arrived in Paris. When Sosnkowski did arrive, in rather heroic mode compared to many senior Polish politicians in Paris, he refused but accepted the post of Presidential successor. This caused umbrage in Sikorski and his followers who had actually hoped that Sikorski would be the designate presidential nominee or at least named as successor.

Raczkiewicz did appoint General Władysław Sikorski to the position of Commander-in-Chief and Prime Minister in the newly-formed coalition Polish Government. But there was a significant modification in the prerogatives enjoyed by the Polish President emanating from the Polish Constitution. Raczkiewicz, much to the consternation of his supporters, agreed that he would not sign decrees without the approval of the Prime Minister. Later that was further modified and extended to the coalition government.

While the actual appointment of Commander-in-Chief during wartime was subject to the President, it was agreed that in fact the C-in-C would exercise his functions with consultation with the Government. When General Sikorski was Prime Minister, C-in-C as well as Minister of Defence and even of Justice, these modifications were cosmetic. They became important after his death in 1943.[1]

When Sosnkowski arrived in France many weeks later there was a certain dilemma of military protocol. Sikorski was already there and was in fact in command of the nascent Polish forces. But he was a lieutenant-general, while Sosnkowski held the higher rank of General of Arms, and came with an aura of having fought. Sosnkowski, always a diplomat, did not make an issue of this but graciously accepted the nebulous post of commanding officer of the Polish Clandestine Forces being formed in Poland.

This was the beginning of the Polish State in Exile and constitutionally the continuation of the Second Polish Republic. Its main external and most visible face was the Polish Armed Forces, which began to be cultivated and nourished by the Poles and also ultimately by the Allies. But the seeds of pre-war political differences not only continued but became more exacerbated, with some politicians calling for a commission to investigate the pre-September leadership for its alleged incompetence and failures. The senior military officer cadre was predominantly pre-war, the majority rooted in the Piłsudski legionary tradition, and while stunned by the September defeat, they resented and were bitter that they were being criticized by many Polish politicians who uttered no condemnation of the French for their failure to act aggressively in September.

The kernel of the Polish Armed Forces in the West, primarily in France in 1939–1940, was the 70,000 Polish military, including 7,000 air personnel, who crossed the southern Polish border into Romania and Hungary and were evacuated in a successful manner to France and the French Levant. The recreated Polish Government in France received military credits from the French and was the recipient of the British

---

1   Reprint of the *Konstytucja Rrzeczypospolitej Polskiej*, Józef Piłsudski Institute of America, pp.30–40.

Government's loan, so long delayed. The fortunate evacuation of close to sixty tons of Polish gold also facilitated the issuance of military (and civilian) credits.

The Polish Naval Headquarters were immediately located in London, since all the Polish warships were based in the United Kingdom. Nearly 40 merchant ships, including four modern large transatlantic liners, were now working with the Allies and also earning monies for the Polish State in Exile. This was overseen by the Polish Transport Committee. Polish legal jurisdiction over the Polish Merchant Marine was implemented initially through Polish consuls and in 1941 by Polish Sea Courts based in the United Kingdom which were in turn legalized by the British Allied Powers Maritime Courts Act of 1941.

PLANS FOR THE CLANDESTINE FORCES IN POLAND

Even as the evacuation of the Polish military from Romania and Hungary was being organized and implemented, the Poles were planning a clandestine force in occupied Poland, and thinking of the manner in which their forces in the West would return to liberate their Homeland.

The strategy was a multi-pronged policy, and involved forming an underground force and arming it, while creating a military in the West, playing a part in the defeat of Germany and working with the Western coalition to liberate Poland.

In the first stages of the German occupation many clandestine military groups of diverse ideological trends were formed. Most quickly joined the official clandestine group accountable to the Polish Government and its military headquarters in France, subsequently after June 1940, in the United Kingdom. This clandestine force had a number of different names, but shortly became known as the Home Army, in contrast to the Army in the West.

The two exceptions were the National Democrats, with their own political agenda, and the Peasant Party, which was strong in eastern Poland around Lublin. Both political parties, while actually represented in the Polish coalition government, maintained their own clandestine military forces. The Communists were completely absent since most had escaped to the Soviet zone and those who remained were pro-Soviet, and in view of the German-Soviet collaboration at the time opposed to the "capitalist" war. This changed after the German invasion of the USSR in June 1941. The communist groups never amounted to much, but did act as receiving points for Soviet agents and saboteurs.

One other prominent clandestine group, the Musketeers, initially attempted to establish direct contacts of co-operation with the British intelligence services by passing the Polish military chain of command, but did not last long, with the majority of its cadre joining the Home Army. It is a speculation, but the initial British reluctance to facilitate Sikorski's request for an air link to his command might have been a wish to rethink the best way forward.

The Polish Government was recognized as the *de jure* government of Poland by the majority of governments outside of the direct orbit and influence of Germany and the Soviet Union. Even Italy and Japan maintained diplomatic relations with the Polish Government until both declared war on Poland's allies, Italy in June 1940 and Japan in December 1941.

Polish war aims, refined throughout the war, were that at the conclusion of the war with Germany, Poland had to emerge as a sovereign state, free of any outside interference in its domestic and foreign policies and with its borders inviolate. But since the Germans had initiated the conflict there had to be consequences and the Poles argued that the so-called 'corridor' to the Baltic had to be widened, particularly on the east side, and Danzig had to be incorporated into Poland, while East Prussia was to be a disarmed area, something the Poles had passionately and unsuccessfully advocated in the Versailles discussions. The Polish Government did not, at that point in time, express a wish for extending Polish territory in the west to the River Oder, the so-called historic Piast lands of the early medieval Polish Kingdom. This was decided by the Big Three at Tehran and Yalta without Polish participation.

On January 23rd 1940 General Władysław Sikorski, in allied France, made the following declaration of Polish war policy – "the recreation of the Polish Army in its greatest size is the most important and essential goal of the Government." In essence this articulated both the political and strategic goals of the Polish Government and focused on the vital importance of the Polish Armed Forces as a fundamental element of the attributes of a legitimate authority as well as of the Polish contribution to the war and thus as the entrance fee for playing a part in the overall war aims of the Allied coalition. Poland had no colonies or extensive worldwide financial institutions and the Polish military became the sole determinant of Polish foreign policy initiatives.

But what is of the essence in understanding the dilemmas and issues of Polish policy in the ensuing years of the war is that by holding the posts of Prime Minister and Commander-in-Chief, Sikorski determined its course. Until his tragic and controversial death in a plane accident in July 1943, Polish strategy was in fact the strategy of a pragmatist – Sikorski.

POLAND'S BALKAN STRATEGY

The fundamental problem for the Poles was how to conceive a strategy which would lead to the liberation of their country not only from the German but also from the Soviet yoke. Both France and Great Britain had declared war on Germany in

accordance with their treaty obligations to Poland, but there were no analogous obligations in respect of the Soviet Union. This was a major challenge to Polish foreign
policy since it was apparent that neither ally was prepared to engage in any action,
apart from words, on Poland's behalf vis-à-vis the Soviets. In fact, in Britain from
the very first, certain political factions worked and hoped to make the Soviets part of
the anti-German coalition, and Polish eastern territory was a seemingly small price
for such an alliance.

But while often distracted by minutiae, and in hindsight criticized for a number
of decisions, General Sikorski was a statesman and superb strategist. As early as
September, 1939, even before arriving in France, he realized that attacking the
German Siegfried Line on the west of the Rhine was a very unrealistic route to liberating Poland.[2]

Sikorski articulated a strategic vision for a grand alliance of the various Balkan
and Danubian countries, based on the old traditional alliance of Poland and Romania,
and that of Poland and Hungary. Throughout the war, first in France and then after
June 1940 in the United Kingdom, the Polish Government's and Polish Military
Staffs planned to liberate the occupied Homeland by military operations from the
Balkans. At the same time Polish diplomatic contacts, in Lisbon, sought to bring the
two Polish southern neighbors over to the Allied side.

Sikorski thus instructed the various agencies coordinating the escape and evacuation of Poles from Romania that a significant number should be sent to French Syria,
rather than to Metropolitan France. This began the nucleus of a Polish Army in the
Levantine Region. The first combat unit became known as the Carpathian Brigade
as it was conceptualized that it would fight its way to Poland through the Carpathian
Mountains.

The Polish military strategy being espoused was to encourage the Western Allies
to attack Germany from the south, the so-called "soft underbelly" of Europe, at
the same time arming a Polish clandestine military organization for an uprising. It
was to be a reprise of the Great War in the Balkans, strategic and political concepts
harking back to the final days of the Great War when the Western Coalition drove
up the Danube from Greek Salonika. Sikorski obviously hoped that this time such
an Allied drive would continue through the Carpathians into south Poland, where
Western forces including Polish formations would join up with the resurgent and
vibrant Polish Secret Army.

This required a robust clandestine force. The embryonic structure of such a clandestine force already existed, having been created on September 27 1939. But to be
strong enough to meet the challenge it had to be armed and that could only come
from the West, and if from the West only by air support.

---

2   Jan Kowalewski, "Cykl Rumuński", *Zeszyty Historyczne* no.6, 1964, p.135.

THE PHONEY WAR

The two Western Allies seemed stuck in a general state of inactivity. This was the period which, in time, became called the Phoney War. The British, as in the First World War, saw the defeat of Germany through an imposed blockade on all goods. Since the British Army was relatively small compared to the French, the British left the latter to make or not to make plans for ground operations. The French, having been even more bloodied than the British in the Great War, were unwilling to attack the far from impregnable German Siegfried Line.

Land armies faced each other and once in a while patrol activity was given publicity. The British Tommy sang about hanging his laundry on the Siegfried Line, but in reality nothing was going on. In the air the activity was even more muted. On the German side, Hitler's enthusiasm to attack the West before the end of the year was effectively slowed by the German generals, who were still rebuilding from losses of the Polish campaign, and concerned about the prowess of the French Army. It was anything but a phoney war for the naval forces, particularly the Royal Navy enforcing the blockade in the North Sea and the beginning of the convoys in the Atlantic.

The Allied governments correctly perceived that a modern military can only function when its industrial base is well provided with oil, iron ore and other metals. The Royal Navy was able to effectively close off the North Sea but the Germans constantly infringed on Norwegian waters, moved Swedish iron ore from Narvik and obtained all the oil needed from Romania.

In this blockade the three Polish destroyer divisions participated. The arrival of the Polish warships in British waters was a direct result of the staff discussions held in Warsaw during the summer of 1939 and antedated the British declaration of war on September 3rd. The three Polish destroyers, (*Grom, Blyskawica* and *Burza*) were a welcome addition to the Royal Navy, strapped for modern destroyers. All three operated out of the British port of Harwich in the stormy waters of the North Sea.

The destroyers had been joined by two Polish submarines ORP *Wilk* and ORP *Orzel*, that had broken out of the Baltic after prolonged operations in nearly impossible conditions.

While in the final analysis the size of the Polish Navy in the West was relatively miniscule, and its contributions to Allied victory absolutely minor, its symbolic role to the Polish cause was far beyond its actual size.

It has to be emphasized that it never played a part in Polish Staff plans for the liberation of Poland, as was the case for the air and land forces. But it earned the little-known distinction of having fought without a break from the first day of the war to its conclusion.

The First World War blockade of Germany and Austria-Hungary did have demonstrable results and brought starvation to the Central Powers. The German situation in the early days of the Second World War was diametrically different since the Soviets were friendly while the Balkans were coerced into providing goods. The Western coalition's focus was on depriving the Germans of iron ore and oil. The first came from neutral Sweden through neutral Norwegian ports, while oil was coming from Romania. But the Western coalition assumed that it was coming from the Soviet Caucasus. There was nothing that a naval blockade could accomplish with the German supply of oil, but much thought was given how to disrupt the shipments of iron ore from Norway.

Yet, underneath the seeming apathetic attitude of the Phoney War there were diplomatic machinations, with the Soviets being solicited as potential allies and at the same time viewed as a potential enemy to be attacked, being seen as purveyors of oil to the Germans.

Quite independently of any Polish plans, the British Government was also trying to come to grips with the seeming stalemate on the Western front. The British also made strategic plans, independently of the Polish ones, focusing on diplomatic efforts to get the Turks to join the Western coalition. There is no archival evidence that the Polish plan was given the time of day, though it would certainly have been forwarded through appropriate channels. The basic fact is that the Churchillian strategy of the soft underbelly of Europe had more to do with saving British lives, and ultimately protecting British interests in the Mediterranean and sea passages to the Middle east and India, than liberating Poland.[3] However, Turkey was more worried about the Soviets than the Germans and at this point neither the French nor the British had much credibility when it came to making and adhering to military alliances.[4]

The Poles did their very best to participate fully at every level to the best of their resources which were always negatively influenced by manpower shortages. To ensure Allied cooperation in his strategic plans Sikorski accepted not just the necessity but even the desirability and political necessity that the Polish Forces would have to be involved in Allied military operations which did not directly affect the liberation of Polish territory. Thus occurred many of the battles and campaigns

THE SOVIETS INVADE FINLAND, AND THE ALLIES RESPOND

All of this was to come to a head when the Soviets invaded Finland in late November 1939, and the close to moribund League of Nations expelled the Soviets. Aid to Finland through Norway offered an excuse for depriving Germany of iron ore. Perhaps nothing illustrates the bankruptcy of both Allied governments in their attempts to somehow

3   Michael Howard, *The Mediterranean Strategy in the Second World War*, Weidenfeld & Nicolson, London, 1968 pp.41–68.
4   Robin Denniston, *Churchill's Secret War. Diplomatic decrypts, the Foreign Office and Turkey, 1942–1944*, Sutton Publishing, Stroud, UK, 1997.

transmogrify a stalemate with Germany into a winning hand. Since it was assumed in the Western capitals that oil was coming to Germany from Russia, then the British wanted Russia to be at least as neutral as possible, or better still, to join the Allied band wagon, and if that could not be finessed, then plans were made to bomb the Batu oil fields of Caucasus. Graham Rhys-Jones' assessment of Western strategy is close to the mark, "a dream world in which the actions follow a logic known only to them-selves and which is almost wholly opaque to us."[5] General Weygand, in command of French Middle East Forces, wanted to grasp the nettle and fight up the Balkans from Salonika. Had Weygand been given his head, and Sikorski empowered in his strategy, the Balkans would have shifted to the Western Allies and Germany would have been deprived of its source of oil from Romania. Greece, Romania and Yugoslavia would undoubtedly have declared, at least passively, for the Allies. Italy would never have gone to war. It is reasonable to argue that the Carpathian mountains might still have proved a major obstacle to Poland's liberation from the south but a Polish Uprising might have tipped the scales.

With the Soviets condemned by the League of Nations on December 14, 1939, the French now became motivated to arm the Poles to fight the Soviets in Finland and suddenly equipment was found. The Poles, de facto, at war with the Soviets, seemed to relish that idea and began to form an air component and a land brigade. But the French went further and wanted to have the Polish destroyers based in the United Kingdom sail into the Barents Sea near Petsamo and assist the Finns. But once the Finns folded and blandishments of Russia failed, the plan to bomb the oil fields of Batu still continued![6] Sikorski, attempting to manage the positions of Prime Minister, Commander–in–Chief, Minister of Defense, and Justice, was clearly overwhelmed, and as was often alleged, swayed by the last man in his office.[7] He did make a number of executive decisions regarding the Polish Clandestine army that was being labo-riously created in the hostile atmosphere of the occupation. He appointed General Kazimierz Sosnkowski to the position of the General Officer Commanding of the Polish Clandestine Army, and also split the command in Poland between the Soviet

5   Talbot Charles Imlay, "A re-assessment of Anglo-French strategy during the Phoney War, 1939–1940," *English Historical Review*, Vol. 119 (2003), pp.333–372; Graham Rhys-Jones, "Churchill and the Norwegian Campaign", *Royal United Service Institute Journal*, Vol.155, No.4, 2010, pp.76–81.

6   Patrick R. Osborn, *Operation Pike. Britain Versus the Soviet Union, 1939–1941*, Greenwood Press, Westport, CT, 2000; Steven Merritt Miner, *Between Churchill and Stalin*, University of North Carolina Press, Chapel Hill, 1988, pp.11–47.

7   Walentyna Korpalska, *Władysław Eugeniusz Sikorski. Biografia Polityczna*, Ossolineum, Wrocław, 1981; Karol Estreicher Jr., *Dziennik Wypadków*. 1939–1945, Towarzystwo Przyjaciół Sztuk Pięknych, Kraków, 2011; Marian Kukiel, *Generał Sikorski. Żołnierz i Mąż Stanu Polski walczącej*, Polish Insti-tute, London, 1970. General Kukiel was a close friend of General Sikorski, shared his political views and became Minister of Defense in November 1942.

and the German zones of occupation. This has been judged to have been a political act, placing Sosnkowski under Sikorski's chain of command.[8]

General Michael Karasiewicz-Tokarzewski, who had been the original head of the clandestine military movement, was seconded to the Soviet Zone, and was very shortly arrested but not identified, while Colonel Stefan (Grot) Rowecki was appointed to head the clandestine forces in the German Zone. Both zone commanders were to report to Sosnkowski in Paris. It proved an unwieldy and relatively shortlived arrangement.[9]

Looking back on the political aspects of Polish foreign policy in exile, there are two inevitable conclusions. Firstly, the options were limited by the geopolitical situation and that while initially the Soviets were treated in a very ambiguous fashion, once they became the allies of the Western nations, the Polish Government was close to marginalized.

The other major issue was a principled divide between two strong political orientations, the pragmatic statesmanship of Sikorski, and the ideological one of Sosnkowski, also shared by the majority of the senior officer corps, and, as it turned out, the Polish Home Army. This divide went back to 1917 when Piłsudski and his inner core, including Sosnkowski, refused to take an oath of allegiance to the German Emperor, went to prison and his legionnaires were disarmed, while Sikorski, wishing to preserve a Polish military, vacillated. This was to repeat itself with the Sikorski negotiations with the British Air Ministry.

Neither the French nor the British paid much attention to the Polish Military, its leadership or September 1939 experience.[10] Nor did the British or the French manifest great eagerness at retraining Poles in Western equipment or actually forming Polish combat units. The British Air Ministry politely resisted all attempts to have Polish Air Force squadrons form in the United Kingdom, while the French were completely lackadaisical in equipping or arming the Poles and some French generals even wished to have the Polish units limited to battalion strength and integrated into French regiments.

Only Winston S. Churchill, at that time First Lord of the Admiralty, showed any interest or gave praise for the Polish Navy and wrote "the young Polish Navy distinguished itself", and "the escape of the *Orzel* was an epic".[11] This led to an early visit by

---

8   Both generals received high British awards on March 15, 1940, General Sikorski, the Honorary Knight Grand Cross of the Military Division of the British Empire [GBE] while Sosnkowski became an Honorary Knight Commander of the Military Division of the British Empire[KBE]. They were the first of a number of senior Polish generals who received honorary knighthoods from the British. Personal communication from the Central Chancery of the Orders of Knighthood.

9   Marek Ney-Krwawicz, *Biuro Generała Sosnkowskiego*, Wydawnictwo Naukowe Semper, Warsaw, 1996.

10   Ernest R. May in *Strange Victory. Hitler's Conquest of France*, Hill & Wang, NY, 2000, writes that, while some discounted the Polish experiences, General Gauche of the French *Deuxiéme Bureau* did prepare a detailed report (p.279).

11   Winston S. Churchill, *The Gathering Storm*, Cassell, London, 1948, p.435.

General Sikorski to the United Kingdom and the signing of the Polish –British Naval agreement.

At this point in time neither the British nor French showed any interest in participating in Polish initiatives to buttress Polish clandestine activity in occupied Poland. One argument advanced was that some politicians in the corridors of powers still hoped for a face saving and peaceful resolution of the conflict. In such a situation, the Polish military, whether in the West or in occupied Poland, might have been a major obstacle. There are no archival trails to explain this reticence, but reluctance there was.

Until Italy declared war on France and Britain in June, 1940, Polish couriers from the West to Poland were able to move with relative ease via Italy to friendly Hungary, and then to Poland across the Carpathians and in some cases even by rail using false papers. But the Polish military wanted to establish a means of moving military material from the West to Poland and this could not be done by couriers.

NEGOTIATIONS WITH THE BRITISH AIR MINISTRY

As early as October 27 1939 Sikorski instructed his Air Force Commander based in Paris, General Józef Zając, to begin negotiations with the British for RAF aircraft for communication and delivery of supplies to occupied Poland. The London-based Polish Air Force attaché in London and the Polish ambassador continued the frustrating negotiations but the British turned down their proposal. The British suggested a civilian aircraft and so the Poles requested the return of one of the Lockheeds of the Polish airlines LOT. The British found all kind of objections to this and two other exotic ideas were broached. One was to use a captured German four-engined Condor, and the other a sea plane, the American Catalina, which could land on the many lakes in Poland. No progress was made, and the Polish plan was essentially buried, for no obvious or recorded reason, since the Foreign Office wrote; "expressed general sympathy with a somewhat nebulous but avowedly urgent Polish project from November 1939". The Foreign Office summarized their position as a "lean to negative", stating "we should not show ourselves as too forthcoming in our answers".[12]

Sikorski also placed great significance on the formation of a Polish Air Force in exile and sought to do so primarily in the United Kingdom. But he was singularly inept in guiding the negotiations with the British Air Ministry for moving some

---

12   TNA ADM 199/1393 80538. This is a long file starting November 1939 and finishing in March 1940. When doing research on the Polish Navy during the Second World War I was surprised to see this material filed under the Admiralty section. I have no explanation for this but a mere guess is that until June 1940 (i.e. the relocation of the Polish Government to the United Kingdom) much of this information went through Churchill, The First Lord of the Admiralty, who was involved in all kinds of unrealistic and fanciful plans for waging war.

Polish Air Force personnel to the United Kingdom. All Polish attempts were met with an uncompromising British stance that the unwritten British Constitution precluded the stationing of foreign military on British soil.

Finally the British made their final offer – two squadrons of the obsolete light bomber, the Fairey Battle, that had been sold to the Poles in August 1939, as long as the Polish airmen were inducted into the Royal Air Force Volunteer Reserve and took an oath of allegiance to the King. This was very reminiscent of the 1917 controversy and Sikorski accepted this in June 1940.[13]

END OF THE PHONEY WAR

The Phoney War came to an end in April 1940 when the Germans marched into Denmark and invaded Norway, while in May and June, French, British, Belgian and Dutch armies were overwhelmed in a period of six weeks, only three weeks longer than the defeat of Poland by the combined German and Soviet armies.

In the short-lived Norwegian campaign Poles participated with the nearly six thousand strong *Podhalanska* Brigade in Narvik. Originally formed to aid the Finns, its mission was on hold, but it did take part in the rather chaotic Allied effort to aid the Norwegians and at the same time cut the iron ore supplies.

Polish destroyers, which had carried out blockade patrols out of Harwich for months, were also engaged in the Norwegian Campaign. One of the first harbingers

France, 1940. President Władysław Raczkiewicz and General Władysław Sikorski reviewing the Podhalańska Brigade on its way to the Norwegian operations in April 1940. (Polish Institute and Sikorski Museum, London, henceforth abbreviated PISM)

---

13   Michael Alfred Peszke, *The Polish Air Force in the United Kingdom, 1939–1946*. Royal Air Force Air Power Review, Vol. 11 No.3, 2008, pp.55–74.

in identifying the German amphibious operations was on April 7th 1940, when the Polish submarine *Orzeł*, on routine patrol in the North Sea, intercepted a German ship and following pre-war protocol (shortly abandoned by all sides), torpedoed the SS *Rio de Janeiro* carrying German troops. The convention was that any merchant ship had to be identified as carrying contraband cargo and could not be sunk on sight. In those Norwegian operations, ORP *Grom*, ORP *Orzeł* as well as the liner MV *Chrobry* carrying British troops were lost. However, Norway was doomed and so was the British Prime Minister Chamberlain, who was succeeded by Churchill.

In British waters, 1940. The famous Polish submarine ORP Orzeł. *Winston S. Churchill, First Lord of the Admiralty, 1939 wrote "the Young Polish Navy had distinguished itself, and the escape of the* Orzeł *was an epic." (PISM)*

BEGINNING OF SIKORSKI'S SOVIET STRATEGY

Early on in France Sikorski became enmeshed with an old political contact, Joseph Hieronim Rettinger, resident in London. It can only be assumed on the basis of many contacts by Rettinger with senior British leaders that he was seen as a discrete and unofficial contact between Sikorski and the British.[14] After resuming contacts in late 1939 Sikorski appointed Rettinger to run the Polish propaganda division in the United Kingdom, bypassing the Polish ambassador. With such an appointment it was natural that Rettinger would have contacts with Litauer, a left-leaning Polish journalist, and it is more than plausible that they discreetly worked with and on Sikorski, to mold and modify Polish policies vis-à-vis the Soviets.

Sikorski's political awareness showed itself when he became aware of the British tendency to solicit a friendly Soviet Union. Even before evacuating to the United Kingdom in June 1940 Sikorski was already thinking about the possibility of the

---

14   Jan Pomian, *Joseph Rettinger. Memoirs of an Eminence Grise*, Sussex University Press, 1972.

Harwich, UK, 1940. Polish destroyers ORP Grom *and ORP* Błyskawica *in Harwich on blockade patrols, early 1940. (PISM)*

Soviets releasing the hundreds of thousands of Polish prisoners in the Soviet Union to the Polish Army. Polish Staff discussions were initiated and British influence was solicited to have the Soviets release the Polish prisoners of war to the West.[15] This initiative was directly in the face of the Sosnkowski faction, who argued that the only uniting and long-term Polish policy was based on principle and not on pragmatic opportunism.

By his actions and policies towards the Soviets Sikorski may be called schizophrenic, but in fact, he attempted to follow the diplomatic path of his powerful Western Allies. With 70 years' hindsight it is obvious that the degree of Polish political and diplomatic maneuver were limited and Sikorski was putting into practice the old adage of policy being the art of the possible. Sikorski was thus working to conform as much as possible to Western policies, which he continued to do till his deadly accident in July 1943, besides doing his best to be a total player in the war, hoping to gain political capital.

However, the anchor on his diplomatic maneuvers was his isolation. The majority of the Poles, whether in the West or in Poland, did not share his views!

---

15   Dwa Memoriały sztabowe na temat Związku Sowieckiego z połowy 1940 r. *Bellona*, 1960, pp.36–46. At this point in time the Katyn murders of over twenty thousand Polish officers by the Soviets were not known.

FRENCH CAPITULATION

The sudden collapse of the French front and the disintegration of the French army's defenses resulted in a French Government crisis which caught the Polish Government by surprise. On June 16 1940 Churchill arranged for Rettinger to fly to France to locate Sikorski and to bring him to the United Kingdom. Sikorski responded to Churchill's invitation, met with the British Prime Minister and it was quickly arranged to initiate the evacuation of the Polish Forces to the United Kingdom.[16]

Sikorski made a speech to the Poles in France, courtesy of the British Broadcasting Corporation (BBC), urging all his military to make for Atlantic ports to be embarked on British and Polish liners, and in some instances on Royal Navy warships. The Polish President was embarked on the Royal Navy Cruiser, HMS Arethuse.[17]

Contrary to all of Sikorski's efforts in his negotiations with the French to have the slowly forming Polish infantry divisions as an organic Polish corps the French reneged. In the midst of their crisis situation the French prevailed and threw the Poles into battle in a piecemeal fashion, even stripping the Poles of their anti-tank batteries to reinforce French divisions. The Polish chief of staff, Colonel Kędzior, resigned in protest. In addition there were two divisions still being formed, but these were short of men and equipment. One armored brigade, whose cadre was the 10th Motorized Cavalry Brigade, the famous "Black Brigade", was also in the final stages of being trained and equipped.

The final result as France capitulated was the complete destruction of the Polish 1st Grenadier Division, while the Polish 2nd Infantry Division was cornered and forced into crossing to Switzerland, where it was interned.

In the air, Polish fighter units were slowly advanced in retraining but even though equipped with all kinds of obsolescent they took part in the French Campaign.[18].

Sikorski's radio message to the Poles in France does not have the wide acclaim that went to De Gaulle's proclamation of a Free France; but it had far more effect in actual numbers of fighting men who flocked to the United Kingdom to fight on. Even so, not all Poles in France heard the message and not all units could act on the message. Some were involved in heavy fighting, others lacked the means to make it to the Atlantic.

Those who could attempted to obey Sikorski's orders. Most of the Polish air units and training facilities had organic motorized transport and were able to make it to the Atlantic or Mediterranean ports and ultimately arrive in the United Kingdom, joining

16 Ernest R. May, *Strange Victory. Hitler's Conquest of France*, Hill & Wang, NY, 2000.
17 TNA ADM 53/111412.
18 Jerzy B. Cynk, *The Polish Air Force at War Volume 1: 1939–1943*, Schiffer, Atglen PA, 1988, pp.94–145. See, also a very excellent bi-lingual book specifically on the Polish fighter units in France during the May/June Campaign, Grzegorz Śliżewski, *The Lost Hopes, Polish Fighters Over France in 1940*, Panda, Koszalin, 2000.

their colleagues who had been arriving in small transports starting in December 1939. This motorized capability was also true for the motorized brigade.

The evacuation of the Polish military to the United Kingdom took place at many French ports. After its combat mission in the Norwegian Campaign the Podhalanska Brigade had been returned to Brittany to buttress the defense of the peninsula. This was a complete French fiasco and only 3,000 of its cadre were saved by boarding British ships at Brest and St. Nazaire. Other evacuation ports were La Pallice, Bordeaux and Marseille to North Africa. But the primary port became the small fishing harbor Saint Jean de Luz, on the Bay of Biscay.

The Poles arriving in Saint Jean de Luz came by the thousands. They arrived in large cohesive and well-armed units but also in small groups and even as individuals. They were army and air force personnel, some well equipped and some only with personal arms. The training base of the Polish Armoured Brigade, the "Black Brigade", was able to facilitate the evacuation of some infantry units but it was a chaotic situation. It is a tribute to the organizing ability of Polish officers who were able to bring order and even a semblance of a chain of command into this inchoate group. The Poles even had to set up a defense perimeter since the Germans were deemed to be close. In fact the Germans were nowhere near, and if anything the danger came from some sycophantic and obsequious French officials and police. Isolated local civilian authorities and occasionally soldiers hoping to prove their allegiance to the conditions of the surrender made futile attempts to stop and arrest small retreating Polish columns. But the Poles were armed and all such attempts came to naught.

The evacuating ships were too big to enter the small fishing port and troops had to be ferried out by fishing boats and other small ancillary vessels. Nevertheless, the Royal Navy came through in its efficient and low-key traditional manner. It also meant that much equipment, trucks, cars, artillery had to be abandoned. On June 25 1940 the last Polish unit, the 2nd Tank Battalion of the 10th Motorized Brigade and last officer – General Burhardt Bukacki – were embarked. This was part of Operation Dynamo in which two Polish liners, Sobieski and Batory, also participated.

The prevailing attitude of the majority of the French to the Poles evacuating was a mixture of anger, guilt, shame, passivity and perplexity and was reflected in an unfriendly posture. There is a story from that time, most likely apocryphal. A Polish military column arriving in a small provincial French town on the way to French Atlantic ports asked for petrol. The answer was that there was no petrol available. The young Polish officer in command of the ad hoc unit in a sad and resigned tone told the town mayor that his community was about to pass into history. The Poles were going to set up a defence perimeter and fight to the last. Petrol was quickly found and the Poles reached the safety of the embarkation ports. I would like to share another side of the French. As civilians my mother and I were refused boarding on the SS Arandora Star since only military were being embarked and once again, for the third time in that war, we said goodbye to my father. Ultimately we made our way through Portugal to rejoin my father in England in July 1941.

The total number of Poles evacuated to the United Kingdom was well over 19,000, but it represented a mere 23% of the Polish military in France. Of this number, over five thousand were transported aboard Polish ships. In the French disaster, the Poles lost most of their ground troops that had been so assiduously and painfully formed. However, the majority of the Polish air force personnel were successfully evacuated to the United Kingdom.

Two different fates awaited the two independent Polish brigades. The Podhalanska brigade, after a credible performance at Narvik, was shipped back to the United Kingdom and had a stopover at Glasgow. It was then shipped to French Brittany where there was hope of forming a final stand. Only three thousand men of the brigade were evacuated from Brest to the United Kingdom. A different fortune awaited the Carpathian Brigade in French Syria. The local French commanders assumed that all the Poles would go along with the French in laying down arms. Once the French realized that the Poles were not going to join them and intended to move to British-controlled Palestine, they demanded that if the Poles were to leave for British Palestine, they had to leave disarmed. The Poles refused, and a fully armed, and highly motivated Polish Brigade joined the British.

There was one other seminal instruction sent to occupied Poland. General Sosnkowski appointed General Rowecki the overall general commanding of the Polish Underground. The declaration of war by Italy against the British made land routes for couriers close to impossible and the chain of command had to be stream-lined. It also made the Polish need for air communication vital.

In July 1940 Colonel Emil (Nile) Fieldorf was dispatched to Poland from the United Kingdom. His fifty-one day journey documents the difficulties faced by Polish couriers. First a flight to Egypt, then under the assumed name of Nile, travel to Istanbul, Bucharest and then to Budapest, which was a major transit point for communications with occupied Poland. Then crossing the Carpathians to Poland. He was involved in fighting the Germans, arrested by the encroaching Soviets in 1944, eventually released, went back to back to Poland, and was again arrested by the Polish Communists, before being executed ! He was one of the thousands of Polish patriots who suffered such a fate, but in this case his fate was well documented.

4

The Polish Government and Military evacuate to Great Britain

Polish Government and Military evacuate to Great Britain – Crisis in the Polish Government over Sikorski initiatives to the Soviet Union – British–Polish Military Agreement of August 1940 – Sikorski's Strategy in 1940 – Anglo-Polish Radio Wireless Research and Manufacturing – Period of Consolidation – Polish Army reformed in Scotland – Battle of Britain – More Polish Squadrons formed – Great Britain survives the Battle of Britain – Britain faces the threat of U-Boats – Polish Forces in Scotland gel into I Corps – Poland on the Seas – Polish Cultural Institutions Formed in the United Kingdom.

The French capitulation in June 1940 was a military disaster for the Poles who lost most of their recently recreated ground forces. But in a paradox, the French debacle was a psychological uplift for the Poles, particularly the officer corps, who had for nine months lived under a barrage of vocal intense criticism for their alleged incompetence in September 1939. This criticism came not just from French sources, which was discreet, albeit blunt, but from some Polish politicians in the coalition government who were vocal and very public. This criticism, directed at their own (i.e. Polish) military, but never at the French allies who failed to meet their treaty obligation, was tacitly condoned by General Sikorski. It led to an alienation of the Commander-in-Chief from many of his own senior military cadre.

The Poles had now all witnessed a proud and self confident, even arrogant, French army humiliated; and saw the British army debunking at Dunkirk and abandoning its equipment. The Royal Air Force squadrons had been decimated and were flying home because their bases had been overrun by advancing German units all too reminiscent of the Polish situation in September, except the Poles could only fly to Romania.

CONTINUED EVACUATIONS

Thousands of Polish military stranded in France continued to trickle to the south of France. Polish consulates, which continued to function in Vichy France until October 1940 when the Germans forced the French to close them, did their best to assist the young men (and women) to leave for British controlled territories. British consulates also assisted in every way possible.

At one point the Poles organized a smuggling ring on French ships but these only carried small groups from south French ports to French North Africa. Since this was a smuggling operation, with hired French hired crews, it was not impervious to leakage and even blackmail. Clearly more needed to be done. Finally the Polish navy mounted an operation out of Gibraltar which used small Spanish fishing boats that picked up parties of men at various small fishing harbors or even beaches in the south of France, and carried them to Gibraltar, thence to the United Kingdom. Over three thousand men, mostly Poles, termed 'evaders' by the British, were evacuated. Goebbels disparagingly called them "Sikorski's tourists", a term which became an accolade.[1]

The Allied forces at this time in the United Kingdom, in addition to the hundreds of thousands British, minus heavy equipment since it had been abandoned in Dunkirk, consisted of Canadians, and minimal forces from countries that were occupied by the Germans, whose governments had also found a home in exile in London. The Norwegians had a considerable merchant fleet, while the Dutch had Asian colonies. The Free French had a symbolic presence but little else since the majority of their military chose to go back to Vichy France. The Polish military presence in the United Kingdom in July 1940 amounted to 27,700 of which eight thousand were air and three thousand naval personnel. It was not just the largest of any of the allied forces but larger than all of the others together.

After their evacuation from France, Polish ground troops were based in Scotland, where eventually they formed the Polish First Corps.

June 1940 began a new chapter for Polish policies and the Polish military. The British government of Chamberlain faced a major crisis and Churchill, not everybody's favorite, became the Prime Minister of a British coalition government. He

---

1   Brooks Richards, *Secret Flotillas. Clandestine Sea Lines to France and French North Africa, 1940–1944*, HMSO, London, 1996, pp.347–551. This is the least known Polish naval operation, yet, the Poles and British had a monopoly of maritime clandestine operations in the Mediterranean till about 1943.

warmly welcomed the Poles in Britain, minuting his staff, "in principle we are to make the most of the Poles. They should be assembled, made comfortable, and re-equipped as soon as possible."[2]

A very euphoric relationship ensued between the Poles and the British. Given all that the British were confronting, on land, sea, air and in North Africa, the amount of time that was devoted to the Polish ally is indeed not merely surprising but even astonishing. But like many a honeymoon, the relationship began to wear thin after the Soviets became a prized and essential ally in the war against Germany. But that was later.

It is probably hard to imagine and grasp the turmoil of those days. For about six weeks there was a seeming lull in actual fighting, except for the British attack on the French fleet, but there were major diplomatic initiatives for some form of a compromise peace. A number of British politicians welcomed such a possibility and a second British crisis was barely averted. When Churchill was assuring the Polish Prime Minister of his absolute commitment to fight to the end, there were some in the corridors of British powers who were exploring other options. Mr. Richard Austen (Rab) Butler, representing the Foreign Office, and the Minster of State, Lord Halifax, met with the Swedish Minister in London and is alleged to have said that, "no opportunity would be neglected for concluding a compromise peace" and that "diehards would not be allowed to stand in the way of negotiations".[3] Churchill managed to fend off the minority in the House of Commons that wished to replace him with Lord Halifax and boldly went on a military and diplomatic attack. The most dramatic and resounding was his order to attack the French fleet at Mers-el-Kébir in the Vichy-controlled port of Algeria. While only partially successful and not involving the Polish Government or its military, it had an indirect effect on the Poles, namely it significantly marginalized the functioning of many Polish agencies in Vichy France.[4] Churchill's other diplomatic efforts went to the United States. Churchill needed American arms and escort destroyers, and blackmailed the United States with a threat that were he not to survive politically, the British fleet might no longer be the bulwark between Germany and the States. Old, most likely nearly useless, American destroyers were traded for extended leases of British naval bases in the Caribbean and Bermuda.

He continued to attempt to inveigle the Turks to the British side and also attempted to convince Stalin that his country was at risk from the Germans and should be less neutral. This began to have indirect bearing on the Poles.

Also following the Dunkirk evacuation of British troops, Churchill created the Special Operations Executive, which began to collaborate with the Polish VI Bureau,

---

2   TNA PREM 712/803781
3   Llewellyn Woodward, *British Foreign Policy in the Second World War, Volume I*, HMSO, London, p.204; John Lukacs, The Duel, Ticknor & Fields, NY, 1991, pp.131–133.
4   Colin Smith, *England's Last War Against France. Fighting Vichy 1940–1942*, Weidenfeld & Nicolson, London, 2009.

in contrast to the earlier lack of British interest in such clandestine activities. But at this point the die was cast and compromise peace was <u>not</u> on Churchill's agenda.

POLISH GOVERNMENTAL CRISIS

Sikorski was less than a passive player in the Soviet inducements and already committed to some form of understanding with the Soviets. This led to a major Polish government crisis.

The Polish chaos during the last days of the French Campaign had stretched Polish nerves. Sikorski was bitterly condemned by his concurrence to the two Polish infantry divisions being stripped of their anti-tank guns and sent into battle helter-skelter. This led to the resignation of chief of staff, Colonel Aleksander Kędzior. Sikorski's final orders, "stay loyal to the French allies", were derided as incomprehensible lack of reality. The loss of the Polish gold and the less than adroit diplomatic attempts by Sikorski to establish relations with the Soviets were resented. There was a reaction to Sikorski and his immediate political, mostly civilian, associates, following the French debacle who had been so vitriolic and unstinting in their criticism of all before 1940. These men had very few friends! Senior officers who had been harassed by a number of coalition cabinet politicians for their alleged incompetence in 1939

Paddington Station, London, June 1940. His Royal Highness King George VI greets the President of Poland, Władysław Raczkiewicz, on his arrival in London in June 1940 from France. (Author's collection)

pointed out the reality of the French debacle and the chaotic evacuation of the Poles from France and Sikorski's absence for a number of days, as he was visiting French front lines, out of any touch, while urging a grand French counter-attack.

The problem of the June 1940 Polish-British air agreement once again came to the forefront. A haste to accomplish worthwhile political goal and coupled with a total lack of English led to an abysmal agreement. The Polish side argued pathetically that it was merely "a temporary agreement" but the British side were understand-ably perplexed and irritated, since nothing alluded to it as "temporary". The Polish air attaché in London warned of what was about to be given away but he was then criticized for the result.

Lower level officers, probably not quite tuned to the high level political issues, were very aware that Sikorski endorsed the agreement to require Polish airmen transferred to the UK in early 1940 to take an oath of allegiance to the King. This was a major issue, which confronted some directly, but all in principle, between the obligation to obey orders, and their innate objection to undertaking an obligation to a foreign state.

Regarding the Soviet initiative, Sikorski, already in London before the rest of the Polish Government arrived, was on his way to meet Churchill, and impulsively accepted an English language draft written for him by the journalist P. Litauer. This English language memorandum to Lord Halifax was in turn to be conveyed though the British ambassador in Moscow to Stalin. It called for a for a detente in Polish-Soviet relations, it was to allow the formation of a Polish Army in the Soviet Union and expressed Sikorski's willingness to cede Polish territories to the Soviets.

Sikorski, in a hurry and not knowing English, asked the Polish ambassador, Edward Raczyński, to read it and translate it. Raczyński was horrified and unaware that the Polish Cabinet had not authorized such an overture. Raczyński urged that such a memorandum could not be hurriedly improved and that no memorandum should be delivered. Sikorski followed this advice but after modifying the most objectionable points, still sent it to Lord Halifax without consulting his foreign minister.

This was a major and critical constitutional issue. In Paris in 1939 Sikorski had demanded that the Polish President refrain from promulgating decrees or making appointments without consulting the Prime Minister, i.e. Sikorski. He was now undertaking foreign policy initiatives without consulting the President or even his coalition Cabinet.

Sikorski went so far as to justify his action by sending a preposterous telegram to the Polish Foreign Minister aboard the HMS *Arethusa* in which he stated that since the minister had <u>voluntarily</u> ensconced himself and was unavailable, important diplomatic actions needed to be taken in London. In fact, wireless contact existed between the British warship and London, and the Polish President sent a telegram to His Royal Highness King George VI through the Polish embassy in London. Sikorski intercepted the telegram and advised the President that it was moot and did not need to be delivered.

At this very time the British cruiser HMS *Arethusa* was in the Gironde Estuary, near Bordeaux, and after boarding the Polish President and Foreign Minister, it stayed, being exposed to aggressive Luftwaffe attacks, waiting for members of the British embassy to be boarded. There was nothing voluntary on the part of the Polish party about staying aboard.

While Sikorski was already in London, rumors were rife about peace feelers through Sweden to the British Foreign Office.[5] This impossible situation reached a crisis point. Raczyński describes a breakfast at the Dorchester, hosted by Major Victor Cazalet, the official British liaison officer to Sikorski.[6] Other guests included General Sikorski, Lord Halifax, and Jozef Hieronim Rettinger. Lord Halifax uttered a generality, described by Raczynski, as "pium desiderium", for Poles in the United Kingdom to avoid internecine conflicts. This British advice agitated Sikorski since he was already aware of the British ambassador, Kennard's suggestion, that the positions of Commander-in-Chief and Prime Minister be assigned to different individuals.

That same day the Polish President dismissed General Sikorski from his post of Prime Minister and appointed August Zaleski to the post.[7] The British Government was immediately alerted and went into crisis management, which documents the obvious dependence of the Poles on the British Government and also British concern about their Polish ally staying pristinely democratic but flexible to British policies.

There were behind the scenes discussions in the British Foreign Office which seventy years later make for fascinating reading of how an established and sophisticated diplomacy works, but also highlight the fact that the British were in a situation of making a decision of which of the Polish political factions most suited their own long term policies. The British ambassador to the Polish Government, Sir Howard Kennard, visited the President and other officials met with Sikorski to allay the crisis. The following is a succinct summary of the many issues which surfaced.

The President rescinded his dismissal most likely as a result of both the British intervention and the diplomatic efforts of Sikorski's rival, General Sosnkowski, who opined that the British would go with Sikorski and that a situation could arise where two groups in the United Kingdom vied for legitimacy, but only one – Sikorski – had the backing of the British. [8]

It is far from clear who was most persuasive. Sosnkowski was strongly criticized by many Polish officers for lacking spine and not seeing the crisis through. A few

---

5   TNA ADM 53/111412.
6   Robert Rhodes James, *Victor Cazalet. A Portrait*, Hamish Hamilton, London, 1976.
7   Maria Pestkowska, *Za Kulisami Rządu Polskiego na Emigracji*, [Behind the Scenes of the Polish Government in Exile], Warsaw, 2000, pp.46–68.
8   A nearly analogous situation developed in late 1944, with the British supporting Mikołajczyk, while the Polish Government began to languish in limbo.

weeks after the crisis the British Government was also advised by Major Perkins of M.I.R. (later head of the Polish Section of Special Operations Executive –or SOE) that Sikorski's reception in Scotland by the Polish land forces was "distinctly frigid" and that most officers were more attached to General Sosnkowski.

After the crisis cooled, the British archives also note that "Sikorski may now feel that he has the backing of the Prime Minister (i.e. Churchill) and Cazalet, and can do what he likes. I understand that he told his cabinet that the Secretary of State (Halifax) insisted he remain Prime Minister." If true, he was no longer a Polish Prime Minister but Churchill's man.

Sikorski's patriotism cannot be impeached but the British Foreign Office archives describe him as having a colossal vanity, and that he should be discreetly advised that he is "not the only pebble on the beach". But, what was important to British policies was that Sikorski was the Polish pebble that was most useful to the British sling at that point of time. The British minutes suggest that in the circumstances the British should work to strengthen the Polish President, who has been hurt.

On the issue which led to the crisis, namely a "Polish Legion" in the Soviet Union, the following minutes by J. Roberts on his meeting with Professor Namier at the suggestion of R. Butler are seminal.

"One of the main weapons used against General Sikorski (i.e. by the Polish President and Foreign Minister) has been his advocacy of better relations with USSR. As instanced by his readiness to consider the proposal for the formation of a Polish legion in Soviet occupied Poland. Professor Namier suggested that it was in the interests of HMG to encourage these ideas of General Sikorski's, since Poland could only exist in the long run assured of either German or Russian support and it was clearly much safer for us [i.e. the UK] if she turned to Russia, rather than to Germany. If such a move encourages the Germans to start German legions, then this could hardly be concealed from the Russians and would also react favorably on British interests."[9]

Roberts comments that "there are serious objections to encouraging the idea of the Polish Legion, although I can see little objection to discreet encouragement of the idea of closer Polish-Russian relations if this is possible."

It would seem in retrospect that Sikorski would have defied his Constitutional President, causing a horrible crisis. The internal Polish governmental crisis was relevant to the whole question of Polish policy and military strategy and absorbed the British Foreign Office. Their archives are a fascinating picture of the many political forces that determined the immediate Polish policy then and in later years.[10]

---

9   TNA FO 371 24474/C7649.
10   TNA FO 371 24474/C/7629/252/55,FO 371 enclosure C. C/7639/262; FO 371 24474/C/7639.

POLISH –BRITISH MILITARY AGREEMENT

As the Polish military were arriving in their thousands on British soil – the Poles called it the Island of Last Refuge – the major legal issue was their status, considering the unwritten British Constitution. Some of this was discreetly finessed by the British, as the arriving army cadres were disarmed and sent to camps in Scotland. Being disarmed they were not considered an armed foreign force on British soil. One American archive refers to them as asylum seekers. The Air Force personnel were a different matter altogether. The British Air Ministry had already recognized that their initial negative attitude to Polish flying personnel was unfounded. In May 1940 their new assessment was reflected in the following memorandum, which addressed the feeling of impatience amongst Polish air personnel being trained on the Fairey Battle light bomber, in the United Kingdom.

> ... at this crucial moment find themselves limited to such duties as foot drill, guarding their station, lectures, etc. This must rankle much more since their compatriots in France are flying operationally and the French express greatest admiration for their efficiency, usefulness and enthusiasm.[11]

This was shortly followed by a June 4 1940 memorandum:

> In view of the present shortage of fighter pilots, D of I has suggested that we should make use of the experienced Polish flying personnel which is now in this country ...

> There are upwards of 70 experienced Polish fighter pilots available. The Poles are apparently willing to agree that these pilots should be taken over by us and used in British fighter squadrons. I think it would be very foolish not to accept this offer".[12]

These experienced pilots were the personnel transferred to man the two light bomber squadrons in early 1940 and had been enrolled in the RAFVR. But the British request and Polish acquiescence was handled expeditiously and by the end of the Battle of Britain nearly a hundred Polish pilots had been inserted in RAF fighter squadrons.

The Air Ministry not unreasonably assumed that the Polish air cadre arriving in June from France, called the French Poles, would also be enrolled in the RAFVR and buttress the sorely tried Fighter Command, and follow the precedent of taking an oath of allegiance to the King. However, the Air Ministry was stunned because the

---

11   TNA AIR 2/4213.
12   TNA AIR 20/1823.

Fairey Battles of Polish 300 Bomber Squadron in the UK, summer of 1940. These were the planes negotiated in the August 1939 military credit granted to Poland by the United Kingdom but never delivered. (PISM)

Polish Air Force General Officer Commanding, Józef Zając, promulgated orders that no further Polish enrollment in the RAFVR was to take place.

The old issue of the British Constitution had to be confronted and the expeditious manner in which the House of Commons accomplished this seemingly great impediment would seem to reflect both a need for the Polish alliance at this critical moment in British affairs, but also confirm that it had been a blatant excuse earlier when dealing with the negotiations on the transfer of the Polish Air Force.

In August 1940 the Poles signed a military treaty with the British. This was the bedrock of all wartime Polish-British military collaboration and addressed a number of major issues – the financing of the Polish Forces by credits to the Polish Government based on need and escrow of the evacuated Polish gold; all salaries and all military equipment used by the Poles was to be debited from the Polish credits. This included the cost of planes, tanks, trucks, heat, gasoline, etc.[13] Polish military law applied in the United Kingdom and its territories for the Polish Army and Polish Navy. One point which became a source of bitter feeling many years later, was that it provided for the Polish Forces being centralized at the request of the Polish Commander-in-Chief.

The Polish Air Force issues were only partially settled in August 1940. The British Air Ministry acknowledged that the Polish Air Force was as much part of the sovereign Polish Armed Forces as the Navy or Army and thus a force of an independent and sovereign state. Polish air personnel were no longer enrolled in the RAFVR,

---

13   TNA T 160/1412.

London, August 1940. The signing of the Polish-British Military Agreement on August 5 1940 in London. From left to right: Lord Halifax, Edward Raczyński, General Sikorski, Prime Minister Churchill, August Zaleski, Clement Attlee. Standing behind Churchill is Anthony Eden. (PISM)

and those in it released back to the Polish Air Force. The oath of loyalty to the King was now a moot issue. But the British Air Chief, Sir Cyril Newall, managed to keep a hand on the Poles and in his cordial memo to the Polish Headquarters, wrote "we would not differentiate the position of the Polish Air Force from that of the Polish Army and Navy, except in so far as operational considerations make a very close liaison with the Royal Air Force essential".[14] From a purely functional point of view this was a justified and logical argument. If the Poles in 1940 had the same resources as the Americans later in the war in the UK with their logistics, then possibly a more autonomous structure might have been argued.

This signing ceremony was given great attention by the British who were represented by Winston Churchill, Clement Attlee, Lord Halifax, Anthony Eden, Sir Kingsley Wood. The Polish side was represented by General Władysław Sikorski, August Zaleski and Count Edward Raczyński. It took place in the Cabinet room at 10 Downing Street.[15]

---

14   TNA AIR 8/295.
15   TNA WO32/2339.

Seventy years later some of these events are probably seen as so minor as to be historically irrelevant. Yet they illustrate the varied motives of both parties and also confirm the good will and intent to bond the alliance at least at the time.

In the middle of the ensuing German Blitz and genuine concern that there could be a German invasion, the British went out of their way to address Polish concerns. The Polish delegate for direct talks with the British on all issues of Polish military was now General Kazimierz Sosnkowski, who continued to be the Minister for Home Affairs, and also, to the discomfort of many politicians in the Polish coalition government, the designated successor of the Polish President. The major Polish contribution to the Allied cause was its outstanding intelligence services on the continent of Europe. The Anglo-Polish Historical Committee published a comprehensive account of this co-operation.[16]

SIKORSKI'S STRATEGY IN 1940

Sikorski now had the following specific military goals.

- Creating a British-based but autonomous radio communication system.
- Recruiting and training in parachute and subversive activities couriers for Poland. The couriers were to be selected on the basis of not merely patriotic motivation, but also on specific skills that were needed by the Underground.
- The creation of a Polish-controlled special duties squadron able to reach occupied Poland with supplies and couriers.
- Finally Sikorski made it his political and military goal to integrate the Polish Underground or Home Army with the strategy of the Western Allies.
- The Armed Forces in the West had the function of serving a reserve and resource for the Home Army, as well as documenting to the world Poland's determination to fight alongside the Allies.

BRITISH SPECIAL OPERATIONS EXECUTIVE AND THE POLISH VI BUREAU

The ground work for this was the memorial submitted by Major Maciej Kalenkiewicz to his Polish superiors when still in France. Kalenkiewicz and his good friend from

---

16   *Intelligence Co-operation between Poland and Great Britain during World War II - The Report of the Anglo-Polish Historical Committee*, Anglo-Polish Historical Committee, Tessa Stirling, Daria Nalecz, Tadeusz Dubicki, eds. Volume 1, Vallentine Mitchell, London, 2005; *Polsko-Brytyjska współpraca wywiadowcza podczas II wojny Światowej. Wybór Dokumentów* [Intelligence Co-Operation between Poland and Great Britain during World War II, Vol. II – Documents], Naczelna Dyrekcja Archiwów Panstwowych, Warsaw, 2005.

cadet school, who was a parachute instructor, wrote a most ambitious plan to raise an uprising in Poland and support it by air. Kalenkiewicz was convinced that clandestine activity was not just possible but realistic. His argument was the ten weeks he had spent in the last Polish fighting unit, the famous Hubal regiment in the Holy Cross Mountains, with which fought the Germans until formally ordered by the Polish command to desist since it was bringing horrible reprisals on the local villagers.

The most senior officer to be inserted into Poland was General Tadeusz Kossakowski, an engineer whose task was to develop underground arms production. General Kossakowski's engineering group in Scotland developed the Polish land mine detector, which contributed to the British victory at El Alamein.

Sikorski was confronted by the reality that his ambition to play a significant role in the Allied coalition was limited by insufficient manpower. Hence his gauche attempts to unshackle Poles in the Soviet Union, quite unaware that by July 1940 horrendous murders of Polish officers had already taken place in Russia, only to be brought to the light of day in April 1943. He also began to make plans for recruiting Polish emigrants in Canada but the response was minimal and barely five hundred Poles volunteered. The Canadian Government was also minimally supportive.

While the Poles were settling in the United Kingdom, and implementing a variety of short and long term plans, the British, spurred by Churchill, created the Special Operations Executive with the purpose of setting Europe ablaze.

The Polish Military Headquarters formed VI Bureau for liaison with occupied Poland and this staff developed a cordial relationship with the British Special Operations Executive, (SOE).[17]

British SOE officers also worked up a plan to spark and support an insurrection in Poland. The British plan was called, "Characteristics of a Modern Insurrectional Movement, Description of a Descent Region and of its work during the Descent".[18]

ANGLO-POLISH RADIO WIRELESS RESEARCH AND MANUFACTURING

Sikorski's energy seemed endless and he managed to negotiate a British-based but autonomous radio communication system for communication with the Polish Home Army. This was supported through the formation of the Anglo-Polish Radio Wireless Research and Manufacturing Company in Stanmore, which made radios that were

17 Józef Garliński, *Poland, SOE and the Allies*, George Allen and Unwin, London, 1969. For a general history see David Stafford, *Britain and European Resistance, 1940–1945. A Survey of the Special Operations Executive with Documents*, University of Toronto Press, Toronto, 1980. See also E.D.R. Harrison, "The British Special Operations Executive and Poland", *The Historical Journal*, 43, 4, 2000, pp.1071–1091.
18 TNA HS4155.

ultimately air-dropped to Poland. In addition the Poles were the only exile military that was tacitly allowed to use its own ciphers.[19]

Congruent with his efforts at forming a Polish-controlled special duties squadron for supply flights to Poland, Sikorski also began to recruit a highly motivated cadre of mostly military men for parachuting into Poland. These men, though there were a few women as well, were to provide technical and skilled knowledge to the AK in areas of sabotage, intelligence-gathering and manufacturing local small arms.

Sikorski now conceptualized a strategy to build up the Polish Clandestine [Secret] Army, now called the Home Army. To accomplish this he had to begin intense negotiations with the British to form a special dedicated air unit for carrying supplies to occupied Poland. This had begun in early in 1940 when still in France but the British had cold-shouldered the initiative.

On October 10 1940 General Sikorski issued orders and promulgated a policy of maximizing all Polish resources in the West to foster the Home Army in its ability to stage an uprising. It should be noted that in his orders to the Minister for Home Affairs – Sosnkowski- and the Polish Air Force Inspector – General Ujejski – Sikorski stated that the <u>first priority for Polish troops was the defense of the United Kingdom</u>, but the Uprising needed to be planned and coordinated with an Allied offensive at some future date. Sikorski outlined his long-term policy as requiring the training and preparation of maximum number of land units for air transport to Poland. Furthermore it mandated planning for Polish air units to Poland to support such an uprising.

On November 5 1940 Sikorski specifically ordered the Polish Air Force Inspectorate to prepare plans for moving up to ten infantry battalions by air to Poland. Sikorski's outline was at this stage of the war quite unrealistic but imaginative, and he even wanted to plan the use of an autogiro.[20]

These Polish initiatives were complemented by the request to the British to help with the formation of a parachute unit, and also to have British bases train Polish couriers. Polish staff and SOE both worked up a plan for fomenting an uprising in occupied Poland. The first fruit of this collaboration was the seconding of a small select number of Polish officers to the British training base at Inverlochy for specific training in sabotage and intelligence gathering.[21] The RAF authority opened the parachute training base at Ringway to Poles, for training couriers for Poland and, very shortly, men for a potential parachute unit.

This RAF base had a number of Polish parachute instructors, all experienced professionals trained in Poland, the predominant ones being Jan Górski and Maciej Kalenkiewicz, who was parachuted to Poland in 1941.[22]

---

19 Zbigniew Siemaszko, *Łaczność i Polityka*, Polish Cultural Foundation, London, 1992.
20 Studium Polski Podziemnej, *Armia Krajowa w Dokumentach, 1939–1945*, Tom I, Gryf Printers, London, 1970.
21 TNA HS4/185 23533.
22 After the Polish Underground forces captured Wilno in 1944, the Poles were surrounded and taken

The specific answer to the Commander-in-Chief's order to the Polish Air Force to prepare plans was the long document, "Plan Użycia i Organizacji Lotnictwa oraz Wojsk Desantowych na Korzyść Kraju" [Plan for the use and organization of Air Force and Airborne Forces on behalf of the Homeland].[23] This was the military goal, a strong and well-armed Polish Underground Army, supported by a timely insertion of the Polish Parachute Brigade to establish a centralized sovereign authority and reinforced by Polish tactical squadrons from the West. William MacKenzie, the eminent historian of the British Special Operations Executive, wrote that the Polish plan made in London by the military staff was "grandiose, but was not absurd.[24]

But even as the staff plans were being made and discussed with the British the war went on. The small Polish Navy continued to play its part in the Battle of the Atlantic. The Polish land forces stationed in Scotland began to be re-equipped and became responsible for the defense of the Eastern Shore north of Edinburgh. This was the First Polish Corps and with time it formed the 1st Polish Armoured Division, which fought in the Battle of Falaise and contributed to the successful liberation of North-West France.

THE BATTLE OF BRITAIN

The Polish Air Force was the crown jewel of the Polish Armed Forces in the West. Being based in the United Kingdom its exploits attracted positive and immediate mass media attention. As noted earlier about seventy Polish pilots already in the United Kingdom in July 1940 and reasonably proficient in English, were embedded into decimated RAF squadrons.

A perfect and notable example of this group was Janusz Zurakowski, who had been already in Poland as an instructor in the Special Fighter Training Unit of the Advanced Flying School, but in 1940 was sent to the United Kingdom from France by the Polish Air Force Command. He wrote that knowing French he was sent to Britain, and being a fighter pilot he was sent to fly bomber planes. He was one of the pilots seconded to the RAF and took part in the Battle of Britain with RAF 234 Squadron. When withdrawn from the air battle that RAF unit had lost fifteen of its original twenty-two pilots.[25] Polish pilots who had fought in France and were in current parlance English-language challenged, were formed into two all-Polish squadrons. These were the 302 Poznański and the fabled 303 Kościuszko. The air victories of the Poles astounded the public and surprised the RAF authorities. Particularly effective was the fact that this battle took place over London and the southern counties, and millions of Britons followed the battle

---

prisoner by the Soviets. Kalenkiewicz assumed command of the remnants but lost his life shortly thereafter.

23   PISM AV II/1a.
24   *The Secret History of SOE. The Special Operations Executive 1940–1945*, St. Ermin's Press, London, 2000.
25   Bill Zuk, Janusz Zurakowski, *Legend in the Skies*, Crecy Publishing, Manchester, 2007.

RAF Northolt, September 1940. During the height of the Battle of Britain, King George VI visited the Polish 303 Kosciuszko Squadron at Northolt. During the visit, the squadron was scrambled. The pilot on the King's right is Captain Witold Urbanowicz, the squadron commander and a successful pilot and ace. (PISM)

during the day, scanning the skies for the contrails of the enemy and of the attacking fighters. Then in the evening they listened to the BBC and in the morning read about what they had seen. One of the messages received by the 303 was in fact from the BBC:

> The BBC sends warm greeting to the famous 303 Polish Squadron with lively congratulations upon its magnificent record and all the best wishes for the future. You use the air for your gallant exploits and we for telling the world of them. F.W. Ogilvie, Director-General Broadcasting House. London, 20th September 1940.

The 303 Squadron has been acknowledged as the most successful fighter squadron in the Battle of Britain and was visited by His Majesty, King George VI, and many other prominent personalities.

The Polish Air Force fighter squadrons made a name for themselves in the Battle of Britain and more than anything else being done, said or written by the Poles in the United Kingdom contributed to a positive perception of the Polish Ally.[26]

---

26 Robert Gretzyngier in *Poles in Defence of Britain. A Day-by-Day Chronology of Polish Day and Night Fighter Pilot Operations: July 1940-June 1941*, Grub Street, London, 2001.

The Polish Air Force grew in size and throughout the war its ten fighter squadrons accounted for about ten percent of RAF Home Fighter Command. In addition to the fighter squadrons the Polish Air Force had four bomber squadrons.

MORE POLISH SQUADRONS FORMED

As originally intended in the early negotiations with the British, the Polish Air Force in the United Kingdom was only to consist of two bomber squadrons, 300 and 301. The influx of Polish personnel in June 1940 allowed for two more to be formed with complete ground crews. These were the 304 and 305 and all four were quickly equipped with the Vickers Wellington twin-engined medium bomber. To support the Polish bomber squadrons the 18 Operational Training Unit (OTU) at RAF Bramcote, Nuneaton near Coventry, was formed, making this nearly an all-Polish base. Finally, the Poles formed an army co-operation squadron on Lysanders, 309, which was based in Scotland and by agreement was to work with the Polish Army's First Corps.[27] Britain survived the Luftwaffe day attacks and the Battle of Britain became the first struggle which the Germans did not win. The Royal Air Force maintained air superiority over the Channel and southern England and that precluded a German invasion. Many in the United Kingdom breathed a sigh of relief, but the Germans unleashed a night-time Blitz on London that was devastating. The British air defenses and the Fighter Command was mostly equipped with Spitfires and Hurricanes, which were not designed or suitable for night operations. The Royal Air Force had a number of night fighter squadrons equipped with Boulton Paul Defiants. Lacking their own radar, the rather strange fighter with a gunner in the rear of the plane was directed to the enemy by ground radar, but then depended on plain eyesight for interception. One of the Polish fighter squadrons, 307 (City of Lwów) flew the Defiants, based on the Isle of Man, and its task was to defend the port of Liverpool.[28]

Alongside London, other British cities including Coventry, Liverpool and the South Coast also suffered severe destruction.

---

27   The most meticulous account of the Polish Air Force was researched and written by Jerzy Cynk - *The Polish Air Force at War, The Official History, 1939–1945*, 2 volumes (Schiffer, Atglen PA, 1998). See also the British official tribute, *Destiny Can Wait. The History of the Polish Air Force in Great Britain*, London, William Heinemann, 1949.

28   The only existing example of that plane is exhibited in the Royal Air Force Museum. It was on the establishment of the 307 City of Lwów Squadron. Later in the war, when the Polish Navy commissioned a British cruiser HMS *Dragon* and wished to rename it the ORP *Lwów*, the British strongly objected and the cruiser served under the Polish flag as ORP *Dragon*. This segue illustrates the Polish-British relations in early 1941 and how they changed in 1943. Lwów was a major bone of contention with the Soviets.

U-Boat threat to Britain

The British Government concern was directed towards maintaining sea links between the British Islands and its empire and North America. Churchill wrote

> The only thing that ever really frightened me during the war was the U-boat peril. Invasion I thought even before the air battle would fail. But now our lifeline, even across the broad oceans, an especially in the entrance to our islands, was endangered. I was even more anxious about his battle than I had been about the glorious air fight called the Battle of Britain.[29]

The ensuing Battle of the Atlantic was not being won, and Allied shipping was losing more vessels than were being built.[30]

Poland on the Seas

In 1939 the Polish Navy in addition to its three destroyers and two submarines had two naval training ships in the Western waters. During the Norwegian operations the Poles lost ORP *Grom* and the submarine ORP *Orzel*. The naval cadet academy [midshipmen school] continued in the United Kingdom, and volunteers from the

United Kingdom, 1940. His Majesty King George VI inspects the Polish naval cadets in the UK. (PISM)

---

29   Winston S. Churchill, *Their Finest Hour*, Cassell, London, 1949, p.529.
30   Winston S. Churchill, *The Grand Alliance*, Cassell, London, 1950, pp.98–137.

Polish merchant marine allowed for a modest expansion. Two fleet destroyers were commissioned by the Poles, ORP *Garland* and ORP *Piorun*. Also two small escort destroyers were manned by the Poles; ORP *Krakowiak* and ORP *Kujawiak*. Finally two small British U-Class submarines were taken over, ORP *Sokół* and ORP *Dźik*, and both were shortly moved to the Mediterranean where they performed brilliantly and became known as 'the Terrible Twins'.

1941 was still a year in which Polish exploits and contributions attracted British mass media attention and were publicized. The action of the Polish destroyer ORP *Piorun* in the pursuit of the German battleship *Bismarck* was given considerable renown.

The Polish Navy never had a place in Polish strategy, since the Baltic was just not accessible. But it was sovereign Polish territory and a great flag shower. Finally the Polish Government issued stamps which were used for mailing from naval and merchant ships.

The Commandant of the Polish Navy, Vice Admiral Jerzy Swirski, was awarded the honorary Knight Commander of the Order of the Bath, Military Division [KCB] for the excellence of his Command.

POLISH GROUND FORCES IN SCOTLAND

By the end of 1940 the Poles had organized their ground forces in Scotland into a cohesive force, well able to play part in the ever-decreasing eventuality of a German invasion of Scotland. As early as July 1940, a bare month after their arrival in the United Kingdom and even before the signing of the August Polish-British military agreement, a battalion of the Polish 1st Infantry Brigade began anti-invasion duties.

The Polish forces in Scotland were called the Polish First Corps. Basic training equipment had arrived, but the Poles were confronting the dilemma of their ambitions for a motorized two-division corps with the reality that they barely had sufficient men for one division. This led to protracted negotiations with the British War Office. The British were also changing their own concepts of the structure of an armored division gleaned from their experiences in France and North Africa.

There was one embarrassing problem which faced the Polish military staffs. There was a surplus of young officers. It was unacceptable for physically able, young men merely spending time learning English, given the fact that all of Britain was still mobilizing for a possible invasion. The Poles with British help targeted the problem with three initiatives. A contract was signed with the British War Office for well over 400 young Polish officers to be sent to officer West African regiments.[31] A small number were assigned to man British armored and anti-aircraft trains, which

---

31   Churchill, *The Grand Alliance*, Cassell, London, 1950, p.686.

Scotland, 1940. The Polish President, Władysław Raczkiewicz, shown visiting the Polish 309 Army Co-Operation Squadron based in Scotland, late 1940. (PISM)

Scotland, 1941. Winston Churchill and General Sikorski review a parade of Polish infantry. The typical Scottish weather is quite evident. (PISM)

Scotland, 1941. General Sikorski hosted the Royal couple on a visit to the Polish First Army Corps. Scotland, early 1941. (PISM)

patrolled areas of Britain that were deemed to be more at risk for invasion. Finally, the rest were formed into officer legion brigades, where the young officers, without losing their actual status as officers, functioned as rifle-carrying privates. One of these officer brigades became the core of the future Polish Parachute Brigade.

This surplus dissipated in 1941 when the Polish Army began to be formed in the Soviet Union, challenged by a shortage of "released" Polish officers. General Sikorski, who always dreamed of leading combat units, organized his field headquarters at Gask in Scotland. Undoubtedly, in a very acute emergency and crisis, General Sikorski could have taken over command of the Polish First Corps, but it eventually became a Scottish-based military camp to which Sikorski could escape from the Polish Headquarters at the Rubens Hotel in London.[32].

During this period, General Sikorski hosted His Majesty King George VI and Queen Elizabeth. This was the first time in British history that the King of Great Britain was officially guarded by foreign troops on British soil. General Sikorski also hosted the British Prime Minister, Winston Churchill and Mrs. Churchill. Sadly, this visit is not mentioned by Churchill in his memoirs. There were other prominent visitors, too many to be mentioned, although Hugh Dalton's visit deserves to be noted.

In addition to the vital issues of girding all resources for war and the feared German invasion of the British Isles, Poles also developed many cultural institutions. Not all were formed in the first year, but most were conceptualized in the first year of the Polish 'invasion'. The most prominent were the Polish Medical School in Edinburgh, Polish University College in London, Polish School of Architecture in Liverpool, Polish School of Law in Oxford, and of course numerous Polish military academies, hospitals, etc.[33]

---

32   The Rubens Hotel on Buckingham Palace Road has a small plaque commemorating the Polish World War II headquarters.

33   J. Rostowski, "Polish School of Medicine, University of Edinburgh", *British Medical Journal*, 28 May 1966, pp.1349–1351.In the two year of its existence, the Polish Medical School trained and graduated 228 physicians.

5

THE POLES BECOME ESTABLISHED IN BRITAIN

The Poles become established in Britain – Polish Planning initiatives – Parachute Brigade – Polish Air Force bomber squadrons bloodied – Sikorski and Churchill meet and discuss the military situation and Sikorski broaches the Balkan strategy and the possible move of Polish troops from the Middle East to Turkey – Sikorski receives a receptive response from Churchill regarding the change of mission for Polish Forces in Scotland – Both leaders discuss the planned Sikorski trip to Canada and USA and Polish hopes for recruiting men for the Polish Forcers – Carpathian Brigade nearly goes to Greece, but instead goes to Tobruk – 3 May 1941 and Churchill's Address to the Polish Nation – Sikorski visits the United States – Germany invades the Soviet Union – The Polish Government and Soviets establish diplomatic relations – A Polish army is formed on Soviet soil – The implementation of Sikorski's Soviet Strategy-Sikorski visits the Soviet Union – British greet rapprochement with satisfaction – British–Soviet Treaty, challenged in British Parliament – Sikorski hosts a conference of Senior Generals in London – Sikorski's Soviet Strategy, British manpower needs, Anders' reluctance to stay in the Soviet Union – Dieppe.

By mid-1941 Sikorski was to some extent on a diplomatic high. His initiatives were being positively and satisfactorily concluded with the various British Governmental agencies. In many ways the Poles had now been accepted by their British allies as valued partners and during the winter months 1940/1941 Sikorski had consolidated his policies

Sikorski, in the words of the Polish ambassador, Raczyński, had set up his own foreign relations apparatus consisting of Rettinger, Litauer and Cazalet.[1] This magnified the ever growing chasm between the foreign policy concepts of Sikorski, playing

---

1   Edward Raczyński, *In Allied London*, Weidenfeld and Nicolson, London, 1962, p.60.

the British card, and the President, his Foreign Minister and General Sosnkowski, still officially the Minister for Home Affairs. It may seem surprising that in a war time and foreign setting there were divisions in the Polish Government. But there were major divisions in the British Government about the conduct of the war as well. The 1942 British-Soviet negotiations on the form and text of their treaty were at times acrimonious but accepted as evidence of a democratic process. This understanding was never extended to the Poles.

SIKORSKI BEGINS TO MAKE PLANS FOR AIDING THE POLISH HOME ARMY

Sikorski worked hard and networked the British successfully in a number of areas. The two immediate issues were the formation of a parachute brigade for action in Poland, and the training of at least eleven battalions from their infantry units based in Scotland for airborne operations, besides training of couriers in parachute technique for drops to Poland.[2]

The British bent backward to be accommodating and on September 23 1941 a cadre of the Polish parachute brigade carried out an air drop simulating a drop in Poland, code named *Mielec*. Mielec, a town in south Poland, had a pre-war aircraft factory taken over by the Germans and possessed a good air base. The landing was supported by Polish 309 Squadron, flying Lysanders. While it remained a cadre unit till about 1942 when new volunteers came from the Middle East after evacuation from the Soviet Union, it was officially named an independent [i.e. free standing] brigade, and began to attract British War Office attention. Polish negotiations with the British War Office regarding a Polish Parachute Brigade were another element in the attempt to strengthen the Polish Home Army, as well as developing a military force which would be in a position to reinforce and build up legitimate military authority in the event that the Germans folded as they did in 1918. The agreement with the British was that it was strictly reserved for action in Poland to buttress the Polish Underground Army and exclusively under the command of the Polish Commander-in-Chief, unlike the other Polish forces in the West which were essentially placed under the overall command of the British in various theatres of operations.

Sikorski had also created III Section of his staff to co-ordinate all such activities with the Polish Underground Army, and appointed Colonel Andrzej Marecki as its director. As part of the Polish co-operation with the British SOE a detachment of volunteer Poles was dispatched to the British No.10 (Inter-Allied) Commando. This relatively small group of men were also parachute trained.[3]

---

2   TNA AIR 8/295/80530.
3   Nick van der Bijl, *No. 10 (Inter-Allied) Commando, 1942–1945*, Osprey, Oxford, 2006.

After training in Wales and Scotland the Polish commando company was the first of the Polish troops to enter combat in Italy in late 1943 and then evolved into a motorized Commando Battalion of the 2 Polish Corps during the Battle of Monte Cassino.

In may be pertinent at this point to outline the developing structure of the ground forces of the Polish Armed forces in the West. The Polish Army eventually had two corps. The first corps created in Scotland in 1940 was always called the "Pierwszy" or First Corps. The forces evacuated from the Soviet Union in 1942 formed the second corps, 2 Corps, which took part in the Italian Campaign and was always referred by the number 2; there was also a Ghost Corps to confuse German intelligence, analogous to the so-called American Army in South-East England in the Spring of 1944. For the ghost corps see the British discussion whether it should be abolished.[4] The British used to call 2 Corps the Polcorps.

POLISH AIR FORCE BOMBER SQUADRONS BLOODIED

While the British War Office was supportive of Polish efforts to create a parachute unit, the Air Ministry and their staff were very negative about Polish endeavors to form a dedicated unit for flights to Poland. The RAF and also many in the British War Office were inherently negative to all kinds of irregular war activities. Finally, and

Scotland, 1942. General Sikorski shown reviewing the Polish 1st Armoured Division in Scotland. May 1942. (PISM)

---

4   TNA WO 204/5608 - "seems a pity to lose an opportunity of encouraging the Germans to keep this
     formation in their Order of Battles lists".

Scotland, 1942. Elements of the Polish 1st Armoured Division. (PISM)

this was the most self-serving British reason, Polish crews were close to vital to keep up the early Bomber Command offensive.

In 1941 the Poles were faced by irreplaceable losses in the four Polish bomber squadrons. The attrition suffered by the Poles was similar to those of the RAF squadrons, but the Poles were scraping the bottom of their manpower resources. Sikorski became very concerned and intervened with a letter of July 22 1941 to Sir Charles Portal, Chief of the Royal Air Force Staff about the losses. He wrote that up to July 10, 1941 the four Polish bombers squadrons had lost 139 men, killed, wounded or shot down and taken prisoner. But that during that time only 120 new air crew had been trained.[5] He failed to point out that the pool of future trainees was nonexistent. Sir Charles responded by initiating a correspondence with the AOC of the Bomber Command, Sir Richard Peirse, whose answer illuminated the reluctance of the Royal Air Force to second Polish crews to a special duties unit. Peirse wrote that he was very much averse to taking the Polish Squadrons off operations or attempting to reduce their present effort:

> Apart from the fact that we want the operational effort we can get just now, it would have a depressing effect on the very keen Polish crews and in any case their new crews, have to graduate through shorter and more simple operations.

Finally, on October 12 1941 Peirse admitted that

5   TNA AIR 8/295 80530.

The casualties [i.e. Polish bomber crews] together with the failure of the squadrons to raise their strength – they have in fact wasted – is having a depressing effect". Portal ends this issue by writing that whatever is the correct assessment of the situation, "we all remember from last year the importance attached to the breakfast table, and I cannot really wonder at General Sikorski becoming uneasy.

The Air Ministry shortly notified General Sikorski that the number of sorties by Poles would be reduced. But still the Poles continued to fly and lose their men, for a total of well over one thousand killed. No wonder all bomber crews called themselves "dead men on leave". This attrition was about one-seventh of all Polish losses in the West, army, air and naval. At their height in early 1942 the four bomber squadrons had an approximate strength of 350 aircrew. A loss of one thousand was three times their establishment.

Their last effort came on May 30, 1942 when all four Polish squadrons and all of the Polish crews in training at the 18 OUT for a total of just over one hundred participated in the first one thousand plane raid on Germany.

Shortly afterwards one squadron was dissolved. One moved to Coastal Command and one to the Tactical Command flying the two-crew Mosquito.

Given the great commitment of Bomber Command in the Bomber Offensive, it is understandable that Polish plans for a special duties unit were constantly shelved. While the British War Office was supportive of Polish plans, the Air Ministry was anything but! The only RAF squadron that was dedicated to supplying clandestine forces and collaborating with the SOE was RAF 138. Initially flying the single-engined Lysander, which was admirably suitable for flights to France and landing on short grass strips, it could not fly to Poland even one way.

The RAF then decided to use the antediluvian and very slow Whitley, which could in winter months, when nights were long, make the round trip to Poland (approximately 2,000 miles). At the strong urging of the Poles, and thanks to the support from the British SOE a RAF mission was flown to Poland in February 1941 code named Adolphus. The mission was to drop the first batch of Polish couriers. The navigator became completely lost and the Polish couriers were dropped over Germany. The Poles managed to make their way to Poland, but all the supplies were lost and the Germans alerted to the new threat.

A real hot correspondence now ensued, with some officers in the RAF insisting that they could not operate unless they had radio location beacons – Rebecca-Eureka, in Poland. The Poles were stunned by this reasoning, and the British unawareness of the situation. If a radio location beacon could guide an Allied plane to a drop zone, it could also do the same for a German ground patrol or fighter plane. Furthermore, the system was too bulky to be moved in a clandestine and surreptitious manner.

It worked perfectly in situations such as major airborne parachute drops where the ground was captured and was not going to be abandoned within hours. It also worked well in carrier operations, where the receiving target, an aircraft carrier, was in safe and stable hands. And perhaps most crucial was that the decision as to which Polish receiving Committee would in fact be the recipient of the drop was made after the plane was off the ground, and a number of such receiving committees were on standby and had to be ready, usually defended by a covering force from random German patrols, not knowing where the plane would come. This would have required as many as ten such Eureka Rebecca location beacons. The Polish receiving commit-tees travelled by foot, occasionally by a horse cart or bicycle, to the most outlying meadows or fields, facts just not appreciated by the RAF senior officers.

The Poles insisted that their crew could find drop zones places in Poland, since they knew the topography of the country. Some of the debate between the two sides became very pernickety, the Royal Air Force insisting that a good RAF navigator was as good as a good Polish one, and a bad one as bad as a bad Pole. The Poles on the other hand argued that this was not a question of astral navigation, but of ability to read maps and recognize Polish ground topography at night which was second nature to pre-war trained Polish aircrews.[6] The Polish argument for a dedicated Polish unit, with its own mechanics, was refuted by saying that not all nights or months were suitable for operations to Poland, and thus such dedicated aircraft would not be well utilized, and the RAF could not afford such redundancy.

All parties were agreed that the Whitley was just not a suitable aircraft, being a discard from combat operations. In August 1941 General Sikorski wrote a three page memorandum to Sir Charles Portal citing his conversations in June 1941, with Prime Minister Churchill and the Minister for Air Sinclair. This is also the first time that the Poles made a formal request for American B–24 Liberators, as being the most suited for such long range operations. It is of some import that the messages between Sikorski and Portal in the Polish SOE files (HS4 specifically HS4/173) are only iden-tified by scrawled initials.

In October 1941 Sir Charles Portal advised Sikorski that three Halifax bombers would be seconded to RAF 138 Squadron and modified for carrying and dropping parachutists. This memo does not mention Liberators but clearly Halifaxes are very much superior to Whitleys.[7] Sir Charles also agreed that three Polish crews would be seconded and accepted to RAF 138, but a separate Polish flight would not be authorized.

This began another period of marginal success and acrimonious debate. The RAF 138 Squadron commander did not appreciate the manner in which the Poles related to his overriding SOE-determined missions. The decisions where the drop would be

6   TNA HS4/173.
7   TNA HS 4/173.

made were literally last minute, which also bothered the RAF officers, who decried the presence of Polish land army staff officers giving instructions in Polish on a RAF base. The RAF argued that this caused unreasonable disquiet in the crew. Probably what he meant was his disquiet, since he did not understand a word that was being said and would have noted that Poles talking together often sound irritable.

The Polish crews seconded to RAF 138 had completed their 30-sortie tour of bomber missions and were volunteering for a unit to deliver supplies to Poland. They were incensed at the poor quality of maintenance of their planes by the RAF mechanics, too often hostile, as opposed to the dedication of their Polish pre-war trained personnel who worked in bomber squadrons. Polish crews complained that for long fights, often nearly twelve hours to Poland and back, the automatic pilot was not a luxury but a necessity, and too often it did not work. Missions to Poland were often canceled due to bad weather but flown to places like Austria or Czechoslovakia. The Polish Air Force authorities attempted to establish the real issue, while the British SOE supported the Polish crews. An internal SOE memorandum comments: "In order to find a way round the Air Ministry brick wall of no-cooperation I have been investigating every possible means of giving support to inside Poland." The writer comments that now that the Poles have signed Lend-Lease act with the Americans "surely the Poles are at liberty in buying direct." He concluded, "Do you think that in view of the fact that the Air Ministry will, after all, still hold every trump in the pack as far as we are concerned, it is worth while investigating this line?" The SOE representative in a scrawled comment responded, "I must say I doubt it. This would only put the Poles in badly with the AM (i.e. Air Ministry) and on balance not worth it".[8]

By February 1942 the Polish crews in RAF 138 Squadron had carried out a total of three missions on Halifaxes. The first was a successful drop but adverse winds forced the plane to land in Sweden, where the crew destroyed it. This crew eventually made it back to once again confront difficulties with the RAF base commander who had received a replacement Polish crew and now had four Polish crews – one too many, according to his RAF establishment! He wanted them out of his base.

Once again the SOE attempted to square the impossible circle. Options were offered, a Polish flight, Polish navigators to help with missions to Poland on RAF planes. A memorandum dated February 2, 1942 from *MP* comments that the integration of the Poles into a RAF squadron was not working. It should be emphasized that many Polish crews served in mixed RAF transport units and Polish pilots in fighter RAF squadrons had no difficulties. This problem seemed to be an idiosyncratic subjective dislike of the base commander to foreign crews, but the focus was the three Polish crews.

---

8   TNA HS 4/173.

The memorandum also makes the following comment about the situation. "Overlooked entirely is that it was eventually though the medium of the Poles that they [i.e. RAF 138] obtained Halifaxes." It was definitely Sikorski's intervention through the Prime Minister and Sir Archibald Sinclair which led to the attachment of these three Halifaxes to 138 Squadron. Once having obtained possession of the three Halifaxes, 138 considered these aircraft their own to be used how, when and where most convenient for their own needs "This is not only disloyal to the Poles but dishonest".[9]

GREECE AN OPTION FOR THE BALKAN STRATEGY

During this period of June 1940 to the middle of 1941 there were no major issues for the Poles and no controversies. But Sikorski, ever alive to the future of a Balkan strategy, on February 16 1941 met with Prime Minister Churchill and Mr. Duff Cooper. Sikorski, still English language-challenged, was accompanied by the Polish ambassador, Edward Raczyński. Sikorski once again promoted his Balkan strategy and offered the Polish Carpathian Brigade, based in the Middle East, for possible deployment to Turkey. He also raised the issue of upgrading the mobility and equipment of the Polish forces in Scotland, and re-assigning their mission from a passive coastal defence to a mobile counter-attack force. He met with a sympathetic response from Churchill. Sikorski also discussed and asked for British support in his mission to Canada and the USA primarily to seek recruits for the Polish Forces.[10]

The conflict in Greece stressed British forces in the Middle East to their limit. After invading and occupying Yugoslavia the Germans moved south into Greece. Churchill decided that combat forces had to be move into the Greek mainland to help the Greeks and keep a buttress between the Germans and the Turks.

On March 14 1941 he met with Sikorski and asked for the Polish Carpathian Brigade based in Palestine to be sent to Greece.[11] Sikorski acquiesced and undoubtedly hoped that this would be a first step in his Balkan strategy. But the Germans overwhelmed the Greek and British forces before the Polish Brigade could even be transported to the mainland. Greece was occupied and one more government in exile created, although this one stayed in Cairo. This was one more fiasco on Churchill's part coming after the Norwegian campaign.

One of the most immediate results of this was a seeming dearth of any further Polish Balkan plans. The Turks and Germans signed a non-aggression pact on June 18 1941, a few days before Hitler attacked the Soviet Union. However, very shortly

9   TNA HS 4/173.
10   TNA FO 371/26735.
11   Winston Churchill, *The Grand Alliance*, Cassell, London, 1950, p.95.

afterwards the Polish Carpathian Brigade was moved to Egypt and moved by sea to reinforce the beleaguered Tobruk. It joined the predominantly Australian garrison and earned the accolade of "rats of Tobruk".

3 MAY 1941 AND CHURCHILL'S MESSAGE TO THE POLISH NATION

Churchill was urged by Hugh Dalton to reach out to the Polish Nation. He picked the perfect day – Poland's 3 May Constitution Day, commemorating the 1791 signing of Europe's first written constitution . His speech, as all Churchill's speeches were, was emotional and touched the Poles.[12]

THE GERMAN INVASION OF THE SOVIET UNION

The German attack on the Soviet Union in June 1941 was greeted by Churchill with a sigh of relief and an immediate offer of help to Stalin. The divergence of Polish governmental policy in regard to the Soviet Union came immediately to center stage. The British considered that restoration of relations between their Polish ally and the Soviets were of paramount importance. This encouragement, many actually called it pressure, actually fell on fertile ground, since Sikorski had as far back as May 1940 looked for some form of détente with the Soviets, liberating Polish prisoners in the Soviet Union and enhancing his meager military manpower.[13]

From October 1939, when the Polish Foreign Minister visited the United Kingdom, the Poles had been discreetly discouraged by the British from getting into a war of words with the Soviets. This was even at a time when the British were thinking of bombing Baku. This is probably the reason why the Polish Government did not raise the issue at the League of Nations. It was raised in December 1939 when the Soviets invaded Finland and the Soviets were censured, and all countries were urged to give assistance to the Finns.

Sikorski was eager and the Polish Foreign Minister, Zaleski, willing to establish diplomatic relations with the Soviets, conditional on the Soviets declaring that the Soviet-German Treaties of 1939 were null and void, that the Soviets confirm the Polish-Soviet Treaty of March 18, 1921, and finally that all Polish prisoners and internees be released.

---

12 Charles Eade, ed. *The Unrelenting Struggle. War Speeches by the Right Hon. Winston S. Church-ill, C.H., M.P.*, Cassell, London, fourth edition, 1946, pp.115–117. This speech is not mentioned in Churchill's memoirs.

13 Anthony Eden, Earl of Avon, *The Memoirs of Anthony Eden, Earl of Avon*, Houghton Mifflin Company, Boston, 1965, pp.314–316.

Negotiations began on July 5 1941 in London under the auspices of the British Foreign Office, composed of Eden and Cadogan with Strang as a technical advisor. They were the catalysts to ensure a satisfactory result. The Soviets were represented by Maisky, the Soviet ambassador in London, who was in constant touch with Moscow regarding specific points. The Polish side initially was composed of Sikorski and Zaleski, with the presence of the ubiquitous Rettinger. Eden suggested that the Polish side dispense with Zaleski. While the reason is not stated in any archives it seems intuitive that given what happened his attitude must have been perceived as an impediment to a quick and thus from a British position satisfactory conclusion of an agreement.[14] Stalin agreed to the British-sponsored rapprochement with the Poles simply because his back was to the wall in mid-July 1941. But the London-based Soviet negotiator, while conceding that the German-Soviet treaties were no longer relevant, absolutely refused in any manner to allude to the Riga Treaty of 1921. The final agreement did not mention the Riga Treaty but accepted the principle of *pacta sunt servanda*, which Sikorski chose to see as accepting the Riga Treaty. The Soviets also agreed to amnesty all Polish citizens detained on Soviet territory. Since the definition of a "Polish citizen" seemed obvious to all Western parties, namely that they were citizens of the Polish Republic, it was not defined, but in later years it was defined by the Soviets.

General Sikorski achieved many of his desiderata, with his priority being the release of Poles and the formation of a Polish Army under the control of the Polish Government. Initially Stalin wished to have a "Polish Legion" and some form of national committee in Moscow. The British supported Sikorski in completely refuting this in 1941, but as history will show, eventually Stalin achieved both goals. The Soviets, after initial balking, agreed that the "amnestied' Polish military would form an army under a Polish commander appointed by Sikorski with the concurrence of the Soviets.[15] Sikorski was between the hammer and the anvil. He was strongly motivated by his desire to have an increase in the Polish military, very much in line with his initiatives in midsummer 1940, and undoubtedly also moved by his humanitarian concerns regarding the hardships of the Poles in the gulags of the Soviet Union. He was also under strong British pressure. Finally, while discreet in his public comments, it is clear from many comments attributed to him that he saw the revision of the Polish-Soviet boundary as inevitable but the retention of Lwów in Poland as non-negotiable. On the other side the Polish President (Raczkiewicz),

14   Edward Raczyński, *In Allied London*, op. cit., p.95–98.
15   Wacław Jędrzejeiwcz, ed. *Poland in the British Parliament, 1939–1945* Vol. I. Piłsudski Institute, New York, 1946, pp.469–475; Sir Llewellyn Woodward, ed. *British Foreign Policy in the Second World*, Vol. II, Chapter XXXV "Great Britain and Russo-Polish relations from the German attack on Russia to the end of 1943", HMSO, London, 1971; Anna M. Cienciała, "General Sikorski and the Conclusion of the Polish-Soviet Agreement, July 30, 1941. A Reassessment", *The Polish Review*, XLI, 1966, pp.401–434.

Foreign Minister (Zaleski), Minister of Justice (Seyda) and Minister for Home Affairs (Sosnkowski), objected strenuously that until the Soviets absolutely agreed to the pre-war frontiers and formal acknowledgment of the Riga Treaty the agreement could not be supported. The three cabinet ministers resigned and the Polish President refused to countersign the agreement which, in reality, became a mere protocol.

The British came partially to Sikorski's support but in reality buttressed the Polish opposition. The British Secretary of State (Foreign Affairs) Anthony Eden, according to his statement to the House of Commons, handed a note to General Sikorski stating that "His Majesty's Government do not recognize any territorial changes which have been effected in Poland since August, 1939".[16] But a question in the Commons about possible British guarantees of Polish boundaries elicited the following reply from Eden – "the exchange of Notes which I have just read in the House does not involve any guarantees of frontiers by His Majesty's Government."

The British greeted the Polish-Soviet agreement with great approval and, for that phlegmatic nation, surprising enthusiasm.

THE POLISH GOVERNMENT AND SOVIETS ESTABLISH DIPLOMATIC RELATIONS, AND A POLISH ARMY IS FORMED ON SOVIET SOIL. THE IMPLEMENTATION OF SIKORSKI'S SOVIET STRATEGY

The Polish Government had to organize an army, establish an embassy, organize help for the civilians, women and many orphans. The ever-present Rettinger was sent to Moscow as Poland's first *Chargé d'Affaires*. A few months later Stanislaw Kot, the first Polish ambassador, arrived in Moscow.[17] With considerable difficulty Poles in Soviet camps or in many rural gulags began to be released. In the first months of the rapprochement the difficulties in implementing the concrete aspects of the agreement had more to do with local Soviet commissars and directors of factories, farms, mines or lumber camps rather than central obstructionist policy. Often the loss of Polish slave workers faced the local camp managers with inability to meet the centralized and mandated production targets. In many instances the Poles, men, women often with children, were either not told about their amnesty or not given information as to where to seek Polish camps. Even if informed they were not given any financial assistance. Furthermore, as Woodward writes, many Poles in Soviet camps were told "their misfortune was due to lack of interest or to obstruction of on the part of the Polish Government and its embassy".[18] General Sikorski appointed one of the

16 Wacław Jędrzejeiwcz, ed. *Poland in the British Parliament, 1939–1945* Vol. I, Piłsudski Institute, New York, 1946.p.473.

17 Stanisław Kot, *Conversations with the Kremlin and dispatches from Russia,* Oxford University Press, London, 1963.

18 Llewllyn Woodward, *British Foreign Policy in the Second World War*, Vol. II, HMSO, London, 1971,

"amnestied" Polish generals, Major General Władysław Anders, to be the overall commander of Polish forces in the Soviet Union. Anders was a major general, one of a number of senior Polish officers who had been "amnestied", but far more senior was Lt. General Michel Karasiewicz-Tokarzewski. However, Tokarzewski had been a Piłsudski legionary, while Anders had opposed the Piłsudski *coup d'etat* in May 1925. This influenced Sikorski. After close to two years of Soviet prisons Anders had little love for them and made an erroneous judgment that the Germans would defeat the Soviets. He miscalculated and underestimated the prodigious military assistance which went to the Soviets from the West to Russia through Iran and shortly thereafter through the Arctic Sea to Murmansk and Arkhangelsk.[19]

The agreement set a new course and hope for Sikorski's political and military strategy. Liberating Poland through the Balkans was now replaced by liberating Poland alongside the Soviets! It also accentuated the chasm in the Polish political scene. Sikorski became an even more important statesman as far as the British were concerned; while the Polish President and General Sosnkowski, and August Zaleski (the third cabinet member did not carry much weight even in Polish circles let alone British opinion) were now seen as obstructionist. It is interesting to note that Eden, who ignored Sikorski's death in 1943, described him as "intrepid" on this issue.[20]

The Maisky–Sikorski agreement, shortlived as it was, led to the release of many thousands of Poles from Soviet gulags. Many other thousands were victims of Soviet obfuscation and did not get the requisite information, or permission to leave the work camps. Many were told "you have a choice, stay and be fed – or leave and starve". But those who heard of the Polish forces being formed left their work camps or in some cases were released from prison.

By the end of 1941 the released Poles formed an army of close to 40,000, however, the concern about missing officers, close to 15,000, was brought to the attention of the Soviet authorities. In addition to the missing officers Polish archives surmise that over 100,000 of the rank and file of the Polish Army captured in September 1939 were never accounted for. The official Soviet reply was always the same until 1943, that all Poles had been released and the missing officers must have escaped. After two divisions of Polish troops had been formed the Soviets stopped further supplies of food, uniforms etc. The Soviets limited Polish formations to 30,000 men, forming two light infantry divisions and only equipped with small arms. The extra men were not on the "books" and thus not supplied by rations, or uniforms.

---

pp.612–617.

19   Joan Beaumont, *Comrades in Arms. British Aid to Russia, 1941–1945*, Davis-Poynter, London, 1980; David Wragg, *Sacrifice for Stalin. The Cost and Value of the Arctic Convoys Re-Assessed*, Pen and Sword, Barnsley, 2005; Alexander Hill. "British Lend-Lease Aid and the Soviet War Effort", *Journal of Military History*, Vol.71 No.3, pp.773–808.

20   Anthony Eden, Earl of Avon, *The Memoirs of Anthony Eden, Earl of Avon*, Houghton Mifflin Company, Boston, 1965.

As the winter war went on the conditions of the "amnestied" Poles deteriorated. Given all the problems Sikorski, who was by every account a hands-on general, decided to make a personal visit to Stalin and inspect the Polish formations. On his way to the Soviet Union Sikorski visited the beleaguered island of Malta and gave a Jolly Roger to the jubilant crew of the Polish submarine, ORP *Sokól*, at that time operating in the Mediterranean and based in Valleta. But even more characteristic of Sikorski's martial temperament was his visit to the Polish Carpathian Brigade in besieged Tobruk. Sikorski's visit was unique! He was in the front line trenches and experienced the life of the Polish soldiers who proudly called themselves the "rats of Tobruk".

He then flew to visit Stalin. The visit was a relative success, since Stalin promised to feed the Polish military and even agreed to the Polish request to increase the establishment of the Polish Forces. It was also agreed that air force personnel, and there were some who had in 1939 crossed into Lithuania and been taken over by the Soviets in 1940, would leave for the Middle East. But the problem of the missing officers was not clarified.

The next months are historically important because the Soviets survived the winter of 1941 and Stalin became assured of his importance in the Allied strategy. Mention has to be made of the completely destructive policies of Beaverbrook who failed to support the Polish request that aid destined to the Poles in Russia should go to the Poles. John Colville wrote "Beaverbrook was captivated by Stalin's insidious charms. Thenceforth he became as stalwart a supporter of Russia as any member of the Communist Party and, as time went by, a dedicated enemy of the Free Polish Government and its gallant divisions of hard fighting soldiers under General Anders."[21]

The ominous disappearance of thousands of Polish officers began to be brought to notice. Their correspondence with relatives in Soviet-occupied Poland had come to an abrupt end in April 1940. Most Poles viewed this as a portentous sign. The surfeit of Polish officers in the West was now addressed as they were moved to the newly-formed units in the Soviet Union. Polish contract officers with the British West African Regiments were released and seconded to Russia, understandably not to every young officer's delight!

The visit to the Soviet Union was seen at the time as a success in every respect, but in reality its consequences, positive as they were, were short-lived. Stalin seemed in a mood to accommodate most of the Polish requests. Size of the army was to increase to seven light infantry divisions and food was to be provided. It was agreed that Polish air force personnel would leave for the Middle East. These men were to bring the Polish Air Force in the United Kingdom up to establishment levels.

However, the political side, while seemingly jovial, went nowhere. Sikorski, seemingly buttressed by Eden's statement that territorial changes would not be recognized if not mutually agreed on, refused to be engaged on that topic. Stalin refuted any

---

21 John Colville, *Winston Churchill and His Inner Circle*, Wyndham Books, NY, 1981, p.106.

Moscow, December 1941. Josef Stalin and General Sikorski signing a memorandum regarding the enhanced recruitment of Poles to the Polish army in the Soviet Union. (PISM)

knowledge of the missing officers, stating categorically that all had been released. In reality Stalin spoke the truth, all live Polish officers had been released. When pressed on the subject he replied that they must have escaped. Sikorski, stunned, asked "to where?" Stalin, without batting an eyelid, responded "to Manchuria".

Sikorski also visited the Polish military camps and the masses of civilians huddled around the food provided by the soldiers. Photographs of the visit are heartbreaking. Thousands of the civilians and military were sick and hundreds dying.[22]

BRITISH GREET RAPPROCHEMENT WITH SATISFACTION

Initially the British military chiefs were as excited about the release of the Poles as Sikorski was hopeful. But while Sikorski visualized a Soviet base, the British chiefs minuted an overestimated optimistic assessment and their own agenda. "I should like to stress the importance which I attach, for military reasons, to the evacuation of as many Poles as possible. We want 10,000 in this country [i.e. UK], 2,000 in the Middle East.

---

22   Sarah Meiklejohn Terry, *Poland's Place in Europe*, Princeton University Press, Princeton, 1983, pp.199–244. This has an excellent chapter describing the vicissitudes of the "rapprochement" between 1941 and 1942.

The successful withdrawal of the remainder – I believe that something like 150,000 are involved – would be a great contribution of good fighting men to our cause".[23]

The Poles were still convinced that not all Poles had been given the opportunity to join the Polish forces. Also there were now the first Soviet hints that they were determining the definition as to who a Polish citizen was. Soviet authorities decided that all Belorussians, Ukrainans and Jews, even if citizens of Poland before the war, did not qualify. The limits on the number of actual places in the Polish forces were limited.[24] The Soviets also manipulated the bureaucracy, telling the Poles that Jews were not Polish citizens and did not qualify for 'amnesty" while assuring the Jews that the Poles did not want them. Regrettably until it was decided later in 1942 that all the Polish forces were going to be moved to British-controlled Middle East, Polish Jews, in general, showed minimal interest in joining the Polish Army.

The commanding officer of the Polish Forces in Russia, General Władysław Anders, was convinced that the Germans would break through the Soviet lines in the spring of 1942; also he was aware of the dire circumstances of his forces. They were short of food, short of uniforms and living in unheated tents. Many were sick and the death rate was high. Food rations barely met the needs of the soldiers, but in addition there were thousands of civilians who flocked to the Polish military looking for help and escape from the Soviets. There were also thousands of orphans who could not be abandoned and had to be fed out of the rations apportioned for the 40,000 soldiers.

BRITISH –SOVIET TREATY CHALLENGED

The summer saw a major diplomatic event, namely British-Soviet negotiations for a treaty. This event is not given anything as much analysis as the Tehran Conference. But it had major significance for the Sikorski strategy and is not well known. The Soviet Commissar for Foreign Affairs, Vyacheslav Molotov, visited London to initiate discussions between the British and Soviets about a treaty.

It is far from obvious a half century later what the British really hoped to achieve. It has been argued that there was a fear that Stalin might come to a compromise peace treaty with Hitler. But it was obvious what the Soviets wanted, namely a signed commitment that their pre–1941 territorial aggrandizement had been approved and arrange for a post-war settlements. The Soviets immediately wanted to have a secret protocol and in their ensuing discussions which went on in the same vein proposed a quid pro quo which would entitle the British to have bases in Norway and Denmark. This chapter is captioned "Acceptance of Russian Demands. Significance of British

---

23   TNA WO216/19 3026.
24   I knew of one pre-war Polish officer from the Wilno Region of Poland who was denied a place in the newly-formed Wilno Brigade. All slots had been taken. He managed to find a position in the Lwów Brigade and eventually fought with them through the Monte Cassino campaign.

Surrender". The British Government acquiesced in the incorporation of the three Baltic States by the Soviets.[25] The Eden papers are bland on this topic as behoves a consummate diplomat.[26] The diaries of his permanent under-secretary of the British Foreign Office, Sir Alexander Cadogan speak volumes. When referring to his political superior, Anthony Eden, he comments "determined to go ahead, gallops gaily over the ground, which will give way under him, one of these days. We're selling the Poles down the river" and "treaty which I hear is beginning to cause a stink amongst MPs – egged on by Victor Cazalet MP".[27]

Victor Cazalet MP, an Etonian, was a liaison officer to Sikorski, traveled with him to Russia and became strongly pro-Polish. Sikorski requested his "services' on July 3 1940 in a letter to Winston Churchill.[28] He privately published a book, *With Sikorski to Russia*, (London, 1942) which caused major angst among many in the corridors of power since it deviated from the British official portrayal of the new ally. Cazalet had no inherent diffidence in writing to Sir Anthony Eden, another Etonian. He expressed grave concern about the British diplomacy, and exhorted Eden to stand firm, reminding him of his courageous stand in 1938.

> I have little doubt that you will get it through. In the present state of hysteria about Russia, you will probably get an overwhelming backing from the Press. With the government control of the BBC the case against it will go by default. The opposition to it may not be much larger than the opposition, which you so courageously maintained almost all alone before the war for so many months against concession to aggressors.

With this introduction, which also speaks volumes on the British mass media enthusiasm for Stalin and his system, Cazalet concludes "for the first time this country has publicly and voluntarily, without even a protest or apology, handed over territory which is not ours to give, to another state, which is not even in occupation of it."[29]

The Polish Government was acutely concerned and did its best to attempt to deflect the British from such a step. Cazalet's opinions were in fact shared by many in the House of Commons and the Foreign Affairs Committee of the House of Commons expressed its strongest opposition.[30]

In March 1942 Sikorski made his second trip to the United States. His first one in April 1941 was prior to the Pearl Harbor attack (December 1941) and antedated

25   Llewellyn Woodward, *British Foreign Policy in the Second World War*, Vol. II HMSO, London, 1971, pp.244–254.
26   Eden, op. cit., pp.334- 352 and 378–383.
27   David Dilks, ed., *The Diaries of Sir Alexander Cadogan, 1938–1945*, G.P. Putnam's Sons, New York, 1972; Eden, op.cit., pp.446, 448.
28   TNA FO 954/19.
29   TNA FO 954/19B.
30   TNA FO 954/19.

America becoming a belligerent. That had been a public relations visit and was quite successful, except for the communist press, which called him "warmonger representing capitalism and Wall Street –Downing Street axis." This one was a business visit. It was preceded by a visit of the acting Polish foreign minister, Edward Raczyński, who had meetings with his counterpart Mr. Berle. The latter presented a future world "utopia" in which only four countries would determine international conduct, and essentially alluded to the sanguine state of Costa Rica protected by the United States as a model for a future Poland under the umbrella of the Soviets. This kind of talk did not reassure the Polish foreign minister. Sikorski flew to the United States seriously concerned that the British – particularly Sir Anthony Eden – were in discussions with Stalin and appeared to acquiesce in the Soviet annexation of the three Baltic States. Even though Eden strongly stated that these negotiations did not include Polish boundaries the Poles were not reassured. Churchill was ambivalent, reluctant and referred the matter through the British ambassador Lord Halifax to the Americans for an opinion allegedly recommending that in the case of an attacked party – the Soviet Union- there should be an exception to the Atlantic Charter. Churchill was worried that the Soviets might sign a separate peace treaty with Germany if they did not get their way.[31] The Soviet ambassador to the Polish Government in London, Aleksander Bogomolow, warned the Poles that their attitude was unfriendly and that after driving the Germans out from Poland the Soviets might halt their military operations, essentially hinting that this would leave Poland under German control.

Sikorski received a much more reassuring welcome and the finale of this diplomatic dance was that the British resisted Soviet pressure to include a mention of boundaries in their twenty year treaty. Not all the British coalition partners in the War Cabinet were for the treaty but the spotlight for success was shone on Sikorski and to some extent Victor Cazalet.

In spite of what Sikorski still hoped for, namely a good working relationship with the Soviets, based on mutual interest, it was beginning to unravel.

SIKORSKI HOSTS A CONFERENCE OF SENIOR GENERALS IN LONDON

In April 1942 Sikorski convened a conference of all his senior generals in London. Present were Generals Marian Kukiel (GOC I Corps in Scotland), Władysław Anders (GOC Polish Army in the Soviet Union), Stanisław Sosabowski (commanding officer Parachute Brigade), Józef Zając (GOC Polish Forces in the Middle East), Gustaw Paszkiewicz, Stanisław Ujejski (Inspector General of the Polish Air Force), Stanisław

---

31   Steven Merritt Miner, *Between Churchill and Stalin. The Soviet Union, Great Britain and the origin of the Grand Alliance*, University of North Carolina Press, Chapel Hill, 1988, pp.138–225.

Kopański (commanding officer of the Carpathian Brigade), Tadeusz Klimecki(Chief of Staff) and Admiral Jerzy Swirski (Commandant of the Polish Navy). The conference lasted two days and was punctuated by a Sikorski meeting with Churchill.

Everyone represented a different view of strategy. Kukiel based in Scotland and Klimecki in London opined that all should be moved to the United Kingdom since it was from the British Isles that the invasion of France would originate and the United Kingdom offered the best training ground. Anders countered this by arguing that such a move would guarantee the Soviets stopping any further release of Poles in the Soviet Union. Ujejski argued the merits of increasing the numbers in the Air Force to make the Polish squadrons less dependent on RAF supporting services. To make the Polish Air Force an autonomous force required an additional increment of 30,000, but Sikorski promised a mere four thousand. Perhaps the most prophetic words came from Paszkiewicz who strongly opposed building up the Parachute Brigade because the British would break the agreement and demand to include it in their order of battle for the invasion of Europe. Paszkiewicz made a very cogent argument that the Parachute Brigade should stay as a cadre unit of officers. If flown into Poland to support operations the rank and file would come from the ranks of the clandestine forces.

Anders strongly voiced the opinion that his forces should be evacuated from the Soviet Union to the Middle East and then be joined by forces in the United Kingdom. He was supported by Zając. Both still thought in terms of the Balkan strategy. Sikorski came up with a compromise, 'a few here and few there', but with Anders' Polish Army to stay in the Soviet Union.[32] The British also had their own plans. Their earlier overtly optimistic assessment of the potential addition of Poles to Allied forces was modulated. But the British had now suffered the disaster of Singapore, and the decision of the Australian Government to pull back their forces from the Middle East to defend the home country left that region desperately short of troops. The British worst case nightmare scenario was the Afrika Korps breaking through the Suez Canal, a German victory in the Caucasus pushing into Turkey, and the Turks going over to the German side as they had in the First World War. German control of the Middle East would mean the restive Iranians and Iraqis also defecting and the loss of oil.

SIKORSKI'S SOVIET STRATEGY, BRITISH MANPOWER NEEDS AND ANDERS' RELUCTANCE TO STAY IN THE SOVIET UNION

Field Marshal Lord Alanbrooke wrote in his dairies of British concerns in the Middle East and hopes for Polish reinforcements, "There are two opposed camps in the Poles now. Sikorski and those in England wish to transfer a large contingent home here, the others [i.e Anders] wish to form Polish forces in the Middle East. Personally I am in

---

32   PISM A. XII. i/129.

favour of the latter. Any forces in the Middle East this summer will be a Godsend to us".[33] It is understandable that Anders now became a British *favorite de jour* and that shipping shortages were cited as precluding major moves.

Sikorski was still pinning his strategy on some form of accommodation with the Soviets. He was well informed of the state of the Polish troops in the Soviet Union, and he had seen them in December 1941. He was also more than aware of the attitude of Anders. His policy of conciliation with the Soviets was not getting the support from the Polish Underground. But Sikorski was convinced that the future of Polish foreign policy depended on keeping good relations with Stalin, and even more importantly on having a Polish Army alongside the Soviets. On May 1 he cabled a long message to Anders. He opined that the victory over Germany would to a large extent depend on the Soviet Armies.

> I strongly desire that that you grasp my intentions regarding the Polish Armed forces, and because of that I am summing up my views in writing, to enable you to see my opinions on the general military situation and the plans for the organization, disposition and use of the Polish Armed Forces.
>
> I have full understanding of the feelings of the soldiers in Russia under your command, especially after the last evacuation. [presumably Sikorski was making a reasonable assumption that those left behind were feeling forsaken] I appeal to their patriotism and their will which has so well stood the test. They should remain in absolute discipline in a post so important for Poland.

This last point was undoubtedly addressed directly to and at Anders, who had during his visit to London in April of 1942 shown a certain degree of independent thinking and was dismissive of the accomplishments of the Poles in the United Kingdom. Sikorski continued,

> There are three factors on the Allied side which will be decisive for the final outcome of the war. They are:
>
> • Soviet Armed Forces.
> • Allied Armed Forces. In particular those of Great Britain and the United States, and at their side a portion of the Polish Armed Forces.
> • The subjugated countries of Europe.

Sikorski showed his grasp of the international scene and geo-political strategy by outlining in a very brilliant manner Polish options and desiderata.

---

33 Alex Danchev and Daniel Todman, eds., *War Diaries, 1939–1945. Field Marshal Lord Alanbrooke*, University of California Press, Berkeley, 2001, p.252.

Our war effort, carried on unceasingly and with increased intensity, has but one aim: Poland, Poland only, a Poland which might be sounder, safer and stronger than the Poland which so resolutely started to fight against the barbaric aggression of our secular enemy.

Which is the shortest way to Poland? From Russia, the Middle East or Great Britain ? Nobody can answer this now. However, what matters most is that at least a portion of the Polish Armed Forces, staying outside Poland, should reinforce the Home Army with modern weapons, in order that the latter may become a centre of order and authority and enable us, in the most efficient way to take hold of East Prussia, Gdansk and the German part of Upper Silesia, removing the Germans from these provinces. In this decisive histor-ical moment only accomplished facts will count.

The Polish Armed Forces must be posted on the existing and future war fronts in such a way that they would be able, in any case to reach Poland within the shortest possible time.

Heretofore, the Polish soldiers have fought on all the war fronts. However, I have neither the right nor the intention to risk a concentration of the whole or major part of the Polish Armed forces on one theater of the war, where a possible misfortune could bring about their excessive, if not complete, destructions.[34]

The British shortage of men in the Middle East bordered on the desperate. They formally enquired as to what was happening with the evacuation of Poles from the Soviet Union to the Middle East and what could be done to speed it up. The British need and Sikorski's strategy were on a collision course. Stalin was still to play his card!

Anders wanted out of the Soviet Union. His men were becoming a major concen-tration of semi-starved and dying men! The British wanted him out to beef up their anemic forces in the Middle East, and Stalin by now had realized that he would much prefer to deal with his own "Polish" creatures, and that Anders was anything but.

One can assume that even if the treaty negotiations with the British did not quite go as Stalin wished, probably the last time he was thwarted, it was a watershed moment and perhaps more importantly showed the opposition to Soviet appeasement as rela-tively marginal. It also made Victor Cazalet its spokesman.

Kukiel writes in his rather panegyric biography of Sikorski that in June, 1942 Sikorski and Eden met in London and apparently indulged in self-congratulations on the positive final outcome of the British-Soviet discussion. Eden attributed the success in dropping territorial concessions to Sikorski and vice versa.

---

34 *Documents on Polish-Soviet Relations, 1939–1945*, Heinemann, London, 1961 and 1967 (2 vols), pp. 344–347.

For the Poles, it was at best a pyrrhic victory and a misreading of the long term American policy and complete misunderstanding of Roosevelt's long-term utopian goal of a United Nations and of the four policemen of the world. For the British it was a mere bump in their inexorable and still difficult to understand accommodation of Stalin.[35] In the meanwhile other events were unfolding, namely the future of the Polish Army in the Soviet Union and Sikorski's Soviet strategy. It is assumed that it was during the visit of Molotov to London that the question of Polish divisions in the Soviet Union being moved to the British controlled Middle East was raised. In July 1942 Churchill sent Stalin this grateful message:

> I am sure it would be in our common interest, Premier Stalin, to have the three divisions of Poles you so kindly offered join their compatriots in Palestine, where we can arm them fully. Those would play a most important part in future fighting as well as keeping the Turks in good heart. The Four Polish divisions when trained would play a strong part in delaying a German southward advance. If we do not get the Poles, we should have to fill their places by drawing on preparations now going forward on a vast scale for the Anglo-American invasion of the continent.

The conclusion of his message was, "The Levant-Caspian front is almost bare."[36] In 1942 the British still feared that the Germans would break the Soviets and that the Turks might side with the Germans. This would have imperiled the Middle East oil supplies. Stalin was happy to do this favor for Churchill. The British got enough men for a two-division corps, Stalin got rid of the Poles, and Anders and his Poles were thrilled to be out of the Soviet Union.

Sikorski's policy was in ruins.

Did it have any chance of success ? Given the nature of Stalin and the explosive news about the Katyn massacre that would shortly break, probably not.

POLISH AIR FORCE IN DIEPPE LANDINGS

Having survived the Battle of Britain, the Royal Air Force slowly went on the offensive. Various incursions over France were made and the tempo built up to the British and Canadian landings to capture Dieppe. The operations was anything but a success, and proved that a direct amphibious invasion on a German-held port had little chance of success.

---

35   Marian Kukiel, *Generał Sikorski. Żołnierz i Mąz Stanu Polski Walczącej*, Polish Institute and General Sikorski Museum, London, 1970, p.189.
36   Churchill, *Hinge of Fate*, Cassell, London, 1948; Woodward, op.cit., p.617. See also TNA WO 208/1736.

The air operations went well and the Luftwaffe, while still present, was not comparable to the Luftwaffe of 1939.Some of his was because much of it was on the Eastern Front.

These operations were the first in which the Polish fighter squadrons fought as a one major wing under Polish command. Major Stefan Janus commanded the First Polish Wing, consisting of 302, 303, 306, 308 and 317 squadrons with spectacular results. The Poles flew 224 individual sorties, achieved sixteen victories, which composed 18% of all Allied victories, and only lost two Polish pilots. Major Janus received the Distinguished Service Cross, and four pilots the Distinguished Flying Cross.[37]

---

37   Norman Franks, *The Greatest Air Battle, Dieppe, 19th August, 1942*, Grub Street, London, 1992.

6

The Polish Clandestine Directorate

General Administrative Issues – The Polish Clandestine Directorate states its case – Polish Headquarters in London fail to communicate all the facts about the Polish Home Army – Sikorski's visit to the United States – Polish presence on the Combined Chiefs of Staff – Messages to the Home Army from Polish HQ at variance with political reality in the West- Lisbon Talks with Romanian and Hungarian diplomats –Katyn – Sikorski killed in plane accident.

Criticism has been leveled at the Polish Government for its alleged military character and, by inference, a lack of a democratic process. The first was easily disposed of by the British ambassador Sir Owen O'Malley in his report to the British Foreign Office, which gives the biographies of all the members of the Polish Government. Sikorski, appointed by a civilian president, was the only one of two serving officers in the Government. The other was the Minister of Military Affairs, General Marian Kukiel. All the others were civilians, including the successor to Sikorski as prime minister, Stanisław Mikołajczyk.[1] But even though the Polish Government was in exile it sought whenever feasible the opinion and concurrence of the Clandestine Delegatura which was not loath to express its opinions, at times quite strongly. But it was always a question as how much they appreciated the ever-decreasing Polish political room for maneuver. Their proffered opinions were not always what "Polish" London wanted to hear, but what is even more vital is that the British were given these opinions and were often discomfited.

In early 1943 we have a formal typed report to the British War Cabinet regarding an interview with a "representative of the Polish Underground". While the name of

---

1   TNA file FO 371/34591 7480 dated May 1943.

the 'representative' is not mentioned in the formal report, it is most likely to have been Jerzy Lerski. The following points of significance are noted by the British:

What became the primary issue was Polish policy towards the Soviet Union. The Directorate expressed its support for the Sikorski July 1941 pact with the Soviets, contrary to the opinion of the Polish President and General Sosnkowski, but also affirmed in the strongest terms that no territorial compromise should be made with the Soviet Union.

- No one has any idea of setting up a rival government in Poland <u>unless General Sikorski were to cede territory to the USSR</u>, in which case a national government would be set up on the lines of the revolutionary government of 1863.
- As regards the political situation, my informant said that the four principal parties which support General Sikorski's Government, the Socialist, Peasant, National Democrats and Labour parties, were working harmoniously together in Poland.

The report concludes that although Soviet parachutists have been introduced into Polish territory, they had carefully refrained from fighting against the Germans but had merely incited the local populations, and so encouraged German reprisals. In these circumstances, the Poles could not regard Soviet policy as that of a loyal ally.[2]

Sikorski had been stalled in his hopes for a Soviet strategy. His opponents made it clear that they never expected anything else. But Sikorski did not give up hope and there were indications that Churchill was strongly backing his efforts to reconcile with Stalin. But Stalin was not paying much attention to Churchill either, since he correctly believed that were it not for Roosevelt, the British would have signed off on his incorporation of the Baltic States. He intended to have them anyway and knew nobody would stop him.

Sikorski now concentrated on simple, tactical issues which he felt he could develop and influence. During the rest of the 1942 and into early 1943 Polish efforts were focused on building up the Polish Home Army. Discussions were also held with the Soviet military mission in London for potential collaboration of the Polish Home Army with the Soviets. The Poles offered the Soviets major sabotage activity in the Eastern Polish territories and in turn asked that the Soviet make their landing bases available for shuttle runs with supplies. The Poles suggested that planes from the West would fly in couriers, radio and sabotage equipment, and on the way from Soviet bases, deliver captured German small arms. But by this phase of the war, the Soviets were anything but interested in collaboration and were already creating their own partisan units in Eastern Poland and even parachuted their agents into Warsaw to seek out communist sympathizers.

2   TNA CAB 66134 /108655.

This began a bitter, acrimonious and controversial episode of competing and tragically bloody struggles in occupied Poland. The history of this is outside of the scope of this monograph and outside of the research that I have pursued in British and Polish archives. But competing ethnic groups have their own strongly held and argued explanations, regrettably filled with accusations against other ethnic groups for the internecine conflicts that ensued.

The Polish Home Army Command under the leadership of the indefatigable General Stefan (Grot) Rowecki were constantly informed and consulted by the Polish authorities in London. Given what eventually happened it is a matter of major polemics and controversy whether the Poles in the occupied country were sufficiently advised as to the unfolding and ever negative Polish diplomatic situation in the West. It is a well documented fact that they were often at the receiving end of relatively optimistic and at times even grandiose facts regarding the status and allegedly high esteem of the Polish Government in the West, and of the size, build up and strength of the Polish Armed Forces. These reports inevitable exaggerated Polish military potential in the West and this was particularly true regarding the Polish Parachute Brigade and its commitment for Poland. Note, too, the fact that the growth and success of the Polish Air Force in the United Kingdom was not commensurate with its ability

Scotland, 1943. A group photo of the men of the Polish Parachute Brigade. "The Polish Parachute Brigade is now composed of the best material and is reserved in the hands of the Polish Commander-in-chief for operations in Poland". (British War Office Allied Quarterly Report, TNA WO 193/42 80751)

Scotland, 1944. Colour party of the Polish Parachute Brigade with their brigade standard, embroidered by the women of Warsaw in 1944 in occupied Poland, and flown out of Poland on Wildhorn I. (PISM)

UK, 1944. General Kazimierz Sosnkowski, who succeeded General Sikorski as Commander in Chief, visited the Polish Parachute Brigade and inspected the pack artillery. In the photograph, General Sosnkowski is the only officer wearing the Polish four-cornered garrison cap; immediately to his left is General Stanisław Sosabowski, Commanding Officer of the Parachute Brigade. The only general wearing a forage cap is General Stanisław Kopański, the Polish Chief of Staff. (PISM)

to function autonomously let alone at such a long distance as Poland from Western bases. Another fact that was not shared with the Home Army was that while the Polish Parachute Brigade was becoming a fine fighting unit, there was no available air transport.[3]

The Polish Home Army Command may be forgiven for not appreciating that seminal point because the following British staff memo, dated May 1942, to Sikorski, was not shared with the Home Army.

> We have been reluctantly forced to the conclusion that the physical problems of transporting materials for secret armies in Eastern Europe is insuperable. I hope, however, that in September it will be possible to resume on an increasing scale, the dropping of a limited number of personnel and stores for diversionary activities.

> The Chiefs of staff are fully alive to your desire that preparation should be made for a Polish airborne force to be dispatched to Poland when a general rising takes place. This question has been fully considered and the conclusion has been reached, with regret, that the dispatch of such a force is not a practical possibility in the foreseeable future, bearing in mind, among other actors, the long distances involved and the severe shortage of suitable aircraft and gliders.[4]

This was as clear and fair statement as one could expect, even if disappointing. There was even less excuse for not appreciating the situation of the Polish Air Force in the United Kingdom by the Home Army, since they were advised repeatedly by Polish Air Force HQ through the medium of relatively senior air force officers parachuted into Poland.

The Polish Air Force Headquarters was repeatedly given general directives for air support of an uprising in Poland. The staff spent hours going over all possible options for such an operation and the inevitable final conclusion was always the same. Unless the Royal Air Force made a total commitment of its resources or if the German Army of occupation became so demoralized as to cease all military activities, there was nothing possible that the Polish Air Force could do for the Home Army.

This staff planning consumed energy and also led to expressed frustration by the air force officers in a handwritten exasperated comment about one of the suggested plans emanating from the C-in-C staff. It simply said "don't fool the country".[5]

In January 1943 a small cadre of air force officers headed by Colonel Roman Rudkowski was parachuted into Poland. Rudkowski had completed thirty bombing

---

3   The British Quarterly Report: "organized in four battalions with supporting arms has been reinforced and is now composed of the best material and is about 2,500 men strong. It is reserved in the hands of the Polish Commander-in-Chief for operations in Poland". TNA WO 193/42 80751.
4   TNA WO 193/42 80751.
5   P.I.S.M. LOT AVII/1b.

missions and then flew a number supply missions as part of the Polish section of RAF 138 Squadron. He was instructed by his air force superiors to ensure that the Polish Home Army were absolutely informed about Polish air force limitations. The parameters were that it did it not have the requisite aircraft for a one way flight to Poland, nor the kind of aircraft that could operate on primitive air strips. In 1944 the British developed special metal mats that could be unrolled and would allow planes to operate out of basic field strips in Normandy, but these were still a good year off.

It would seem that to some extent the British either did and said things to keep the Polish spirit alive, or were even in some instances guilty of being disingenuous. But when they supported the Poles, it can be assumed that there was always an option that after the "foreseeable future", events might be different. For example, the Royal Air Force facilitated the training of Polish officers on captured German planes. This was the highly secret "Enemy Aircraft Circus", and the Poles, all experienced and veteran pilots, became acquainted and flew the German Heinkel 111, Me 110 and Ju 88.[6] These officers with their own long experience underwent basic indoctrination to German planes and were assumed to be competent enough to operate captured German planes and possibly train others in Poland.

SIKORSKI'S THIRD VISIT TO THE UNITED STATES

The Polish hope for a Balkan strategy was far from dead. In December 1942, Sikorski made his third (and last) trip to the United States. He was accompanied by Józef Rettinger. Sikorski met with President Roosevelt and the American military leadership and the talks were directed at specific military and general political issues. The major Polish goal was to secure American political support in the intensifying war of words with the Soviets, which had just publicly announced that all Poles had left the USSR and the rest were Soviet citizens.

Sikorski also argued the merits of a Balkan strategy and also attempted to negotiate directly for American Liberator bombers to serve as long-range supply planes for the Polish Underground.

While Sikorski was treated royally in the United States, the only concrete achievement was the inclusion of a Polish officer, Colonel Leon Mitkiewicz, in the Combined Chiefs of Staffs in Washington and a suggestion by Roosevelt to Churchill to make some Liberators available to the Poles. Colonel Leon Mitkiewicz described his unsuccessful attempts at integrating the Polish Underground into overall Allied strategy.[7]

---

6   TNA AIR 29/868.
7   Leon Mitkiewicz, *W Najwyzszym Sztabie Zachodnich Aliantów, 1943–1945,*, Veritas, London, 1971. Mitkiewicz's own archives are in the Yale University library.

The White House, Washington DC., 1942. In 1941 President Roosevelt hosts the Polish Prime Minister and Commander in Chief, General Władysław Sikorski. (PISM)

Archival evidence shows how strongly Sikorski made his case, and speaks to his strategic and political foresight. He analyzed the situation as offering the Western Allies two major options, a Northern route though Norway, Denmark into Germany, or a Southern Route, the Balkan strategy. Sikorski shared the British disquiet about a head-on invasion of Western Europe (i.e. France) and argued the strategic merits of an invasion which would drive a wedge between the German concentrations in the West (passively defensive) and the East. Sikorski was convinced that both Romania and Hungary would go over to the Western side in such a case if the Allies landed in Greece and Yugoslavia.[8] At the same time as Sikorski was meeting with President Roosevelt his chief of operational staff, Colonel Andrzej Marecki, met with American staffs. Marecki also strongly argued the Balkan strategy but apart from a courteous reception it made no impact.

The Americans saw the war against Germany as a secondary issue to be settled as quickly as possible and then to confront Japan. To Americans, the Pacific was of immense geo-political importance while Europe, particularly East-Central Europe,

---

8   Robert Szymczak, "Sikorski Strategy Memorandum, President's Secretary's File: Diplomatic Correspondence"; Mieczysław Bolesław Biskupski and James S. Pula, eds., "General Władysław Sikorski and the Allies", *Poland and Europe: Historical Dimensions* Volume 1, East European Monographs, 1993, pp.145–153.

was of negligible significance. In the next two years this became obvious, and only President Roosevelt's concern about the Polish-American electorate and his 1944 re-election campaign kept the embers of Polish diplomatic hopes alive.

Sikorski returned to the United Kingdom from his prolonged stay in the United States and Canada, followed by a short visit to Mexico. He was obviously a conflicted statesman. Estreicher writes of General Sikorski's general despondency after the trip.[9] At the same time he attempted to promote optimism, which perhaps muddied the clear thinking of the Polish Home Command – the old saying being that if wishes were horses ...

One of the political couriers expedited to Poland was Jerzy Lerski, and he carried the following message to the Polish Home Army Commander from Sikorski.

> Assure him we are doing our best to increase, as he requires, the supply of weapons and ammunition from the air. For this purpose I have just secured in Washington the delivery of a squadron of American Liberators to replace the smaller and slower British Halifaxes. The First Polish Airborne Brigade is being trained in Scotland to parachute in support of the forthcoming Uprising at home.[10]

According to Estreicher Sikorski was far from convinced that the Poles would get any Liberators.[11] But he had reason to hope. His memo about a "squadron", usually defined as twelve planes, was absolutely beyond reality. The categorical and assured statement about the Airborne Brigade (in fact Parachute Brigade) is completely at odds with the message in 1942 from the British Staff that air transport for moving a large number of men was just not available in the "foreseeable future". So what is one to assume about the obvious discrepancies between clear and blunt British policy statements, and Sikorski's optimistic and one could even categorize as grandiose communications to the occupied Homeland?

The tenor of the cited message is confirmed by the message carried a month later by Captain Jan Górski, who was a pre-war Polish parachute instructor and enthusiast of airborne and parachute operations. He had also been an instructor for nearly two years at the British Parachute Centre, Ringway, where he was involved in the instruction of the cadre of the Polish Parachute Brigade and couriers destined for Poland. The message carried by him was:

> ... acquaint the Home Army with new proposed plans for Air Force support of the Uprising. Because of his personal background he is to develop plans

---

9   Karol Estreicher, Jr., *Dziennik Wypadków*, Kraków, 2001, p.1943.
10   Jerzy Lerski, *Poland's Secret Envoy, 1939–1943*, Bicentennial Press, NY 1988, p.75.
11   Karol Estreicher, Jr., op.cit., p.1943.

for the parachuting of the Polish Para Brigade to capture a base or complex of bases.[12]

Messages of that tenor carried by various couriers, army and civilian, were contrary to what the Polish Military Headquarters knew. But the only voice of reality came from the Polish Air Force. There was a major difference, if not chasm, between the reality-bound air force staffs and close to fanciful army officers in the VI Bureau of the C-in-C Headquarters.

It may be pertinent at this point to comment on what was becoming a significant cultural difference between the senior officers of the Polish Air Force and of the Polish Army. The army officers literally lived and worked in a Polish setting. Polish air force officers were constantly, at every level, functioning in a British [RAF] setting. They developed a British manner of administrative practice, a British way of looking at military issues to the point that the Polish army brass disparagingly referred to them as Anglicized.

The Home Army command can be forgiven for picking and choosing those which seemed to offer the most hope in a situation of brutal repressions and terror. But the question remains why did Sikorski contribute to this basic and unqualified confusion, that in 1944 led directly or indirectly to the tragedy of the Warsaw Uprising? The fact that many described him as arrogant and conceited is insufficient to explain this posture vis-à-vis the Home Army.

It would appear that Sikorski was genuinely concerned about losing control of the Home Army and worried that other nationalistic groups might take over the control of the Polish State. The consequences of this could have led to many different political directions.

LIBERATORS FOR THE POLISH SPECIAL DUTIES FLIGHT

The process of obtaining Liberators proceeded. Was it because of the support from Lord Selborne, or the letter to Churchill from Roosevelt? As early as June 1942 the British staffs opined that "we should support the Poles in acquisition of the six Liberators in addition to our own allocation."[13] In December 1942 the British became aware that the Americans communicated to them "the US has no Liberators available for additional commitments."[14] But Roosevelt did write to Churchill on January 8 1943 regarding his meeting with Sikorski and the latter's request, as well as his own reservations, since Poland is "within a British theatre of operations and responsibilities". Roosevelt suggested that Sikorski's "proposal has a great deal of merit". He

---

12   P.I.S.M. LOTA.V. II/1b.
13   TNA AIR 19/18 80530.
14   TNA AIR 19/18 80530,

concluded "you might perhaps be able to spare him six out of the total of 398 B–24s [Liberators] allocated from US production under the recent Arnold-Evill-McCain-Patterson agreement."[15] The British archives document the Air Ministry reserva-tions, which are reasonable but rather unfocused. Eventually a memorandum from Air Ministry to RAFDEL in Washington, dated January 13 1943, emphasizes that the British should not support Polish requests for Liberators, but reviewed and cites Polish arguments for the new aircraft.

The Poles argued and the British agreed that the "number of Halifaxes allotted specifically for Polish tasks is insufficient to undertake high priority requirements". Furthermore the Poles argued that the "range and speed of Halifax insufficient to carry long range tasks during short nights and even in most favourable conditions aircraft unable to reach certain objectives." The Air Ministry then vacillated and stated that the Poles would get improved Halifaxes, and in the future, when flame dampening problems has been solved in the British share of Liberators, the Poles might get some of these aircraft. The facts are that the Air Ministry and the Chief of the Air Staff were conflicted and under pressures from their own political leaders, who were sympathetic to the Polish request.

The B–24 Liberator, like all American heavy bombers, was a day bomber, and intended to fly in defensive box formations rather than follow the tactics of the RAF, whose bombers were intended for night missions and essentially flew solo, finding their target by a variety of radio beacons and in the final approach by multi-colored markers dropped by skilled navigators – the pathfinders.

Finally, the Air Minister, Sir Archibald Sinclair, wrote to the Polish Prime Minister (General Sikorski) in February, 1943, stating:

> Both the Americans and ourselves are doing everything possible to over-come the technical difficulties, but I am afraid there is little to prospect of reaching a satisfactory conclusion before June at the earliest. In the mean-while I hope you will accept my assurance that everything is being done to ensure that you are provided with the most suitable type of aircraft available to enable you to maintain the morale and equipment of your gallant armies now fighting in Poland.[16]

The Chief of the Royal Air Force, Marshal of the Royal Air Force Portal, was also still possessive and protective of his limited resources. He made it clear that the Poles could not have three Liberators and still keep their Halifaxes.

---

15   TNA ADM 199/1393 80530. Again note the paradox of these files being in the ADM series.
16   TNA ADM 199/1393.

LISBON TALKS WITH ROMANIAN AND HUNGARIAN DIPLOMATS

The direction of Polish Balkan policy and strategy was not just limited to negotiations with London and Washington. The Poles also displayed a major initiative in Lisbon with semi-official and discrete representatives of the Italian, Romanian and Hungarian governments, who were all seeking a way of jumping ship and abandoning their ally, Germany. This was a natural evolution of Poland's foreign policy before the war which had attempted to craft a coalition/federation of East/Central European Countries. The Polish foreign minister, Beck and his deputy, Szembek, saw Hungary and Romania as the obvious partners. One of the major Polish negotiators was Lt Colonel Jan Kowalewski, who had held important inter-war posts as military attaché Moscow and Budapest.[17]

In the United Kingdom, Sikorski pursued a policy of reconciliation with the leadership of the Czecho-Slovak state and finally managed to seal an agreement with Beneš.[18] It was understood by the Poles that this confederation would also be joined by two of Poland's closest, pre-war, partners if not actual allies, Romania and Hungary. The dilemma was that both Hungary and Romania had thrown in their political fortunes with Germany, not against the United Kingdom, but against the Soviets. Aware of the abject failure of the British to honour their mutual assistance treaty with Poland, and witnesses to the British inability to help Yugoslavia and Greece, it seemed logical to them to assume that the Germans would decide the fate of Europe. Furthermore in the case of Romanians, they had been forced to cede part of their territory to the Soviets in 1940 and wanted that land back.

The Polish Government was particularly interested in subverting the Romanians and Hungarians over to the Allied side. The Polish negotiations were carried out, absolutely unofficially, by one of Poland's pre-war senior diplomats, Szembek, in neutral Lisbon. In turn he kept the Polish Foreign Office in London advised and in turn so were the British. The latter were intrigued but at best cautious and insisted that the Poles should also be not forthcoming since the Balkans were viewed by the British as within the Soviet sphere of influence. After the Tehran Conference the Romanians grasped the reality that the Polish connection added nothing to their hopes of loosening the chains of the German alliance. The Western call for "Unconditional Surrender" also turned their heads if not their hearts to Moscow. Finally the British formally requested in 1944 that the Polish secret negotiations in Lisbon cease. It has to be assumed that they became aware of the Soviets being knowledgeable of this, and that these countries had been settled as being in the Soviet sphere of interest.

---

17 Tessa Stirling, Daria Nałecz and Tadeusz Dubicki, eds., *The Report of the Anglo-Polish Historical Committee*, Volume 1, Vallentine Mitchell, London, 2005, Chapter 54, "Lt. Col. Jan Kowalewski's Mission in Portugal", by Jan Stanisław Ciechanowski.

18 Piotr S. Wandycz, *Czechoslovak –Polish Confederation and the Great Powers, 1940–1943*, Indiana University Press, Bloomington, 1956.

The British rationalized this with some justification, that since these countries were fighting the Soviets, it was up to the Soviets to 'sort them out". Had the Polish plan for the Balkans been completely supported by at least the British, it would have led to the following probable strategic scenarios. Allied troops including Poles, would have landed in the Dalmatian coast, joined with the Royalist Yugoslav partisans of Draża Mihajlowicz and immediately caused the Hungarian and Romanian armies to go over to the Allies. In such a scenario it is inevitable that the Turks would also have thrown in their lot with the Western Allies. It is likely that the Slovaks would also have thrown in their lot with Western Allies, since their Fall 1944 uprising against the Germans proved their mettle. It is also predictably regrettable that the Czechs would not have participated and with the Carpathian chain between the Balkans and Poland, the final outcome for the Poles would not have necessarily succeeded, unless the Germans morally collapsed as they did in 1918.[19]

Churchill also never lost his eye on the Balkan strategy though the British never had sufficient political or military clout to impose this strategy on the coalition of the "United Nations". In August 1943, when meeting Roosevelt in Hyde Park, he attempted to interest the President in the Balkans while at the Quebec meeting (Quadrant) he urged that the Italian campaign be prosecuted. This was the time when Churchill seemed to do all he could to delay *Overlord* and the American military chiefs were perturbed. Churchill "became excited" by a possible landing of 75,000 Polish troops and possibly 2nd New Zealand Division on the Dalmatian coast. The Polish Corps was still in the Middle East but was moved to the Italian front in December 1943.[20]

The Americans viewed the European war as a necessary nuisance to be disposed of before their major war with Japan. The Americans were on pace to become the major power in the Pacific, the European balance of power was of little concern, and Churchill's grand strategy was perceived as outdated colonialism and imperi-alism. The paradox was the British as well as French and Dutch colonialism was condemned, but the Soviet expansion into neighboring states was condoned as a benign development analogous to American interventions in the Caribbean region. Both Anglo-Saxon powers were concerned lest Stalin sign a peace of some sort with Hitler; but the Americans on a practical level hoped for Stalin's help in defeating Japan, while Roosevelt, with an idealistic and utopian view, hoped for a world run by the great powers which would help preserve peace. To some extent this harked back to what many saw as the great success of the Congress of Vienna, 1815, a view still

---

19   Tadeusz Piszczkowski, *Miedzy Lizbona a Londynem,* Polish Institute, London, 1979. This is a mono-graph based on the archives of the Polish Institute in London. This is a magnificent account of Polish wartime diplomatic initiatives, rather strangely omitted from the Bibliographical Essay in Piotr S. Wandycz, *Polish Diplomacy 1914–1945. Aims and Achievements,* Orbis Books, London, 1988.
20   Hastings, Sir Max, *Winston's War. Churchill 1940–1945,* Alfred A. Knopf, NY, 2010, p.317.

entertained by many after the collapse of the Soviet Empire in Eastern Europe in 1989, and given what happened in 1815 not shared by the Poles.

One of the most influential American statesmen, William C. Bullitt, also favored a Balkan strategy. He was of the opinion that had the Allies moved quickly to exploit the Italian surrender then they might have been able to establish a viable presence in the Balkans, since the Romanians, and other small countries of the region would have changed sides.[21]

This was obviously the last thing the Soviets wanted! It would be foolish to make the argument that Churchill looked with favor on the Balkan Strategy because of Polish hopes. He clearly wished to ensure that the Mediterranean area remained under British control. But the Americans became close to phobic about any suggestion that forces should be diverted to anything but the cross channel invasion of France – *Overlord*.

FINAL TALKS BETWEEN THE POLES AND THE SOVIETS IN MOSCOW

In early 1943, just before the break down of diplomatic relations between the Poles and Soviet, the Polish ambassador in Moscow, Tadeusz Romer, in conversations with Stalin attempted to address the deteriorating situation, and offered Soviets the help of the Polish Home Army. Romer stated that the Poles could stop all German rail transports in Eastern Poland heading for the front. Stalin discouraged such a move as one likely to bring major reprisals on the population. Since that conversation the Soviets had expressed contemptuous opinions on the Polish Home Army and were constantly critical that the Western Allies were flying in military supplies, even though they were limited to sabotage and intelligence work. Nevertheless, the Polish side always offered to participate in the liberation of Poland. Later in 1944, to prove that the Polish Home Army existed, a major operation was undertaken, codenamed Julia.

---

21   Orville H. Bullitt, ed., *For the President. Personal and Secret. Correspondence Between Franklin D. Roosevelt and William C. Bullitt*, Houghton Mifflin Company, Boston, 1972, pp.590–597. Post-war two senior American generals confirmed the major strategic issues and their own political analysis. General John R. Deanne wrote, "Stalin wanted the Anglo-American forces in Western, not Southern Europe; Churchill thought our post-war position would be improved and British interest best served if the Anglo-Americans as well as the Russians participated in the occupation of the Balkans. From the military point of view there can be no doubt of the wisdom of the American Chiefs of Staff in urging a cross-Channel invasion as preferable. From the political point of view hindsight on our part points to foresight on Churchill's part (*The Strange Alliance*, Viking Press, NY 1947, p. 43). General Albert Wedemeyer commented regretfully, "If we could get through the Balkans I foresaw the accomplishment of my ulterior but quietly guarded political objective of keeping the Russians from overrunning Central Europe. If could get Anglo-American forces up into Poland by attacking from the south, the Mediterranean, I would gladly jump at the chance. But after careful scrutiny of all possibilities, couldn't see a chance of success. The terrain was against it." (*Wedemeyer Reports*, Henry Holt and Company, NY, 1958, p. 228).

1943 – the year of Polish calamities

1943 was to be a calamitous year for the Poles. It began in April when the Germans stunned the world by announcing the discovery of the bodies of thousands of Polish officers in large unmarked graves at a place that has gone into Polish history –Katyn. It finished with the infamous Tehran Conference of the "Big Three" in which the Polish future was decided by Stalin and Roosevelt with Churchill becoming aware of the relative impotence of Britain. Only in retrospect is it obvious that this was the year that Poland finally lost the war and not just a major campaign.

Even before the discovery of the Polish dead at Katyn, the Polish-Soviet relations were becoming sour. The Soviets incrementally ratcheted up their diplomatic war with the Poles. All Polish pre-war citizens who had lived in territories annexed by the Soviets in 1939 were now officially declared to be Soviet citizens. Stalin made it clear that the Polish Government in London was not democratic, that it was unfriendly to the Soviets and needed to be changed.

A Polish Communist Committee was formed in Russia and recruitment began to a Polish communist army under Colonel Zygmunt Berling whom Stalin shortly made a general in the Polish Army. All of these moves were a test of how much anti-Polish propaganda the Western Allies would tolerate. It was tolerated, and Stalin correctly assumed that he could do what he liked regarding the Poles. The first major open crisis was indeed the Katyn graves.

Katyn was a small Russian town near Smolensk and in 1943 under German occupation. Preliminary photographs distributed by the Germans with great glee and enthusiasm showed mounds of corpses in Polish uniforms. Later it turned out that this was only one of many sites of horrible atrocities committed against Polish prisoners of war by the Soviets. While it was obvious from the distributed photographs that the men had been shot in the back of the head, the controversy which erupted had to do with who was the perpetrator. As far as the Poles in the West were concerned, this was proof of what they had dreaded since 1941 when unable to locate close to 15,000 active duty and reserve officers.

The Polish Government and overwhelming majority of Poles suspected that they had been lied to by Stalin when told that thousands of men had escaped. The Polish Government, without pointing a finger, requested the International Red Cross to investigate the graves without accusing any one. Stalin, who had all along disclaimed all knowledge of the Polish officers, now claimed that the Germans were obviously responsible and was insulted and broke off relations with the Polish Government. After the war Churchill wrote about the revised Soviet version in his memoirs:

> This version to be believed involves acceptance of the fact that nearly 15,000 Polish officers of whom there was no record since the Spring of 1940,

passed into German hands in July 1941, and were later destroyed by the Germans without one single person escaping and reporting, either to the Russian authorities or to the Polish consul in Russia or to the Underground Movement in Poland. When we remember the confusion caused by the German advance, that the guards of the camp must have fled as the invaders came nearer, and all the contacts afterwards during this period of Russo-Polish co-operation, the belief seems an act of faith.[22]

The British ambassador to the Polish Government, Sir Owen O'Malley, wrote a report which left no doubt as to who was responsible but attempted to address the consequences for the British Government. As a result of the report and of Stalin's decision to break off the very recently established relations with the Poles there was considerable angst in the British Government. All members of the Foreign Office were clearly convinced as to Soviet responsibility but attempted to minimize damage to the relationship with an important ally. Churchill advised President Roosevelt but whatever the latter believed he made it clear that as far as he was concerned the party responsible were the Germans and refused to discuss the issue.[23] This was the end of Sikorski's political plans for a working relationship with the Soviets.

GENERAL SIKORSKI IS KILLED IN A PLANE ACCIDENT

This year of calamities continued when in July 1943, returning from an inspection of the Polish Forces in the Middle East, Sikorski was a victim of a controversial plane accident at Gibraltar.

General Sikorski flew to inspect the Polish Forces in the Middle East. The majority of the Polish forces in the Middle East were from the Eastern Polish territories that had been annexed by the Soviets in 1939, and most had gone through the Soviet gulags before being "amnestied" in 1941 and evacuated. All watched with great deal of anxiety the complete regression of Polish-Soviet relations. It would be an exaggeration to say that the forces were becoming demoralized, but some were becoming disenchanted with what they saw as Sikorski's ineffectual attempts to preserve a relationship with the Soviets. About that same time Churchill wrote to his Deputy Minister of Defense, General Ismay "time has come to bring Polish troops from Persia in to the

---

22   Winston Churchill, *The Hinge of Fate*, Cassell, London, p.680. The story of this tragedy was shaped by the communist authorities in Poland to follow the Soviet line. The best histories of both tragic events were written by Polish historians in the West. The first was Janusz K. Zawodny, *Death in the Forest, The Story of the Katyn Forest Massacre*, University of Notre Dame Press, South Bend, 1962. Also, see George Sanford, *Katyn and the Soviet Massacre of 1940*, Routledge, Taylor & Francis Group, NY, 2009.

23   Laurence Rees, *WWII Behind Closed Doors. Stalin, the Nazis and the West*, Pantheon Books, New York, 2008. pp.242–250.

Mediterranean theatre. Politically highly desirable, as the men wish to fight and once engaged will worry less about their own affairs, which are tragic".[24]

General Sikorski decided to visit the forces, and there is some indirect evidence that he hoped that while in the Middle East he would arrange a visit to Stalin and attempt to address the problems. As so often the source for this was Rettinger in a meeting with one of the SOE operatives, Peter Wilkinson. All were becoming apprehensive about the future role of SOE in a standoff between the Polish Home Army and the encroaching Soviet armies. Wilkinson was supposed to accompany General Sikorski to the Middle East, but at the last minute because of Churchill's request he was dropped in favor of Major Victor Cazalet. It is perhaps a coincidence, but Rettinger did not accompany Sikorski on this trip. Wilkinson writes "At one of our periodic dinners at the Ecu de France, Rettinger told me that Sikorski was becoming very anxious about future Polish-Soviet relations and proposed shortly to visit the Soviet Union to discuss these matters personally with Stalin."[25] There were also rumors in Polish circles in London that Sikorski was so discouraged by

London, July 1943. General Stanisław Sosabowski, commanding general of the Polish Parachute Brigade, leads a detachment of the Brigade through the streets of London to Westminster Cathedral for the funeral service of General Sikorski. (PISM)

24 Winston S. Churchill, *Closing the Ring*, Cassell, London, 1952. p. 573.
25 Peter Wilkinson, *Foreign Fields. The Story of an SOE Operative*, I.B. Tauris Publishers, London, 1997, p.129.

American and British lack of support that he planned to follow Beneš, the Czech leader, by making up with Stalin. There is no archival support for this, but it a most plausible possibility. But if in late 1941, with the Germans at the outskirts of Moscow, Stalin allegedly reached out to Sikorski to sign some form of agreement with the Poles ceding Eastern Poland, one can assume that by mid-1943 any such arrangement would not have been of any interest to Stalin.

The possible visit to the Soviet Union did not take place but by all accounts the visit to the Polish Forces went well and Sikorski boarded his plane for the United Kingdom. After a sort stopover in Gibraltar on July 4 1943 his plane crashed minutes after taking off. All aboard except for the pilot were killed. This very important and tragic accident is discussed briefly in Appendix B. In this disaster the Poles also lost their Chief of Staff, Major General Tadeusz Klimecki, as well as Chief of III operations, Colonel Andrzej Marecki. Also killed was Lt. Colonel Victor Cazalet.

7

New Polish Prime Minister

New Polish Prime Minister and new Polish Commander-in-Chief –
Continued Negotiations over Air Support for Poland's Home Army –
Combined Chiefs turn down Polish plans for arming the Polish Home Army
– events leading to the Tehran Conference.

Change of Government and of Strategic Policies

Immediately on receiving news of the accident and death of the Polish Commander-in-Chief, the President asked the Deputy Prime Minister, Stanisław Mikołajczyk, to act as an interim chair of the cabinet. The President also embarked on consultations with all the members of cabinet representing the various political parties. It was obvious that even if Mikołajczyk was nominated by the President to the post of Prime Minister and approved by the whole cabinet, the posts of Prime Minister and Commander-in-Chief had to be separated. The most senior general in the West was Kazimierz Sosnkowski and he was the obvious nominee. In fact, by all logic he should have been appointed to that post in October 1939.

But political and personal issues surfaced. General Anders in the Middle East found Mikołajczyk to be too closely identified with Stanisław Kot.[1] Anders sent a message through General Michel Karasiewicz-Tokarzewski, who was attending Sikorski's funeral ceremonies, that he adamantly opposed the nomination of Mikołajczyk for prime minister but expressed strong support for Sosnkowski as C-in-C.

---

1 Stanisław Kot, who as Polish ambassador in Moscow, when Anders was attempting to form a Polish army in the Soviet Union, had earned his loathing. Kot was one of the first politicians to rush back to communist Poland then made slanderous remarks about Anders.

In turn supporters of Mikołajczyk for Prime Minister went on record that Sosnkowski was unacceptable. Most regrettably the Mikołajczyk faction, in the person of Kot and Litauer, turned to the British for support.

This contemptible move by some Polish politicians again opened the door for British interference in Polish politics. Churchill called in Rettinger for consultation. We have no archives for the discussions and only self-serving memoirs. In general the British were less than pleased with the selection of Sosnkowski probably because of his adamant opposition to the 1941 Sikorski–Maisky agreement. But Anders' opposition to Mikołajczyk did not pass unnoticed in the British cabinet or by Mikołajczyk.

In general, the British did not like the Polish constitutional position of Commander-in-Chief and would have preferred the Poles to model the British system of a war cabinet. But the Polish Constitution stipulated that post, even though given the dispersion of Polish Forces in many places, it was an anomaly. Therefore, in the Polish situation it was a much more political position than intended in the 1935 Constitution and inexorably became a political center significantly independent of the Polish coalition cabinet.

After discussions with the representatives of all the political parties, the Polish president nominated Mikołajczyk to be Prime Minister. This was unanimously approved by his coalition cabinet. The President also nominated Sosnkowski to be C-in-C. In his new cabinet Mikołajczyk dismissed Raczyński as foreign minister and appointed Tadeusz Romer.

Given Kot's *claque* to the British for support in the final details of Polish governance, it is not at all surprising that shortly afterwards, when Stalin demanded a change in the Polish London based government, it did not meet with the categorical rejection on the part of the British, but merely an acquiescence to discuss it with Mikołajczyk.

It was also at that time that the General Officer Commanding the Polish Underground Army, General Stefan (Grot) Rowecki, was captured by the Germans. The new commander became General Tadeusz (Bór) Komorowski.[2]

It would be simplistic and naïve to explain all of the problems which confronted the Poles in 1943, and later, as due to the lack of mutual conception of strategic goals between the Prime Minister and Commander-in-Chief. But the fact is that the Prime Minister before the war had been an active member of the Peasant Party and a small-holding farmer. He was shrewd, pragmatic, and in his discussions in Moscow in the Fall of 1944, showed great political skill, dignity and nerve. He did not allow himself to be brow beaten by an irate and guilty Churchill and a wily Stalin. By all accounts, he grew into his role though he also had many political enemies. Churchill assumed that he would be pliable in his hands, but there is some evidence that he was more resistant to flattery than Sikorski had been.

---

2   *The Secret Army. The memoirs of General Tadeusz (Bór) Komorowski,* Frontline Books, Barnsley, UK, 2011.

Mikołajczyk came from Western Poland and believed that since the Poles had defied Germanization for well over a century they would survive the Russians, who were far less culturally advanced. But like many uneducated men he had a chip on his shoulder when it came to came to dealing with men who had been born with a silver spoon in their mouth and in particular if they had been in the corridors of power of pre-war Poland, like the President, General Sosnkowski or Ambassador Raczyński.

Mikołajczyk's attempts to work with Churchill, and agree to many of Stalin's initial demands and his ultimate failure in the rigged elections of 1947 resulted in his being secretly whisked out of Communist Poland.[3]

Sosnkowski on the other hand was a sophisticated and analytic ideologue, often criticized for a Hamlet-like inability to act quickly on important events or to confront controversial issues. In 1940, during the last government crisis, he was bitterly criticized by many senior Polish officers for not taking a determined stand against British involvement in Polish politics and their protégé Sikorski. Sosnkowski espoused nothing short of complete Polish sovereignty, motivated by a sense of Polish history which he saw in centuries and not years. Sosnkowski was imbued with the national sense of disgrace at the part played by many Poles in contributing to the partitions in the late 18th Century. Whatever might happen to Poland, he was determined that the Poles would not play any humiliating role in it or contribute to it.

Very shortly, after the appointments had been made and General Sikorski laid to rest in the Polish military cemetery at Newark, joining hundreds of Polish airmen killed during training and operational missions, the Polish President invited Mr. Churchill to lunch at Claridge's. Other guests were Mr. August Zaleski, Sir Owen O'Malley and Count Edward Raczyński. Churchill discoursed on many important aspects of current world affairs, essentially tacitly admitting to his belief as to the Soviet responsibility for Katyn. He also made it clear that British policy had to defer to the Soviets who were gutting the German armies. Churchill summarized the situation as unsettled and that the Soviets had not deserved "British gratitude but its admiration", and warned the Poles not to provoke Stalin. The final statement was that Great Britain was under a legal obligation to restore Poland, but also made it clear that this did not mean support of the pre–1939 boundaries.[4]

CONTINUED NEGOTIATIONS OVER AIR SUPPORT FOR POLAND'S HOME ARMY

For the Poles it was no longer simply a Balkan strategy but a diplomatic initiative to integrate the Polish Home Army with the Western strategies. In simple terms,

---

3   Andrzej Paczkowski, *Stanisław Mikołajczyk. Czyli Klęska Realisty* [Stanisław Mikołajczyk. The catastrophe of a realist], Omnipress, Warsaw, 1991.
4   *Documents on Polish-Soviet Relations*, Volume II - 1943–1945, Heinemann, London, 1967, pp.25–28; Raczyński, *In Allied London*, op.cit., pp.159–160.

the Poles urged that an Allied military mission be sent to the Home Army, push for recognizing it as a formal belligerent force and send in the Polish Parachute Brigade as a concrete confirmation of Poland's sovereignty and its allegiance to the constitutional government. The question of the military mission foundered on British concerns about a Soviet response.

There was a continued back and forth between the Polish Commander-in-Chief and the various British authorities regarding enhanced air support for the Polish Home Army. The Polish side argued for more planes dedicated to such flights while the British were to some extent constrained by the realities of the distance, and political concern about Soviet reaction to arming a clandestine force in an area which the Soviets claimed as backwater.

Furthermore, the Air Ministry were quite negative about the benefits of such diversionary activities and the relocation of valuable aircraft to such activities. It was one thing to use outdated Lysanders to fly and land in France, but Liberators and Halifaxes were valuable planes, demanding extensive maintenance and ground support as well as frequent engine changes. Finally, flights to Poland were constrained to a period when the nights were long enough to ensure relative safety and this "season" only extended from September to April. It also needs to be emphasized that during the winter months all planes were subject to the danger of icing.

The Poles attempted at all levels to elevate the standing of their Home Army to the same status as the Polish Forces in the West. In spite of the sympathetic posture of the British Minister for Economic Warfare, Lord Selborne, who had succeeded Hugh Dalton, General Sosnkowski's attempts to have the issues of the Polish Home Army negotiated at the level of the British Chiefs of Staff came to naught. The British insisted that this was the function of the SOE "who are best fitted to discharge" these functions.[5] So Sosnkowski turned all his energies to engaging Lord Selborne in his endeavor and found a sympathetic ear. He urged that 600 support flights were the absolute minimum to provide material for the Home Army. Lord Selborne supported the Poles in his memorandum to the Air Ministry but opined that the figure of 600 was unrealistic. He suggested that the goal should be 300 flights. This is when that number of 300 originated. Lord Selborne also proposed that the Polish Special Duties flight be moved to Italy, which would to decrease the danger from German night fighters and also spread the depth of range to various drop zones in Poland.

He also urged the Polish position, so far received with a tin ear, that the Polish flight be earmarked strictly for flights to Poland and not used in other areas of the Balkans. This also was in a major disagreement with both the Air Ministry and the Chiefs of Staff, who felt that these planes belonged to them for their most utilitarian use. Lord Selborne wrote this most evocative memorandum on Poland's behalf:

---

5   TNA WO 293/42 80751.

The season during which the night is long enough to infiltrate men and equipment to Poland by air from the UK extends from September to April. In August last General Sosnkowski pressed us for acceptance of a programme of 600 successful sorties during the coming season, i.e. 75 a month. We said it was impossible, but that we hoped to achieve 300 in numbers of operations, i.e. 35–40 in number a month. General Sosnkowski now says that he never accepted this figure. In effect we were only able to achieve 16 in number operations in September and so far only 7 in October. The reason for this failure is the increase in the German night fighter force in NW Germany. During September we lost 6 aircraft in 22 sorties and in October 1 out of 8. These losses compelled the Air Ministry to route SOE aircraft on a more northerly course. The effect of this is to increase the mileage that the aircraft can only reach the NW of Poland, whereas General Sosnkowski wants his equipment delivered all over Poland and has a large number of men standing by to receive them.[6]

In the circumstance, I do not propose to ask for an increase of allotment of aircraft for SOE work now but I shall feel bound to ask shortly for more aircraft for 1944 and the claims of Poland will occupy a prominent place in my case, I confess to great sympathy with the Polish standpoint. They braved Hitler in 1939 on Britain's guaranteed support. They have been crucified. They have not winced. Alone among our occupied Allies they have no Quisling. They have incurred considerable casualties in very successfully attacking Germany's organized army of 250,000 in Poland which only need equipment. To be told that Britain cannot afford them more than six aircraft is a bit hard. The case for increased assistance to Poland rests less on strategy than on Polish morale, to which I attach great importance. I also think that the very difficult role we may later have to play with them in regard to their Eastern Frontier may perhaps be facilitated with success in making some response to the appeal which General Sosnkowski has addressed to me. To the Poles the war is in Poland and this is their last chance of fighting there.[7]

I feel, and I am sure you will agree that we have a heavy responsibility towards the Poles concerning the reception committees. The Polish heroes composing them have to tramp or bicycle long miles from their homes to the rendezvous and there exist in hiding among the rigors of a Polish winter. This is bad enough when they a buoyed up by the hope of successful operation but, as night success night and disappoint continues, the strongest may be forgiven if their will to continue resistance becomes impaired. The

6   TNA AIR 19/815 80530.
7   TNA AIR 19/815 80530.

plan on which these Committees work cannot be switched or cancelled at a moment's notice in a way that orders to air force with full base facilities at its disposal can be a varied.

In the circumstance is it really fair for a C-in-C Bomber Command to force us to tell the Poles that the route from the UK is so dangerous that it cannot be contemplated by Bomber Command? If we add to such a statement an excuse that we are not satisfied with the integrity of their organization in Poland until an enquiry into the matter has been concluded, in spite of all the evidence that exists of the splendid work the Resistance Groups in Poland are doing, then I feel we shall indeed have placed ourselves in a most humiliating and unenviable position and one which we shall really no answer whatever to the resulting Polish outburst.[8]

Lord Selborne, the British Minister of Economic Warfare, was a strong advocate of the Polish endeavor. He reminded Sir Archibald Sinclair, the Minister for Air on repeated occasions of the importance of this for the Poles and even on one occasion commented that given the Polish contribution of fourteen squadrons to be told that "Britain cannot afford them more than 6 aircraft is a bit hard."[9]

It should be noted that in addition to the fourteen squadrons there were 275 Polish pilots, 55 navigators, and many other aircrew in the RAF Transport Command. So there were Polish aircrew trained and experienced in operating large aircraft.

By the end of 1943 three Liberators joined the three Halifaxes of the Polish Special Duties flight (not squadron) which was moved to south Italy, near Brindisi.

In the Combined Chiefs of Staff, Washington

Colonel Mitkiewicz, the Polish representative at the Combined Chiefs of Staff in Washington, presented this outline of Polish strategy on June 30 1943:

Immediately after the occupation of Poland, a secret army had been formed in the country which was centered in the Warsaw, Cracow, Lódź and Lublin area. This army was in contact with the Polish Government in London and under the command of General Sikorski. Liaison was maintained by radio and by a Polish flight of a British squadron. Men, particularly officers, small arms, signal equipment and demolition material have been flown into them. General Sikorski considered this secret army as the main force of Poland since it was situated in the country and supported by the people. The

8   TNA AIR 19/815 80530.
9   TNA AIR 19/815 80539.

intention was to coordinate action by this secret army with that of the Polish forces abroad and with Allied plans. It was important the closest liaison be maintained with this army since its tie with the Polish General Staff had to be strengthened, and the interests of the Allies in its well being and operations demonstrated. Unless the ties were close, there was danger of an ill-timed movement started without direct coordination with Allied Command. The geographical situation of this army was immensely valuable. It separated the main German forces on the Eastern Front from their bases in the Reich and was in a position to cut their lines of communication should Germany wish to draw forces from the East for action in the West. General Sikorski's conception was to seize control of central Poland with the secret army, then to reinforce it by the transfer of Polish air forces and the Polish parachute brigade from the United Kingdom. Later, if possible, Polish land forces would be added. All these plans required the use of considerable air transport, and further, it was essential that they be coordinated with and form part of the Allied offensive in Europe. In addition to severing German concentrations between the Eastern front and the Reich, the secret army would engage considerable German forces and a very important area in Europe would be under allied control.

The Polish General Staff deem the recognition by the Combined Chiefs of Staff of the plan for the immediate preparation of the Secrete Army in Poland as vitally important to the overall war effort. Poland and occupies a central position in the region defined in the West by Germany proper, in the North by the Baltic sea, in the East by the German East Wall and the Black Sea, and in the South by the Mediterranean. In consequence of the development of Allied operations in southern Europe the whole of the above determined area had acquired preeminent strategic significance.

While these territories are held by the enemy, there remains a strong potential resistance which requires only means and direction for timely activation. The countries of this German hegemony are to a greater or less degree preparing for open military revolt. With adequate assistance they could undoubtedly precipitate the fall of the German European defenses. These forces would at the same time provide for Allied military security against chaos and organized movements, either from within the Reich or from elements of the Wehrmacht dispersed throughout Europe.

In this area Poland has retained and advanced military organization operating under the orders of the Polish General Staff in London. Recent military progress both in Eastern Europe and in the Mediterranean area brings forward a demand for determining strategic responsibility with regard to the territory of Poland. In active operations the Polish Armed forces in the UK will probably be employed under a joint Anglo-American command. The purpose and employment of the Secret Army in Poland are of primary strategic interest to the Allies, engaged in military operations against Germany. In accordance with the requirements of coordinate leadership, the Polish General Staff, therefore, consider it essential that the entire Polish Armed Forces should be placed under a common Allied Command, and the area of Poland should be considered one of joint strategic responsibility.

Equipment is flown from the UK for the maintenance of subversive activities, sabotage, and intelligence conducted by the Secret Army.

It has now become essential to intensify considerably the scale of these activities. Moreover, it is necessary to transfer to Poland a sufficient quantity of arms for the seizure, at a given signal, of certain points of subsequent reception for the bulk of combat equipment.

The performance of this task requires 500 operational flights to Poland before April 1944. The execution of 300 has been agreed upon by the British Joint Staff. In order to cover the remaining 200 flights and for reasons of increasing liaison requirements, the Polish General Staff, recommend the establishment of a Special Squadron of 18- 20 B–24 bombers.

The success of the general rising of the Secret Army will be conditioned upon the supply of sufficient combat equipment to the points previously captured and secured by the initial insurgent groups. The development of the operation will mainly depend upon the extent of equipment and reinforcement supplied from abroad.

The insurrections should occur when the bulk of the German forces are fully engaged, and when the rears are demoralized by facing an apparently hopeless struggle. The German High Command will then be incapable of directing and coordinating actions against an organized rising on its own rear and on hostile soil. The determination of a propitious opportunity for the rising by the Secret Army will be difficult. It will, however, become inevitable in order to prevent the rising from being occasioned an uncontrollable flow of events. Nor should this decision under any circumstance delay or influence the execution of the plan. Timely preparation and assistance will assure the direction of the military effort of Poland in conformance with Allied intentions." [10]

---

10   National Archives, College Park, USA, CCS 334 218.

The final reversal of Polish fortunes came from the Combined Chiefs of Staff in Washington who politely but categorically turned down all Polish requests to integrate the Polish Underground with Allied strategy and limited aid by air to sabotage and intelligence equipment.[11]

EVENTS LEADING UP TO TEHRAN CONFERENCE

The British began to be pre-occupied with the immediacy of Polish-Soviet problems in late 1943.They entertained a hope, which in retrospect was proven naïve and not shared by the majority of Poles, that were the Poles to finally compromise on frontiers, and make changes in their London-based government to suit Stalin, then all might be well. General Sosnkowski, General Anders as well as the Polish President were identified as the main recalcitrants but it was also finally understood that the whole Polish clandestine State was united in opposing any loss of historic Polish lands.

The question that was not readily apparent and the Polish military in London were not forthcoming on was as to the position of the Home Army in regard to the advancing Soviet armies. This was not merely a reluctance to share intelligence and policy data, but to some extent the London-based Headquarters were not always sure of the local Polish policy and reaction.

Some of the strategic concepts and Polish diplomatic efforts through the British Government to resume relations with the Soviets had a continuity even after Sikorski's death. The Polish Government in London was now under great pressure from all sides. But the Soviets firmly held to their line that all Polish citizens, resident in those parts of Poland that had been occupied by the Soviets in 1939, were Soviet citizens, since there had been a plebiscite in which 99% of the people voted to join the Soviet Union. They expressed reluctant acceptance of British and American pressure to resume diplomatic relations with the Poles, conditioned on the Polish Government agreeing to the Curzon Line, and significant changes in the Polish Government. The British pressured the Poles to agree to the Curzon Line with the variation that Lwów would remain Polish. Internally the Poles were under pressure from their Clandestine Delegatura that no territories could be forfeited to the Soviets. Finally, the soldiers of 2 Corps all came from territories that were being claimed by the Soviets, and tacitly conceded by the British, and many still had family members in the Soviet Union.

These ultimately very flawed discussions went nowhere, since the Soviets realized that the British were at best lukewarm in supporting their Polish ally, while their own strategic situations was improving with every day. After Stalingrad it was inevitable that the Germans would be defeated.

---

11   National Archives, College Park MD. CCS 334 218.

Finally, Raczyński met with Eden and informed him that the British and American governments were both to state unequivocally that they had agreed to the Soviet territorial demands (Lwów staying Polish while Wilno going to the Lithuanians) and both Western powers guaranteeing Polish independence of the Soviets, then reluctantly the Poles would agree to such a *force majeure*. Eden grasped this straw but the Americans refused to either guarantee future borders or to discuss changes during the war. Eden could not persuade the Soviets to resume diplomatic relations with the Poles who had now began to accuse the Poles of conspiring with the Germans. The Soviets also strongly alleged that the Polish Underground really did not exist except for Gestapo agents masquerading as Poles and killing Soviet partisans.[12]

Woodward in his account of the actions of the British Foreign Office states that Eden on October 1943 circulated a memorandum on the question of the Soviets approaching the Polish borders and the Polish Home Army. He seemed to assume that the Soviets would expect the Polish Underground (Home Army) "to harass the Germans". He admitted that at this point the British Government would "find it difficult to continue our policy of discouraging premature risings". This is an admission, one of many, that the British did not want to have the Poles stage a major uprising and that their commitment to supplying the Polish Home Army was in fact limited by policy to intelligence gathering and sabotage.

The Foreign Office had to face the question of arming an army of 65,000 since "hitherto we had done nothing to arm them". The War Cabinet was advised that the Combined Chiefs of Staffs in Washington on September 17, 1943 had rejected a Polish appeal for equipment, and it was assumed by the Foreign Office that the primary reason was " shortage of aircraft", but he also took the position that Poles could not be expected to agree unless the Poles and Soviets resumed diplomatic relations; and that changes in the Polish Government under Soviet duress were unreasonable.

This necessary segue into political issues goes to the heart of the matter and the fact that the British Government fully realized the machiavellian manipulations of Moscow. Stalin wanted the Polish Government to get rid of its President and of General Sosnkowski. Eden fully realized the impossibility of changing the President but commented that if Sosnkowski was dismissed the only candidate to replace him was General Anders, even more of a *bête noire* to the Soviets. Anybody else would lead to a state of extreme anxiety and demoralization in the Polish Armed forces.[13]

---

12 Llewellyn Woodward, *British Foreign Policy in the Second World War,* Vol. II, HMSO, London, 1971, pp.627–657. For details of the Curzon line see pp. 657–662.
13 Woodward, op.cit., p.649.

8

TEHRAN AND ITS CONSEQUENCES

Consequences of Tehran – British Support for the Poles – Mass media war against the Polish Government – Polish Government reacts – Polish Maritime Exhibit in London -Polish Naval involvement in Operation Neptune.

POST-TEHRAN

The Big Three Decision reached at Tehran involved more than the Polish territories but in the context of this monograph they were critical and decisive to the future of an independent Polish State.[1] It was obvious that Germany was on an inevitable slide to defeat. But the other invaders of Poland in 1939, the Soviets, were showing an ever increasing and blatant enmity to the Poles. The Soviet armies, generously supported by Western airpower, which was never acknowledged, were tearing the German armies to shreds on an inevitable road to accomplishing ideological and territorial ambitions that had been temporarily thwarted in 1920.[2] The leaked news of the Tehran Conference was horrible but many Poles refused to believe that the Western democracies would abandon them. Those who were sanguine and those who were not had no alternative but to fight to the end. Raczyński, in his notes as early as July 1943, shortly after the break in diplomatic relations with the Soviets, perhaps best described the overall attitude of the Poles, as:

1   Keith Eubank, *Summit at Tehran. The Untold Story*, William Morrow and Company, New York, 1985; Jan Karski, *The Great Powers and Poland. 1919–1945. From Versailles to Yalta*, University Press of America, Lanham MD,1985.

2   Adam Zamoyski, *Warsaw 1920, Lenin's Failed Conquest of Europe*, Harper Press, London, 2008. This is an account of the Polish victory at the gates of Warsaw which threw the Soviets back and led to the Treaty of Riga.

The game was bound to be lost for us whatever the Polish Government in exile and the Polish armies might do, either in Poland itself or on the battle-fields of the Alliance. I personally had no illusions and few hopes. But I believed that the game should be played through to the end, to the last polit-ical card and to the last shot.[3]

The Soviet war against the Poles was waged in many ways. Once the Soviets crossed into Polish territory in their pursuit of the retreating Germans the Soviets began to round up and arrest Polish Home Army units that had attempted to co-operate with them. But these were discrete and secret actions, hidden by distance and the lack of any credible Western military missions. Only Polish Home Army radio communica-tions reported these facts to the West and the Poles in the United Kingdom were not being given any publicity.

On January 3 1944 Sir Owen O'Malley, British ambassador to the Polish Government, and genuinely pro-Polish, but representing the views of the Government of the United Kingdom, met with the Polish Prime Minister and indicated that the Poles needed to make territorial concessions, pointing out that "frontiers are not sacro-sanct", also using the worn-out argument that the area between the Riga Treaty, from 1921 and the Curzon Line, which was actually drawn up by Namier (Namierkowski) on behalf of the British Foreign Office, was of a mixed ethnic population.[4] O'Malley further made a philosophical statement that the whole trend in modern history is "in the direction of homogeneity of states". How adding Belorussians and Ukrainians to a Soviet giant improved the homogeneity of the USSR defies logic. Nonetheless Poles were constantly being given good advice. The British also showed little respect to that homogeneity philosophy by tacitly agreeing to the Soviet absorption of three little and ethnically non-Slav Baltic republics.[5]

On January 20, 1944 there was a meeting of Mikołajczyk, the Polish foreign minister, Romer, and Raczyński with Churchill, Eden and Cadogan in which the British Prime Minister urged as strongly as possible that the Poles abandon Eastern Poland since this was a condition demanded by Stalin before resuming diplomatic relations with the Poles.[6]

The dispiriting reality of the Tehran Conference was confirmed by Churchill at the House of Commons debate in February 1944. Churchill made complimentary remarks about the "heroic Polish race" but opined that the Soviets had security reasons to move their borders further West. Churchill apparently had no memory or wish to

---

3   Count Edward Raczyński, *In Allied London*, Weidenfeld & Nicolson, London, 1962, p.155.
4   Norman Davies, *Lloyd George and Poland, 1919–1920*, Wydawnictwo Uniwersytetu Gdanskiego, Gdansk, Poland, 2000.
5   *Documents on Polish Soviet Relations*, Vol. II 1943–1945, pp.122–123. It should be added that Sir Owen O'Malley was a good friend of the Polish people.
6   Ibid., pp.144–149.

remember that it was the Soviet decision of 1939 that brought Germany to the Soviet borders. A most lively debate followed, with many for and some against the conclusions of the Conference regarding Poland and British policy, but it would appear that the majority of the members were caught between the anvil and the hammer.[7]

The British Ambassador, Sir Own O'Malley, while representing the views of His Majesty's Government to the Poles, also presented his own views to Anthony Eden.

> The real choice before us seems to me, to put it brutally, to lie between on the one hand selling the corpse of Poland to Russia and finding an alibi to be used in evidence when we are indicted for murder; and on the other hand putting the points of principle to Stalin in the clearest possible way and warning him that our position might have to be explained publicly with equal clearness. In the second alternative we might indeed fail to deflect him from violent and illegal courses, but it would be on record that we had done our utmost. [8]

Sir Owen probably expressed not just his views but the opinion of the majority of Poles. They all at this point began to realize that the British were not going to fight a war over Polish Eastern territories. But all were dismayed, many depressed at the eagerness of the British Government and the public to embrace Soviet policies vis-à-vis Poland.

Eden's hand-scrawled comment was, "but would it help Poland?"

The behavior of the British leadership to the Poles was also a mixture of reassurance, some discrete sympathy about the impasse that the Poles were in, calls for Poles to compromise and in some cases support. The minutes of the Defence Committee on Special Operations held in February 1944 document a discussion between Churchill, Eden, Selborne and Portal regarding the basic good will towards their Polish ally.

> Minister of Economic Warfare agreed with the opinion of the Chief of Staffs in their report that the control of special operations in both countries [i.e. Poland and Czechoslovakia] should remain with the SOE in London, subject to the direction of the Chiefs of Staff. As regards Poland the position was as follows. Assistance to the Poles had to be provided from the Mediterranean. The German night fighter strength made SOE operations over Poland based in this country impracticable. On the other hand, the Polish Government was established in London. Relations with the Poles involved many difficult political problems which had to be settled here. In the circumstances it would be inconvenient for the control of SOE operations over that country to be centred in the Mediterranean theatre. As regards Czechoslovakia,

---

7   Wacław Jedrzejewicz, ed., *Poland in the British Parliament, 1939–1945. Volume II, Fall 1941-Spring 1944*, Józef Piłudski Institute of America, New York, 1959, pp.339- 418.

8   TNA FO 954/ 20.

Lord Selborne said that after the assassination of Heydrich the Germans had conducted a terrible campaign of repression and slaughter which had the effect of stamping out the secret army in that country. SOE had made several attempts to encourage the re-organization of resistance, but had met with no success and had received little support or encouragement from the Czechoslovak Government in this country.

Apart from the matters specifically included in the agenda the Minister wishes to raise a few other questions regarding the Polish Resistance Movement. A recent report by the Joint Intelligence Sub-Committee, had criticized the degree of autonomy allowed to the Polish authorities in the use of ciphers and in expenditures of money. He reminded the Committee that in 1940, under the authority of the Prime Minister, a credit had been opened for the Polish Government, for the purpose of fostering resistance in Poland, of L600,000 a year. Up to date a total of only L400,000 had been spent. The Poles had recently asked for money to be released from this credit and he had agreed; but in view of the criticism leveled by the Joint Intelligence Sub-Committee, he had thought it desirable to seek confirmation from the Committee. The Secretary of State for Foreign Affairs stated that he would have like his Majesty's Government to have had the same control over the Poles as they possessed over our other Allies. He felt, however, that this was not a happy moment to make change and suggested that the existing arrangements should for the time being be allowed to continue. The Minister of Economic Warfare next asked the Committee to give directions for an increase in the assistance to be given to the resistance movement in Poland. At present only 6 aircraft had been allocated for SOE work over Poland and lately only 2 of these were serviceable. He was satisfied that the Polish Resistance was most vigorous and efficient. The Poles were experts in resistance, and in this respect compared favourably with the people of any other country occupied by Germany. The Poles themselves claimed that they were containing large German forces. He had heard a figure mentioned of half million men. He urged the Committee to authorize the allocation of 17 aircraft for SOE work over Poland. The Chief of Air Staff said he felt confident that an increase in supplies of Poland could be achieved with the pool of aircraft for SOE operations in the Mediterranean if not restricted as to operations they were permitted to carry out. This pool of 32 aircraft was now available for operations over the Balkans only. If the pool were "unfrozen" he believed that it would pay great dividend. Weather conditions would at some periods make operations possible in some areas when they were impossible in others. The Secretary of State for Foreign Affairs stated that the number of aircraft allotted for SOE work over Yugoslavia, Greece and Poland was only 38. It seemed a very small allocation in view of the importance at this stage of the war of encouraging the patriot forces in those countries to resist the enemy and to contain his forces. The Chief of Air Staff said our supreme task in the air was to sustain the battle which was being waged by Bomber Command, and which might prove decisive if we did not allow ourselves to be drawn away by less essential calls on our resources. If our Bomber crews felt that at this time when the German defense was increasing its efficiency, that they were not receiving support, their moral was bound to suffer. The large scale bombing of the distant parts of Germany was only possible in the months of February, March, and April, which were the same months which were alone suitable for operations over Poland.

The Prime Minister said that he considered it a matter of high public importance that greater assistance should be given by the Air Staff to resistance movements in occupied Europe even at some small expense to other responsibilities of the Royal Air Force. Treble the present allocation of aircraft to Poland should be accorded. The diversion of 12 aircraft from the bomber effort over Germany was a small price to pay. There was danger in rigid adherence to overriding priorities. Priorities should only be considered in relation to the assignment to which they referred. An extra 12 aircraft for Poland at this stage might make a considerable difference. Now that the Russians were advancing into Poland it was in our interest that Poland should be strong and well supported. Were she weak and overrun by the advancing Soviet armies, the results might hold great dangers in the future for the English-speaking people.[9]

This had nearly immediate results for the Polish Special Duties flight and the overall effort, Polish as well as RAF, to fly supplies to the Polish Home Army.

MASS MEDIA WAR AGAINST THE POLISH GOVERNMENT

The real war was fought, and won by the Soviets, in the British mass media. This change of attitude to the Poles, in less than two years, was both a bitter experience for the average Polish soldier, and an outward sign that the British Government had little appetite for confronting the Soviets over Poland, or at least its London-based Government.

That left-wing groups espoused the Soviet position was not at all surprising but in this ever-escalating anti-Polish propaganda war they were aided and abetted by many liberal elements of British society. When Hugh Dalton, as Minister of Economic Warfare, had visited Polish troops in Scotland at Christmas time in 1940, he addressed the assembled Polish officers with the following words: "I tell them that on the day of victory Poland, as the first nation to stand up to Hitler, while others have been grovelling

9   TNA AIR 19/815 80530.

on their bellies, should ride in the van of the victory march".[10] However when in 1944 Dalton met with the socialist members of the Polish Government the situation was dramatically different. "I speak to them rather frankly and tell them unless they make friends with the Russians, who are great favourites in this country, there will be nobody left to back the Poles over here except a few Roman Catholic priests."[11]

Stenton documents the cascade of anti-Polish propaganda orchestrated in Moscow and writes "Soviet ill-will and Zionist antipathy made the Polish question repulsively propagandistic."[12] The Head of the Polish Section of the BBC expressed an opinion that unless steps were taken to counteract the propaganda, "the Soviet suggestion that the Polish Government were a quasi-fascist rump would be widely accepted".[13]

The Jewish Community also became increasingly adversarial to the Polish Government. A number of prominent British parliamentarians such as Mr Driberg, Lord Strabolgi, Mr Shinwell, Mr Strauss and Mr Pritt made repeated interventions in the House of Commons accusing the Polish Army of systemic anti-Semitism.[14] The British Foreign Office became involved as a result of the parliamentarians' questions and Frank Savery's report is a cogent summary.

> The critics have not proved or even sought to prove that anti-Semitism is general yet by these judicious citations of isolated cases they have succeeded in creating an impression which they are content to leave distant from the truth. Impetuous and sensational exaggerations of the few available facts by the Press almost as whole, has created a regrettable myth, and had subjected a credulous public to an invidious propaganda. It has been the unexpected one-sidedness of the British press which has discouraged the average Polish soldier.[15]

In his two-volume study of the relationship of the Polish Government in London and the Jewish community Engel comments that it was much easier to stimulate British and American opinion about allegations of anti-Semitism in the Polish Army than about the reports of the systematic murder of millions of Jews by Germans. Engel touches delicately on the Jewish attitude – "Jewish leaders calculated that their own collective interests and those of the Jewish people as a whole, and demanded that they maintain good relations with the Soviet Union".[16]

10　Ben Pimlott, ed., *The Second World War Diary of Hugh Dalton, 1940–1945*, The British Library of Political and Economic Science, London, 1986, pp.131–133.
11　Ibid., pp.780–781.
12　Michael Stenton, *Radio London and Resistance in Occupied Europe, British Political Warfare, 1939–1943*, Oxford University Press, Oxford, 2000, p.280.
13　Stenton, op.cit., p.291.
14　Raczyński, op.cit., p.201; TNA FO 371/39401 1117445.
15　TNA FO 371/39481.
16　David Engel, *Facing a Holocaust. The Polish Government-in- Exile and the Jews, 1943–1945*, University of North Carolina Press, 1993, pp.173–178.

Even seventy years later in the American Jewish intellectual community there is an odd lack of appreciation of the wrongs inflicted on the Polish nation by Soviet Communism. Hence Polish antipathy to the Soviets and their imposed regime is, in a strange way, equated with a conviction that therefore the Poles must have been pro-German and fascist. Seemingly these were only options for Polish politics or the Polish people. Engel omits to mention that as the Poles were being denounced by British parliamentarians for their alleged anti-Semitism, their own government was doing all it could to prevent Jews in countries such as Hungary or Bulgaria from emigrating to Palestine.[17]

There were other deep currents of policy involved. The British Foreign Office comments in July 1944 that ...

> Considerable Jewish circles in America, mostly Zionist but apparently including some Orthodox as well, are agitating that all the property in Poland which before the war belonged to Jews should be regarded as belonging to the Jewish Community. The American Jews are clearly out to keep this property in Jewish hands. There is I should say, no chance whatsoever that the Polish Government would agree to this suggestion, the result of which would certainly be build up a state within a state in Poland.[18]

This escalating and well-orchestrated campaign of anti-Polish vitriolic and slanderous invectives was beyond the tone of a free press. The Poles were accused of being Nazi sympathizers, of being closet anti-Semites, of doing nothing except living well in the United Kingdom and chasing British girls. The liberal and left-wing mass media made much of the so-called Polish feudal landlords. In response to this the British Ambassador to the Polish Government –Sir Owen O'Malley – analyzed the backgrounds of Polish statesmen and dismissed this as a preposterous distortion. But far more telling to the anti-Polish atmosphere are the comments of the British Foreign Office after receiving their ambassador's dispatch:

> A most useful dispatch. I only wish we could send a copy of it to each of the many ill-informed enthusiasts who write us daily letters protesting against the activities of the 'pro-fascist Polish émigré aristocrats' in this country. There is no doubt whatsoever that the Soviet Govt. have deliberately worked up a completely artificial 'hate' against the Polish Govt. The allegations that they are pro-Hitlerite, collaborationist and opposed to active resistance to

17 On April 7, 1943 Churchill gave the following reply in Parliament: "The Government of Palestine have agreed to admit from Bulgaria 4,000 children and 500 adults, and the necessary negotiations for their release and transport are taking place through the Protecting Power."

18 TNA FO 371/ 39524/10. While unable to find any archives to document this, there was a general rumor in Polish London after Sikorski's third –and last- visit to the USA that he was offered Jewish support in turn for this move. Some of these issues continue to reverberate even in 2012 with the Jewish community of the USA laying claim to all intestate Jewish property in Poland.

Germany, unrepresentative and reactionary landowners and aristocrats. On basis of information supplied by SOE we should challenge the Soviet Govt. over a) by showing them how much is being done in Poland in the way of active resistance organised by the Polish Government. Might we not also, on the basis of the present dispatch, challenge them over b)? Surely we are entitled to show the Russians that we are not taken in by the propaganda which is seeking with considerable success to persuade the world including the British public, that HMG are harboring in this country a mere gang of reactionary and blimpish feudal lords.

The anti-Polish vitriol was manifest in most British mass media. The London *Times* extolled the Union of Polish Patriots in Moscow and the Berling (Peoples' Army) divisions which had been formed by Stalin and officered by Soviets. The *Observer* attacked the Polish Army for its anti-Semitism, while the *Economist* described them as a hotbed of hooliganism, so it was not surprising that the communist *Daily Worker* went beyond insult, and described the Polish Army as a cross between the Nazi SS and a comic opera. The increasing participation of the Poles in the war in the West was all but ignored. The Poles was not merely the butts of insults but the relative lack of any pro-Polish views or objective statements from any of the British press except the *Catholic Tablet* and the *Edinburgh Scotsman,* occasionally the *Daily Telegraph* and *London Illustrated News,* was a bitter experience. The fact that the Polish merchant marine carried more cargo in one month than all the food consumed by the "indolent" Poles was not brought to the fore. The fact that the Polish Air Force bomber squadrons had lost over 300% of their initial cadre was ignored.

The internal archives of the British SOE for 28 April 1944 literally speak volumes as to the propaganda that confronted the Poles:

You may know that the Operation Julia was conceived and carried out, not only because of its tactical military value, but also for a purpose of far greater importance, namely, to prove to the world that the Polish Underground Army is, in fact, under the command of General Sosnkowski, and though him, of the Polish Government in London. It was hoped to definitely and finally, to refute the Soviet claim that the Government has no power in Poland. Every possible precaution was taken in the methods of disseminating the news of the operation. Propaganda was in the hands of the Polish Section at P.W.E. [i.e. Political Warfare Executive]. Mr Moray McLaren. P.W.E. controls the broadcasts on the European service of the BBC and on this service I understand that the news was given its correct value. Mr McLaren liaised with the foreign office on the political directive to the press to accompany the news. I saw this directive, and it did indeed point out the significance of the news of this action.

The news was given out to the news agencies and was, I understand, given its proper importance by them. The newspapers, however, universally refused to afford it the prominence it so richly deserved. There appears to exist, at this time, a very definite ban on anything in the British press, which could in any way be considered as favourable to the present Polish Government, moreover, at this particular time, it is quite definite that the newspapers and the British public are more interested in the news of anti-Semitic incidents which are supposed to have happened in the recent past.

Julia as a propaganda operation has therefore failed. It is to be expected that the effect on the morale of the Poles with whom we are in contact will be considerable. There is already a feeling that the British press and the British people are not maintaining their old tradition of sportsmanship and justice. The anti-Polish campaign and the derogatory reports which have appeared in the press about Jews in the Polish Army will, we fear, have a very definite effect on the war and I suggest that it is time that these matters were put to in their true light, both in Parliament and in the press. I understand that Mr McLaren has already pointed out that the Polish Underground Army is sheltering thousands of Jews at great risk to the lives of Polish Christian citizens.[19]

POLISH RESPONSE TO ANTI-POLISH MASS MEDIA BLITZ

In an attempt to refute the inimical mass media coverage of the Polish Government and its forces, the Polish Government organized a Polish Maritime Exhibition in London and invited the First Lord of the Admiralty to its opening. The Polish Navy was not involved in the overall Polish strategic plans but it was an important symbolic service and a great flag shower. Alexander's comments were well said but probably only heard by a few:

Whenever in the course of naval operations in the present world conflict at sea a great concourse of ships is gathered together, there is almost always to be seen one or more Polish ensigns, worn either by Polish warships or by vessels of the Polish Mercantile Marine, or by both. In view of its small size, the number of operations in which the Polish Navy has taken part is almost incredible. Amongst these operations are Narvik, Dunkirk, Lofoten Islands, Tobruk, Dieppe, attacks on shipping in the Channel, Sicily, Italy, Oran and patrols notably in the Mediterranean and convoy escorting. The recent work of the Polish ships in the Mediterranean has been especially brilliant. Since

---

19   TNA HS 4/167. For a general history of the P.W.E. see David Garnett, *The Secret History of PWE. The Political Warfare Executive, 1939–1945,* St. Ermin's Press, London, 2002. See, also the comment by Churchill elsewhere about the lack of news on the Warsaw Uprising.

May 1943, one Polish submarine sank no less than 18 enemy vessels of a total of 49,000 tons. Other Polish submarines have accomplished equally meritorious work in Norwegian waters and elsewhere, including the sinking of a large German transport ship packed with troops.[20]

The words written in early 1944 did not address the most outstanding work of the Polish destroyers in Operation Neptune in June 1944.[21]

Scotland, 1944. Tanks of the Polish 10th Motorised Cavalry, divisional reconnaissance of the 1st Polish Armoured Division. Churchill minuted his military "Please do not on any account let the Polish Division be out of the battle front. Not only is it a magnificent fighting force, but its exploits will help keep alive the soul of Poland." (PISM)

Operation Neptune was the naval side of the greatest amphibious operation in world history, the invasion of Normandy, codenamed *Overlord*. American, British and Canadian forces landed on five beaches supported by the greatest naval armada ever assembled. Polish fighter squadrons and all but one Polish warship took part in the invasion on D-Day. The Polish Armoured Division went ashore in the second echelon and was assigned to strengthen the Canadian Army. As events were unfolding in a positive and optimistic manner the situation on the Eastern Front was also unfolding in a critical situation for the Poles, albeit disastrously for the Germans.

20   Peter Jordan and Alexander Janta, *Seafaring Poland*, MaxLove Publishing Company, London, 1944, pp.5–7.
21   Michael Alfred Peszke, *Poland's Navy, 1918–1945*, Hippocrene Books, NY, 1999.

9

POLISH MILITARY STRATEGIC ASPECTS

Polish Flight 1586 moves to south Italy – Third Polish-British Air Force agreement – Political Initiatives – Polish-British Lend Agreement- Rettinger inserted into Poland – Extension of Polish-British Treaty of Mutual Assistance – Wildhorn flights to occupied Poland – Sosnkowski makes second visit to Polish 2 Corps – Polish Parachute Brigade in Market Garden.

POLISH MILITARY STRATEGIC ASPECTS

The Polish Special Duties Flight 1586, now reinforced by American B–24 Liberators, was moved to south Italy from the United Kingdom after an interim basing in Tunis from which some supply flights were flown to Poland. It became administratively part of RAF 344 Wing. This unit was also tasked with flying supplies to Balkans and other clandestine groups including Poland. The Poles were expected to participate in supply missions to other countries, and the RAF crews were expected to fly to Poland when weather conditions and other requirements allowed. From what can be ascertained at the level of the Wing, relations were excellent between the Poles and the RAF but somewhat strained with senior RAF officers who were always disenchanted with the irresistible Polish unit's tendency to independence.

This new base shared with the RAF 344 Wing allowed flights much deeper into Poland and permitted supplies to be dropped in a wider area. It should be noted that because a successful drop was achieved, the actual supplies and even couriers had to be dispersed from the drop which immediately attracted German attention, often including radar and wireless surveillance. In an occupied Poland, with ubiquitous German patrols it was always a challenge to move clandestine supplies or people. But the move to the magnificent warmth of south Italy was not all bliss. Flights to

Poland from the United Kingdom took about twelve hours and had to face the odd German night fighter. From Italy, the flights were shorter, but still over ten hours and the planes had to fly over the Austrian Alps and Carpathian mountains. There were no German fighters but there was the deadly phenomenon of icing.

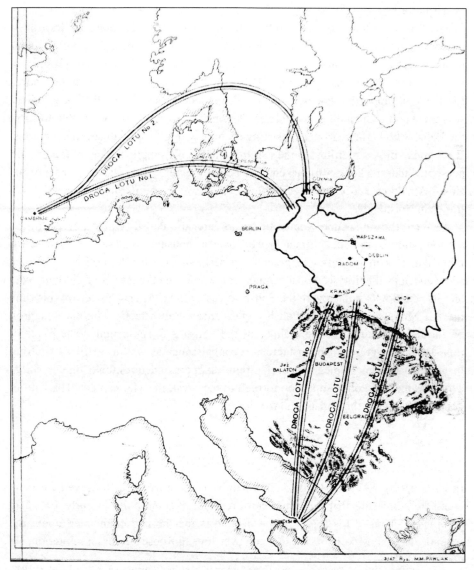

Map showing routes of special duties flights to Poland from the UK
and then from Italy.

THE THIRD POLISH–BRITISH AIR AGREEMENT, APRIL, 1944

With some political clouds emanating from concerns and apprehensions about the Soviet reaction, the RAF re-negotiated the Polish-British Air Force Agreement in April 1944. Polish Air Force personnel were now only subject to Polish military law and could only be commanded by Polish officers. Numerous Polish Air Force officers were assigned to many RAF Groups and the Inspectorate renamed Polish Air Force Headquarters.[1]

The Royal Air Force showed itself more supportive of Polish plans for forming a tactical group than for a Special Duties Flight. This was to be a fully Polish independent tactical group able to function from field bases with complete supporting services. The British disquiet, fully justified, was the lack of Polish personnel cadres to fill all the supportive slots vital to an independent tactical group. But the goodwill was there and ultimately just before D-Day the Polish Air Force were able to form the Polish 18th Fighter Group, consisting of three wings – a total of seven squadrons. RAF goodwill was manifest in the fact that the British supplied many of the ground personnel that the Poles still lacked. The Polish Fighter Group was to be part of the Royal Air Force 2nd Tactical Air Force, which was going to support the invasion forces in Normandy.[2]

At about the same time women began to enter the Polish Armed Forces. In the air force this increment, ultimately well over a thousand, released many men for other duties or merely allowed greater logistical support for the Polish squadrons. The sudden availability of Polish women came from the thousands of civilians who had left the Soviet gulags with the Polish forces in 1942. Approximately at this time the Air Ministry granted the Polish request that a Polish tactical fighter squadron be formed and moved to the vicinity of the Polish 2 Corps in Italy. The pilots of this squadron were trained for tactical reconnaissance as well as artillery spotting in addition to their typical roles of ground support and traditional fighter skills. This was the last Polish squadron formed in the West, the 318, named "The City of Gdansk", bringing the Polish total to ten.

POLITICAL INITIATIVES

In early spring 1944 the Polish Prime Minister now turned to Roosevelt for help, completely unaware that the American President at some point in early 1943 had completely changed his mind on the principles that he had enunciated about the Atlantic Charter. Mikołajczyk had made overtures to Roosevelt for an invitation. He

---

1   *Destiny Can Wait. The Polish Air Force in the Second World War*, William Heinemann, London, 1949, pp.383–389.
2   Jerzy Cynk, *The Polish Air Force at War, 1943–1945* Vol. 2, Schiffer, Atglen PA, 1998, pp.394–409.

had been put off by the White House due to the amount of business that Roosevelt had to attend. But the imminent November elections and the political pressure of the Polish-American Congress, about five million strong, until then always voting Democratic and thus possibly a deciding factor in a number of key states, finally led to the visit which took place on June 1944.

The Polish ambassador in Washington, Ciechanowski, described this visit as a "Red carpet for Mikołajczyk". Roosevelt indulged, as was his passive aggressive style when the individual in question was not present, and made some snide remarks about "my poor friend Churchill" and that "he had a nineteenth-century British mentality". Roosevelt's advice to Mikołajczyk was to meet with Stalin and thrash things out – "when things become unavoidable, one should adapt oneself to it". Finally, he stated that if policy demanded that he change his government, he would "if he could inspire confidence in a much stronger adversary and thereby open the door to an understanding".[3]

It is not quite clear whether Roosevelt understood the difference between the American political system and Polish parliamentary democracy, or whether he really cared! Roosevelt, like all American presidents after being sworn to the office of the President, picked his various departmental secretaries. They served at his pleasure. Mikołajczyk was prime minister of a coalition government where each cabinet member represented a political party.

Mikołajczyk brought with him General Stanisław [Tabor] Tatar, who had been extracted from Poland and had been appointed Head of the VI Section of the Polish Military Staff in London. General Tatar has been one of the most controversial individuals in Polish World War II history.[4] While still in occupied Poland and a member of the senior staff of the Polish Home Army, he had been an advocate of the closest co-operation with the Soviet armies. It has been inferred that his political views were so categorical that the Polish Home Army Command wanted him out and thus accommodated to his being extracted. In Washington he met with the Combined Chiefs of Staff and articulated opinions completely at variance with reality, but opinions which fell on fertile ground with the British members of the Combined Chiefs, not so much with the Americans, namely that the Polish Underground and the Soviet were co-operating in a satisfactory manner.

General Tatar gave a sober account of the lack of military equipment of the Home Army and opined that it needed at least 500 supply missions immediately and a further 1,300 in the coming months.

Mitkiewicz, the formal Polish representative to the Combined Chiefs of Staff was stunned since he knew that these numbers were completely out of the question. Furthermore General Tatar talked with the Combined Chiefs of Staff through an

3   Jan Ciechanowski, *Defeat in Victory*, Victor Gollancz, London, 1948, pp.305–315
4   Zbigniew S. Siemaszko, *Działalność Generała Tatara, 1943–1949*, Norbetinum, Lublin, 2004.

interpreter. The concluding remarks from Admiral Leahy thanking him for his pres-
entation and promising a careful review were misinterpreted by Tatar. On returning
to London, he told the British that he had obtained the concurrence of the CCS for his
plans. All of these points came back to bedevil Mitkiewicz.[5] Back in London, General
Tatar was decorated by the British with the Order of the Bath, Military Division.
Siemaszko is of the opinion that this had to do more with his political, pro-Soviet views,
than any accomplishments in the Home Army prior to extraction from Poland. This
award was performed by Lord Selborne, but somewhat uniquely was not processed by
the Chancery of the Polish President, who had to formally agree to a foreign decoration
of a Polish citizen, let alone a serving officer.[6] One of the most perplexing and far from
well-understood events is the donation of ten million dollars to the Polish VI Section
for activities in occupied Poland. One and half million was placed at the disposition of
the Polish Treasury for help for civilians in Poland, and the rest moved to the operating
base in Brindisi. It is assumed but far from proven that the money was intended to help
strengthen Mikołajczyk and his party west of the so-called Curzon Line.

LEND-LEASE AGREEMENT

Finally the Polish and British Governments signed their formal Lend-Lease agreement on 29 June 1944. The Poles had literally kept postponing this move. The British
on the other hand had kept pushing it as minimizing the complicated business of
bookkeeping about military supplies going to the Poles. The British, most likely,
were correct in attributing Polish reluctance to their desire to keep all the equipment
after the war. An excerpt of the letter from Alexander Cadogan to Raczyński, who
were the joint signatories, illustrates the situation, before and after.

> In connexion with the Agreement which we have signed to-day to make
> fresh arrangements for the attribution of expenditures incurred in the organ-
> isation of and employment of the Polish armed forces during the present war,
> I have the honour to inform your Excellency that His Majesty's Government
> in the United Kingdom, desiring to demonstrate in a practical manner their
> recognition of the services, facilities and other material benefits which they
> have received from the Government of the Republic of Poland, propose to
> apply the principles of the aforesaid Agreement to all military supplies and
> services made available to the Polish Armed forces since the opening of the

5   Leon Mitkiewicz, *W Najwyższym Sztabie Zachodnich Aliantów, 1943–1945*, Veritas, London, 1971,
     pp.169–191; Zbigniew Siemaszko, *Działalność Generała Tatara, 1943–1949*, Norbertinum, Lublin,
     2004, pp.45–49.
6   Siemaszko, op.cit., p.50. Siemszko notes that at about this time two other Polish generals received the
     Order of the Bath, namely General Anders following the capture of Monte Cassino by 2 Corps, which
     he commanded, from Field Marshal Alexander, and General Stanisław Kopański from Lord Selborne.

Polish military credit on 3rd June, 1940. The practical effect of this proposal would be that a figure would be assessed to represent the values of all goods and services provide since the opening of the Polish Military Credit which under the Agreement would in the future be provided free of charge, and that this figure should be deducted from the sum already owing to His Majesty's Government under the Polish Military Credit.[7]

THE BRITISH ASCERTAIN THE OPINIONS OF THE POLISH CLANDESTINE STATE

So was the Polish Clandestine State as adamant about boundaries as was reported by the Polish Government? The Poles were beginning to be distrusted, perhaps not so much about their account of the strong opinion of the Polish Clandestine State, but whether the Poles were in fact communicating the political and diplomatic reality to the Homeland. Given the facts, British mistrust was well justified. One of the most enigmatic individuals of Polish World War Two history was now flown to Poland on one of the most secret wartime missions. The British SOE arranged to fly Rettinger to Poland.

Even seventy years later, there is controversy as to who was behind the mission, and its purpose. Logical deduction has only three answers: to share the general political background in the West with the clandestine state, make an independent assessment, or to convey specific instructions. The first assumption is a reasonable speculation. The second possibility, namely assessment of the attitudes, morale and policies of the Polish Clandestine State is also likely if it was being done on behalf of the British. There was no reason for Mikołajczyk to have Rettinger give him information about Poland since he had his own civilian couriers, going back and forth, plus wireless communication. That was even more true for the Polish military. The last hypothetical option can be dismissed immediately. Nobody in Poland, civilian or military, would take instructions from Rettinger.

The original plan was to transport him on the first Wildhorn mission. These were to be flights by DC–2 Dakotas which would land in Poland and also pick up agents. But there was a delay in accomplishing this first Wildhorn flight and Rettinger was flown on the night of 3 April 1944 by a Polish crew flying a Halifax and parachuted at an agreed drop zone, about 26 kilometers east of Warsaw. Rettinger might very well have been the oldest man ever to parachute in a hostile situation. After a three month stint in occupied Poland, where he came down with a serious bout of polyneuritis, Rettinger was extracted by a Wildhorn III mission. He was met by Colin Gubbins of the SOE at the Brindisi base and immediately flown to Cairo to meet with Mikołajczyk on his way to Moscow. Rettinger then flew on to London and became ensconced at the Dorchester Hotel where he was immediately visited by Sir Anthony Eden.

---

7   TNA T 160/399.

All of this was happening as the United Nations, Roosevelt's term for the Allied Expeditionary Force, was landing in Normandy, and as Mikołajczyk was proceeding on his trip to Moscow to meet with Stalin at Churchill's strong insistence.

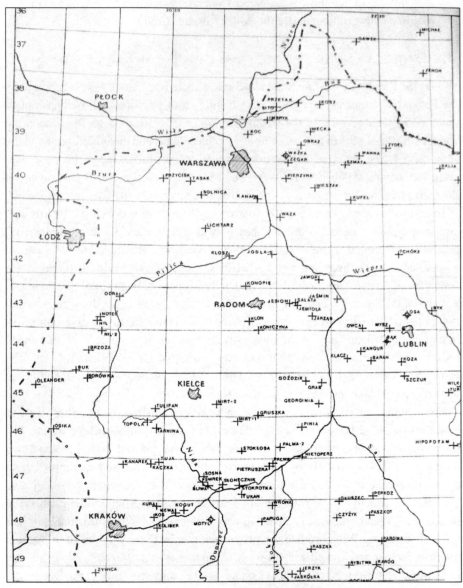

Map illustrating the number and location of different
Polish Home Army reception parties.

EXTENSION OF THE POLISH-BRITISH TREATY OF MUTUAL ASSISTANCE

About the same time, namely March 1944, a question was asked in the House of Commons as to whether it was the intention of the His Majesty's Government to extend the Anglo-Polish Pact of Mutual Assistance for another five years, since it was expiring in August 1944. Sir Anthony Eden, responded "that Article 8 of the Anglo-Polish provided that it shall remain in force for five years, and continue unless denounced six month before the period of expiration. Therefore there is no question of this Agreement expiring in August 1944 and no need for any extension of the Agreement at that time".[8]

WILDHORN (*MOSTY*) MISSIONS

The availability of the American Dakota and also the ever increasing skills of the Polish Underground to arrange landing places in Poland led to a number of flights where important people were flown in and out. In Wildhorn I the most senior and important person extracted was General Stanisław Tatar. He had been a senior officer in the Polish Home Army and was sent the United Kingdom to assume the post of Chief of VI Section of the Polish Staff dealing with the Home Army. A total of three such flights were flown, though a number more were planned. In Wildhorn II the most important passenger inserted was General Tadeusz Kossakowski, whose function in Poland was to organize secret arms production. Wildhorn III was the most important. It took place on 25 July 1944, a bare week before the onset of the Warsaw Uprising, and its most important passenger inserted was Jan Nowak, who was returning to Poland. While in London he had met with Raczyński, probably the most astute and sophisticated Polish statesman, with the British ambassador to Poland, Sir Owen O'Malley and Colonel Perkins, the head of the Polish Section of SOE. He had been advised by all responsible parties that Western help could not be expected. From London to Italy he flew with General Sosnkowski, who insisted on flying with a Polish crew.

Flown out of Poland on Wildhorn III were Rettinger, as well as the Polish Socialist leader, Arciszewski, and, of vital importance, parts of a German rocket that had gone astray and been secreted by the Polish Home Army.

At this time Lord Selborne commented about the Polish Home Army,

> A fresh instance of their efficiency has just occurred. The aerodromes in Poland from which parts of the German secret rockets were brought back last week by SOE were seized and held by a brigade of the Polish Secret Army for the purpose of this operations.[9]

---

8   Jedrzejewicz, *Poland in the British Parliament* Vol. 3, p.418.
9   TNA HS 4/156. See also, Józef Garliński, *Hitler's Last Weapons. The Underground War against the*

General Sosnkowski only flew with a Polish crew. (PISM)

POLISH POLICIES BECOME REACTIVE NOT PRO-ACTIVE

While many Poles were discouraged, many still pinned their hopes on the prom-
ises heard from the leaders of the Western Powers and at the very best took a stoic
stand that the final events might turn out more positively. The Polish Government's
desire to make some compromises related to a stipulation that Soviet claims could be
accepted as an interim Soviet administrative boundary, pending a peace treaty and
full Polish Parliamentary accord. But the Polish Government in London received a
"Resolution" from the Council of National Unity and the Delegate of the Government
in occupied Poland, "we object firmly to any discussion with the Soviets with regard
to revision of the Eastern boundaries".[10]

Furthermore, the Soviets also demanded changes in the Polish Government and a
return to the 1921 Polish Constitution. It is a sad commentary that this outrageous
demand was not rejected out of hand by the British. Even if there was support for such
a move in the Polish Government, how was this to be accomplished by a Government
in Exile and a country under occupation? Soviet insistence on these ultimatums can

---

V1 and V 2, Times Books, New York, 1978, pp.153–159.

10   *Documents on Polish-Soviet Relations*, Vol. 2, pp.179–180 .

only be understood by a very machiavellian policy of breaking up the connections between the Polish Government, and its armed forces and most importantly demonstrating to the occupied Polish nation and its civilian and military leadership the futility of expecting the Polish Government to represent its interests. Opposition to any territorial compromise was also the overwhelming feeling of 2 Polish Corps and its G.O.C. Anders, who all hailed from the Eastern Polish territories and had all experienced Soviet treachery and prisons. Many, if not most had families either in Soviet gulags or still living in Eastern Poland. As the Poles were being moved into positions in the Italian front they were assigned to the British Eighth Army, known by its Crusader Crest. The new GOC of the Army was Sir Oliver Leese, had just replaced General Montgomery, who went to the United Kingdom to assume command of the 21st Army Group in preparation for the invasion of Normandy. Anders met with Leese to discuss the Polish deployment but pointed out how inappropriate and disconcerting it was for his troops to be greeted by an article in their *Eighth Army News Letter* upholding the Soviet position about borders and with Moscow slanders directed at his men. Shortly Anders received this impertinent telegram from Leese:

> Since our last meeting at Agnone I have thought over in detail the point of view you expressed during that meeting with regard to the actual Polish problems. In my capacity of Army Commander I have to point out how superfluous it is for a Corps Commander to express in public opinions concerning political situation, in particular at the present moment.[11]

In a number of English histories critical of the alleged involvement of Polish military in political matters this has become an oft-cited exchange. But what was superfluous? Was it that Anders was concerned about anti-Polish and slanderous propaganda directed at his troops entering battle or the "present moment"? Leese would never have dared to write such a message to an American general and Leese obviously did not know that Anders was much more than a Corps Commander in the Polish Army. Anders had face to face intense discussions with Stalin and a confrontation with Churchill. He had argued with two of his own commander-in-chiefs about Polish troop dispositions and prevailed. Numerous photographs show Anders meeting with Attlee, Churchill, Eden and MacMillan. He was not just a corps commander in 1943 or later in 1946. Sir Oliver Leese had absolutely no disciplinary authority over Polish units, he was merely their Army Commander, and if he was of the opinion that Anders' comments were detrimental to his overall command, then it behoved him to go up the chain of command and then to the Polish Government.

---

11   Władysław Anders, *An Army in Exile*, Macmillan, London, 1949, p.155.

SOSNKOWSKI MAKES SECOND VISIT TO THE POLISH 2 CORPS

As 2 Polish Corps began to enter military operations in the Italian Campaign in early January 1944, General Sosnkowski exercised the privilege and responsibility of his office to visit his forces. Sosnkowski looked with ever increasing concern on what he perceived as a tendency to compromise Polish frontiers on the part of the Polish Prime Minister, Mikołajczyk. His concern was actually unwarranted since the Polish Premier was still strongly upholding Polish rights to the Eastern Territories. But the pressure on Mikołajczyk was ever greater and mounting.

Sosnkowski saw the Polish Corps as the one really independent Polish center. Aware of the disquiet in it, and also wishing to make his own judgment on the situation Sosnkowski flew to visit the formation in Italy. The report to the UK from Italy was that the visit was satisfactory. Given what was to happen in the next few months the extract of the British report is seminal.

> General Sosnkowski is much more popular with his troops than General Sikorski ever was and is in many respects a better C-in-C. He certainly seems to have been very helpful on this visit. The outstanding feature of General Sosnkowski's tour was the amount of interest, time and trouble he devoted to the private soldier, and the resulting confidence and enthusiasm which this appeared to produce. No mountain post was too inaccessible for the Polish C-in-C if there were two or three Polish soldiers manning it with whom he could smoke a cigarette and talk of their daily life, their families and the ultimate liberation of Poland.[12]

As a footnote, it is relevant to add that he insisted on flying in a Polish-crewed plane from RAF Transport Command, which had hundreds of Polish personnel. His visit was militarily timely and his wish to inspect his one full corps in operations more than justified, but there are indications that this was also an inspection of political issues, and not just military morale.

One of the less known events occurred when Sosnkowski was informed by General Anders on his arrival that it had been agreed following a British request that the Polish Corps be the third allied formation to attempt to storm Monte Cassino. After evaluating the tactical situation Sosnkowski remonstrated with Anders that his acquiescence should have been delayed until his own arrival on the scene; and he pointed out what was nearly evident to all, that a front attack on the craggy mountain was unnecessary and that the monastery should be bypassed. Anders replied that it was time to show what the Polish soldier could do given all the scurrilous remarks coming from so many quarters about Poles being Nazi sympathizers.

---

12   TNA WO 216/167.

The Poles did storm the craggy slopes of Monte Cassino, suffering significant losses. The Polish cemetery near the monastery is a silent tribute to their hero-ism.[13] Sosnkowski was right, the Goums of the French Moroccan division ensured the success by the very maneuver proposed by Sosnkowski. The Poles have taken great pride in this tactical success, but the official BBC announcement merely stated that "Allied troops have captured Monte Cassino." Churchill wrote in his post-war memoirs,

> The Poles triumphantly hoisted their red and white standard over the ruins of the monastery. They greatly distinguished themselves in their first major engagement in Italy. Later, under their thrustful General Anders, himself a survivor from Russian imprisonment, they were to win many laurels during their long advance to the river Po.[14]

The next and most successful battle for the Polish Corps was the capture of the important and undamaged port of Ancona on the Adriatic and then onto Bologna.[15]

On flying back to the United Kingdom Sosnkowski had to confront the issue of the disposition of the Polish Parachute Brigade. The British had made a formal request, in March 1944, to amend the existing agreements and release the Polish Parachute Brigade for operations in North West Europe. This was made by the British General Grasset representing SHAEF (Supreme Headquarters Allied Expeditionary Force). Grasset acknowledged that under the "existing agreement the Polish Parachute Brigade is unreservedly at your disposal for operations in Poland". Grasset also made a complimentary remark about the "fine fighting material" of the Brigade. But he made this plea – "we are now faced with the probability of the most formidable oper-ations of War of all times and one that will require the employment of the maximum efforts and resources at the disposal of the Allies. In this operation we must not fail." Grasset also stipulated that if combat losses exceeded 25% the Brigade would be withdrawn immediately, before concluding:

> … when an opportunity arises for employing this Brigade in Poland, it will be placed at the disposal of the Polish Commander-in-Chief . It is not possible at this stage to give definitive guarantees on the subject of aircraft, but every effort will be made to release aircraft for the transport of the Brigade to Poland.[16]

---

13 Mathew Parker, *Monte Cassino: The Hardest–Fought Battle of World War II*, Doubleday, New York, 2004. The title may be a major hype, but it was probably the most bitter battle in Western Europe. See also E.D. Smith, *The Battles for Cassino*, Charles Scribner's Sons, New York, 1975, specifically Chapter 16, "The Poles come to Cassino".
14 Churchill, *Closing the Ring*, p.530.
15 Timothy R. Brooks, *The War North of Rome, June 1944-May 1945*, Castle Books, Edison, New Jersey, 2001.
16 P.I.S.M. AV 20/31 18.

For a while the Poles resisted and attempted to negotiate a lower percent of casualties (15%) and a better assurance about the future provision of aircraft and gliders plus fighter escort and logistical support for Polish operations. The answer was predictable – " I feel sure you will appreciate the position of the British Chief of Staff and recognize their inability to commit themselves specifically at this stage of the war".[17]

The conundrum for the Poles was that refusing the British request inexorably led to losing any prospect of possible future British assistance. Finally the Polish Commander-in-Chief consulted the Polish Home Army, obtained their probably less than well informed consent, and finally sent the matter to the Polish Government for opinion. He recommended that British goodwill needed to be cultivated and that there were benefits to having a battle-experienced brigade. The coalition government approved and Sosnkowski placed the Polish Parachute Brigade unconditionally in the order of battle of the Allied Airborne Army on June 6 1944.commanded by the American General Lewis H. Brereton.[18]

Sosnkowski received a most gracious letter from Dwight Eisenhower:

I can assure you that I greatly appreciate the efforts which you and your Government are making towards the war effort of the United Nations".[19] Churchill's minutes to General Hollis of June 23 1944 are intriguing:

I consider that the Polish Parachute Brigade should not be lightly cast away. It may have a value in Poland far out of the proportion to its actual military power. I trust these view may be conveyed to General Eisenhower, and Montgomery, before the brigade is definitely established in France.[20]

A number of airborne operations were planned by the Allies for North-West Europe, but the German retreat was faster than the Allies' pursuit. Finally Market Garden was planned – the largest ever airborne operation. It was intended that the Allied Airborne Army would capture a number of bridges over major rivers in Holland and secure a back way into the German heartland for Montgomery's land forces. The whole operation was flawed in every respect. The main problem which impaired the Western Allies from possibly finishing off the war in the West in late 1944 had to do with logistics. Failure to secure Antwerp before developing an attack against the German back door ultimately had serious negative consequences.[21]

---

17   Ibid.
18   *The Brereton Diaries: The War in the Air in the Pacific, Middle East and Europe, 3 October 1941– 8 May 1945,* Morrow, New York, 1946.
19   PISM AV 29/31 18.
20   Winston S. Churchill, *Triumph and Tragedy,* Cassell, London, 1954, p.592.
21   Peter Beale, *The Great Mistake. The Battle of Antwerp and the Beveland Peninsula September 1944,* Sutton Publishing, Stroud, UK, 2004; Denis Whitaker and Shelagh Whitaker, *Tug of War. The Allied Victory that Opened Antwerp,* Stoddart, Toronto, 2000.

The Allied Airborne Army was composed of two corps, an American one consisting of the 101st and 82nd US airborne divisions, and the British corps consisting of the British 1st Airborne Division and the Polish Parachute Brigade. The British Corps was commanded by General Frederick 'Boy' Browning, a great advocate of parachute forces and by all accounts desperate to see action before the war finished. Lloyd Clark writes that "Frederick Browning had a desire to impress his superiors for his own ends and to take what was likely to be his final opportunity to lead his airborne corps into battle. As result Browning did not question decisions nearly as much as he should have done during the planning phase and took up valuable transportation assets to lift his headquarters, which would have been far more useful in England."[22] Perhaps the most serious criticisms are directed at the relative hands-off attitude of General Eisenhower, and the failure by Montgomery to do a set battle plan for which he was justifiably famous. One does not need to be an admirer of Montgomery to intuitively know that he was much better tactician than the sorry result of the "bridge too far". It has to be believed that the actual goal of his attack had to do with the concentration of V–1 and V2 firing sites in north Holland which were beginning to wreak havoc and affect morale in London among a population tired after five years of war. If this was the reason, or at least one of the reasons, for the operation, then the unseemly hurry might make tactical sense.

The Polish Parachute Brigade, commanded by General Stanisław Sosabowski, was used in Market Garden and suffered significant losses, never to fight again. Prior to insertion it was cannibalized by having its anti-tank elements glider-borne and dropped as part of the British 1st Airborne Division on the north side of the Rhine near Arnhem. Their pack artillery never arrived. The Polish paras were dropped on the south side of the river after a delay due to bad weather and then tasked with fording the river for which they had no equipment.[23]

Following the complete destruction of the British forces the British senior generals, right up to Montgomery, attempted to put a good spin on the fact that the front had moved the front about forty miles, even though it failed to punch the hole in the German defenses that was hoped for. The pundits placed blame on their failure onto the Polish Brigade and in particular their commander. The British historian William F. Buckingham, devoted a whole chapter in his study of Arnhem to the Polish Brigade, giving it the evocative title, "Plagiarised, Bullied and Hijacked. The 1st Polish Independent Parachute Brigade, September 1941-August 1944". Buckingham concluded that the British charges against Sosabowski, who had argued against the amateurish planning, lacked "a shred of truth" and "was a blatant and shameful attempt to conceal British incompetence that sealed the fate of Market Garden".[24]

---

22   Lloyd Clark, *Arnhem. Operation Market Garden, September 1944*, Sutton Publishing, Stroud, UK, 2002.
23   George Cholewczynski, *Poles Apart. The Polish Airborne at Arnhem*, Sarpendon, New York, 1993.
24   William F. Buckingham, *Arnhem, 1944*, Tempus, Stroud, UK 2002, pp.43–48, 177–183.

Following the operation, the Brigade was reconstituted but never saw combat and eventually joined the Polish 1st Armoured Division in occupation duties of in Germany after V-E Day.

10

Prelude to the Warsaw Uprising

Prelude to Warsaw Uprising – Political issues stemming from British pressure to accommodate to Soviet demands – Mikołajczyk visits to Moscow – Warsaw Uprising – Churchill attempts to mobilize American support for the Polish Insurgents – Aid to Warsaw Uprising.

Prelude to the Warsaw Uprising

As the Soviet advance on the Eastern Front gathered pace and threw back the Germans, the situation for the Poles became increasingly critical. In July 1944 the Soviet armies crossed into undisputed Polish territory west of the disputed Curzon line. The Polish Underground expressed a wish to collaborate with the Soviet forces since they saw no other option. Tabor, now in London, was an advocate of such collaboration. He was not completely delusional, since there was some indirect support.

The Polish Commander-in-Chief General Sosnkowski was very cautious, while Mikołajczyk, the Prime Minister, gave full approval for local decision-making.

In July 1944 a number of German generals who realized all was lost for Germany attempted to assassinate Hitler. There was a feeling that maybe Hitler's thousand year Reich was disintegrating, again analogous to the situation in 1918 when many sailors in the German Navy revolted.

MIKOŁAJCZYK'S FIRST VISIT TO MOSCOW

In July 1944 Mikołajczyk, at the strong urging of both Churchill and Roosevelt, embarked on his visit to Moscow. Even after eighty years it is not clear how much he wanted and expected the imminent Warsaw Uprising to strengthen his hand in negotiations with Stalin. But as Mikołajczyk was flying to Moscow, Stalin upped the ante in his Polish policy. He had already organised a Polish People's Army, mainly officered by Soviets and now he recognized a predominantly Communist Committee in Lublin as the Provisional Government of Poland. On hearing the news the Polish Prime Minister in Cairo, halfway to Moscow, balked at continuing since it was so obvious that this was another slap in the face at the Poles by Stalin. But he was cajoled by Churchill to proceed.

In late July 1944 the puppet 'Polish' Lublin government called for an uprising in Warsaw. Soviet armies were less than twenty miles from Warsaw. The sound of Soviet guns could be heard in Warsaw and the population was eager to grab control of the city. Furthermore, in addition to a restive population raging against the four years of occupation the Polish Home Army Commanders were also concerned that the small communist party might take control of the inevitable uprising of the city and present a *fait accompli*.

It is not surprising that Stalin, the most crafty and successful of the Second World statesmen, also did not want the Poles to have a *fait accompli* by assuming control of Poland's capital. As the events unfolded it became clear how successful his policy was, and how correct Sosnkowski was in all his precautionary warnings about the risks of any such undertaking.

SOSNKOWSKI FLIES TO ITALY TO THE POLISH 2 CORPS

When Mikołajczyk flew to Moscow, Sosnkowski flew from the United Kingdom to Italy to be with the Polish 2 Corps. His projected trip had been obstructed, by both the British and Mikołajczyk. The British excuse for delaying his visit to 2 Polish Corps was ostensibly an embargo on all flights from the UK during the time immediately prior to D-Day. But eventually the invasion had taken place and was no longer a secret so the British were obliged to accommodate the formal request of the Polish Commander-in-Chief to visit his forces fighting in Italy. Sosnkowski was understandably concerned about the potential willingness of the Polish Prime Minister and his Peasant Party colleagues in the Polish Government to go along with the British appeasement. All historians assume that Sosnkowski was prepared to stage his own *fait accompli* with Anders, namely continuing to accept the Polish President as the ultimate authority but no longer recognizing the London-based coalition government if it folded to Churchill's pressure. It is hypothetical as to the position of the Polish

Secret State. About a year prior to that the Secret State had formally noted that if the Polish Government agreed to the loss of the eastern territories, then they would form their own revolutionary government and disavow 'London'. Did they mean it, or was it a bargaining position. Is this what Rettinger reported when he met with Eden at the Dorchester Hotel?

General Sosnkowski was accompanied on his flight to Italy by Jan Nowak, recently extracted from occupied Poland. The flight was again with a Polish crew and the Dakota carried the Polish red and white checkerboard and the name "Spirit of Ostra Brama".

Jan Nowak was about to be re-inserted into Poland on Wildhorn III, which took place July 26 1944, a bare four days before the Uprising. Nowak wrote that he warned the Underground leadership that help from the West could not be expected! His categorical warning was not just a personal and subjective opinion, and one that proved to br correct, but was reached after meeting in London with the British ambassador to the Polish Government, Sir Owen O'Malley, and also Edward Raczyński, as well as the Head of the Polish Section of the SOE, Colonel Harold Perkins.[1]

General Sosnkowski had warned the Underground all along about the Soviets and their malevolent policies and intentions. The tragic fate of the Polish Home Army units that attempted to carry out the orders of the Home Army Commander and collaborate with the Soviets were paramount in Sosnkowski's opinion. Treated cordially by the local front line Soviet generals, they were soon surrounded by NKVD units and disarmed and sent to concentration camps. This was the situation in Wilno and later in Lwów.

Sosnkowski had argued in joint discussions with the Polish coalition cabinet that an Uprising should not even be contemplated, unless there was a resumption of diplomatic relations with the Soviets and joint collaboration; unless the Western Allies promised full support; and unless the German army had totally collapsed. This last point once again alluded to the possibility that the morale of the German forces would collapse and that there would be a vacuum which could be filled by the Polish Home Army disarming the retreating Germans. However messages from the Polish Home Army seemed to indicate that while aware of the Polish Commander-in-Chief's warnings there was a relentless pressure to fight the Germans and to declare themselves to the Soviet field commanders.

On September 5 1944 the Polish Prime Minister, Mikołajczyk, wrote to the War Cabinet urging, one could even say – begging – that a token company-sized unit of the Polish Parachute Brigade be flown into Warsaw. General Gubbins and the SOE were supportive of the Polish effort. It was their position that a military mission

---

1   Jan Nowak, *Courier from Warsaw*, Wayne State University Press, Detroit, 1982.

should be flown into Poland and that elements of the Polish Parachute Brigade could also be inserted.

The War Cabinet clearly gave it serious consideration, the merits being political rather military. Eventually on September 9, they responded to General Gubbins, but seemingly not directly to the Poles, that there was sufficient available air capacity to move one Polish company from the UK to Italy to be inserted into a region of Poland where German forces were less concentrated.

The War Cabinet then went on to qualify their acquiescence by stating that this would be to the detriment of "routine" supply flights to Poland. The clincher was that "the chiefs of staff consider that it will be necessary to consult the Russian Military before taking a final decision".[2]

It would have made no military difference but it would have given an overwhelming status to the uprising and placed it in a different light.[3] At the same time Lord Selborne, in his memorandum to the British Chiefs of Staff, outlines a carefully crafted political suggestion about the minimum of help which could be sent to Poland without presumably antagonizing the Soviets. He does not mention the possibility of a British military mission, which the Poles had requested on numerous occasions.

> Two problems – military and political. Britain as an ally of Russia could hardly take military action in the Russian theatre of war without the concurrence of the Russian Government. In my view the attitude of the Russian Government would largely depend on the outcome of the conversations now taking place between Premier Mikołajczyk and Marshal Stalin. I know that you would wish to do anything possible that would be of assistance to Poland but I thought that you would be anxious to do nothing that would render more difficult a satisfactory outcome of the Mikołajczyk/Stalin conversations . I need hardly as that I should greatly rejoice if it were found possible to do anything to meet the Polish requests. For five years their forces have been fighting alongside ours and have proved good comrades in arms. I do not think it would be militarily very difficult to despatch now to Poland a company of Polish Parachute troops. The air lift is practically within the compass of the aircraft already allocated to the SOE for Polish work, and now operating on that work from Italy. The gesture would have a most important effect on the morale of the Polish Secret Army, not only a signal of British support but also as a demonstration of the identity of the Polish Forces in Italy and England with those in Poland. I also hope that it will be possible to make a declaration concerning the Polish Secret Arm analogous to that

2   TNA HS4/193.
3   David Stafford, *Britain and European Resistance 1940–1945. A Survey of Special Operations Executive, with Documents*, University of Toronto Press, Toronto, 1983, pp.181–185.

just made by General Eisenhower concerning the French Secret Army i.e. that we recognize them as an allied fighting force and combatants under international law. This would give great satisfaction to the Poles and I hope that you will give the matter your sympathetic consideration. Logically it would be very difficult to refuse such a declaration. Our relations with them Polish Secret Army for the last four years have been precisely the same as our relations with the French Secret Army, and of the two the Polish Secret Army is certainly the best organized and most competent.[4]

Sosnkowski cabled the Polish Home Army Command that "in the face of Soviet political pressures and known actions, a heroic uprising would be an act lacking in political value and it could require unnecessary sacrifices. Remember that a heroic uprising and cooperation mean nothing in the face of Soviet lack of goodwill." This was the tenor of all his communications with the Polish Home Army. But there was an element of the Greek tragedy in the unfolding events. Given internal pressures in the Polish populace to get rid of the hated Germans who appeared to be crumbling, given the tacit encouragement of the Polish Prime Minister to use their own judgment, the die was cast. This was the background to the Warsaw Uprising, the last ditch effort to establish a sovereign Polish political center in Poland. All the events in which the Poles participated, either actively or passively, eventually came down to that final struggle.

It was a tragic political act veiled as a military endeavor.

The Home Army Commander on July 26 1944 requested significant help from the Polish Government Allies. He cabled that with the Uprising imminent the move of the Polish Parachute Brigade to Poland and the bombing of German positions near Warsaw were of vital importance. He also reiterated his formal request for a British military mission. It is really quite problematic whether the Polish Home Army were not aware of all the cautionary warnings from the West or whether it was a statement of inevitability and an attempt to confront the West with a *fait accompli*. The Polish ambassador and independently the Polish Minister of Defence transmitted this request to the British. The Poles were advised on August 1 1944 that all such activities would require Soviet concurrence since Poland was in their area of military operations. But there was a glimmer of some hope for the Poles in the memo of the SOE representatives.

It seems therefore, all the more important to get as much material as we can to the Poles in the shortest possible time, because it appears certain that the Poles in the Warsaw area will rise shortly whether or not the British Chiefs of Staff or the Russians approve. There are no less than 250 tons of stores

---

4   TNA HS4/156.

for the Poles already packed in containers in Italy which merely await the
necessary allocation of aircraft – about 200 sorties.[5]

On August 1, 1944 General Tadeusz Pełczyński, Commanding Officer of the
Warsaw Home Army Garrison, after consultations with Jan Stanisław Jankowski,
the head of the civilian Delegatura, ordered an uprising in the City.

In the West the Warsaw Uprising is seen as a tragic, but militarily unimportant
event. Some historians paint it as an irresponsible act of Polish machiavellian dilet-
tanti, some see this as the beginning of the cold war. Many Polish historians are
still engaged in polemics as to who was responsible and why? The eminent British
historian William MacKenzie gave this judgment, "the decision to rise had tragic
consequences, but it was not irresponsibly taken".[6]

Literature on the Warsaw tragedy is extensive but exclusively published in the
West. This was due to the fact that the Polish Communist regime was absolutely
reluctant to admit to the Soviet behavior during the insurgency or, to the role and
importance of the Polish Government which was behind it![7]

This event was of crucial importance, not just to Polish World War Two history
and its catastrophic outcome but to the third event that soured Polish Soviet relations
for well over a half century – the other issues being the Soviet invasion of September
1939 and the murder of thousands of Polish officers.

Warsaw now endured a savage street battle, building to building, with the insurgents using the sewers for moving from district to district. Girl scouts carried mail,
boy scouts ammunition, women cooked for the soldiers, makeshift first aid places
were everywhere. A number of the participants have written firsthand accounts of
the seventy-day battle.[8]

The British Chiefs of Staff had given fair warning that help could not be expected
from the West and with the full agreement of the British Foreign Office reluctantly
refused any assistance. Stalin decried the uprising as irresponsible and completely
dissociated himself from the Polish Home Army. That was certainly within his political domain. It was one thing to refuse assistance or divert resources from other
possible priorities, but Stalin did everything he could to sabotage the Poles. What

5   TNA HS4/147 28181.
6   William MacKenzie, *The Secret History of the SOE: the Special Operations Executive, 1940–1945*, St.
     Ermin's Press, London, 2000, p.523.
7   Janusz J. Zawodny, who was an officer in the Home Army and took part in the uprising, wrote *Nothing
     but Honor, The Story of the Warsaw Uprising,1944*, Hoover Institution Press, Stanford, California, 1978.
     See also Andrew Borowiec, *Destroy Warsaw! Hitler's Punishment. Stalin's Revenge*, Praeger, London,
     2001; Włodzimierz, Borodziej, *The Warsaw Uprising of 1944*, Madison, University of Wisconsin Press,
     2005; Jan M. Ciechanowski, *The Warsaw Rising of 1944*. Cambridge University Press, Cambridge,
     1974. This particular monograph is also written by a historian who, as a very young man, was involved
     in and a witness to the Uprising. He is critical of the Polish leadership for initiating the Uprising.
8   Wacław Zagorski, *Seventy Days*, Frederick Muller, London, 1957; Tadeusz Bór-Komorowski, *The Se-
     cret Army. The Memoirs of General Bór-Komorowski*, Frontline Books, Barnsley, 2011, pp.199–380.

was absolutely criminal was his categorical prohibition of the landing of Polish, RAF, and South African aircraft on Soviet-controlled airfields that were attempting to drop supplies to the insurgents. The Soviet offensive that was rolling up the Germans suddenly stalled in the eastern outskirts of Warsaw. When it resumed after a number of weeks, the Soviets captured the Warsaw region of Praga but found the Vistula (Wisła) river beyond their fording capacity. It is a fascinating comment that at the Tehran Conference, a Soviet marshal tried to persuade the Americans and British that a cross-channel operation was no different than fording a river. Now the sluggish Vistula in August, that had shoals and could be walked over, was too much for the Soviets.

The Soviets impeded Polish Home Army units, usually of about seven hundred to fifteen hundred men in strength, from moving westward to aid Warsaw. These units were surrounded and disarmed.

The German positions engaged in street-to-street fighting were nearly face to face with the Polish Home Army insurgents, but there were also German heavy artillery batteries battering down one building at a time. These were well within the range of Soviet guns and could have easily been engaged and possibly even silenced. But nothing of the sort happened.

The Polish Government and the Polish Commander–in- Chief as well as General Marian Kukiel, the Polish Defence Minister, all made heartbreaking interventions with their opposite British partners. Polish civilian and military leaders were placed in humiliating, impotent and pathetic positions by the decisions, however seemingly inevitable, of other men. Finally on September 1 1944, back in London, and having failed to achieve any significant help from the British for Warsaw Sosnkowski promulgated an order to all Polish military units which was also published in the Polish language press in England. He alluded to the Polish- British treaty of Mutual assistance and stated that the British had reneged.[9]

In 1943 Stalin was insulted that the Poles asked for an impartial investigation of the murders at Katyn. Now the British Government was insulted at the Polish C-in-C pointing out that the Britain were obligated to render assistance to the Poles, regardless of whether Warsaw was in the Soviet theatre of operations or not! Anthony Eden visited the Polish President and essentially demanded for the good of any continued Polish–British relations that the Polish C-in-C should be dismissed since the British could no longer work with him! Similar pressure was brought to bear on the Polish Prime Minister but in this case it fell on well-prepared and fertile ground, since Mikołajczyk had been at odds with the Polish- C-in-C.

This mutual antipathy was reciprocated but the reasons were complex and went beyond mere personal dislike. Mikołajczyk, on taking the premiership, had made

9   Anders, op.cit., p.220; Kazimierz Sosnkowski, *Materiały Historyczne*, Gryf Publications, London, 1966, pp.200–203.

every possible attempt to do away with the position of C-in-C, and also to make the post accountable to the Government and not directly to the President thus limiting his prerogatives. On the other side, Sosnkowski distrusted Mikołajczyk's commitment to Polish sovereignty and was more than aware that the Prime Minister on his visit to Moscow made it clear that he did not like the Polish Constitution of 1935 and would, after returning to Poland, begin the process of a new constitutional convention. But while Sosnkowski coordinated all his decisions with the coalition government, he did not receive the same courtesy from Mikołajczyk. In the ever increasing acrimony and interventions of the British the Polish coalition government unanimously asked the President to dismiss the C-in-C. Raczkiewicz met with Sosnkowski on a number of nearly concurrent days but Sosnkowski refused to resign. Finally on September 30 1944 the President dismissed his old friend, the Polish C-in-C, from his post. It also should be pointed out that General Kopański, the Chief of Staff, also met with the President and offered his opinion that dismissing the C-in-C would be detrimental to the morale of the Polish Military. General Anders, who had spent a couple of weeks in London, also strenuously argued against any such move and was extremely critical of Mikołajczyk for being a passive stooge for Churchill. Finally, the Commander of the Polish Home Army strongly supported the Polish Commander-in-Chief. As Anthony Eden commented, the Polish Home Army had a greater sense of affinity and loyalty to Sosnkowski than to Mikołajczyk.

But while these background events were unfolding, Warsaw fought and bled. Churchill was moved to attempt to help the insurgents. Did he do as much as he could have is a question that perhaps is not easily answered.

Churchill flew to Italy on August 12 1944 and met with Tito and the Prime Minister of the exiled Yugoslav Government in London, Subâsić. Tito expressed an interest in an Allied invasion of Istria.

Churchill wrote to Stalin asking for help for the Poles and he also wrote to Roosevelt to have him join in remonstrances to Stalin.[10] Churchill's memoirs document his attempted interventions, pleas, and the responses. Stalin replied "the Warsaw action represents a reckless and terrible adventure" and "that the Soviet Command has come to the conclusion that it must dissociate itself from the Warsaw adventure". Churchill's call to Roosevelt to join him in an appeal was successful but the Western leaders received the following message from Stalin, "sooner or later the truth about the group of criminals who have embarked on the Warsaw adventure in order to seize power will become known to everybody". Stalin went so far as to say that "there can be no doubt that the Red Army is not sparing its efforts to break the Germans around Warsaw".

---

10   Churchill, *Triumph and Tragedy*, Cassell, London, 1954, pp.113–128.

While in Italy Churchill witnessed the realistic end of his Balkan strategy. He had been very cautious about the invasion of France (*Overlord*) but was adamantly opposed to withdrawing forces from the Italian front to the invasion of South France (*Anvil-Dragoon*). But he still talked about these plans at the Second Quebec Conference which followed shortly after his Italian visit. In June 1944 he had still advocated the invasion of Istria with a direction of Ljubljana and even possibly Vienna. But Americans were adamantly opposed. Macmillan comments that discussing the broad sweep into the Ljubljana Gap with General Marshall, the American responded by asking, "Say, where is this Ljubljana? If it's in the Balkans we can't go there".[11] It's impossible at this point to determine whether American opposition to Churchill's Balkan option was because of a secret deal with Stalin, whether it had to do with American antipathy to getting involved in anything but winning a war, or possibly, as some have suggested, because of Roosevelt's concern about the American public reaction to so-called imperialistic wars.

Such an invasion may also have moved Tito from his pro-Soviet orientation to one which he nearly espoused later, relative independence.[12] Roosevelt refused to countenance such a change from the Tehran Conference decisions but eventually agreed to consult Stalin for his opinion. Churchill did not follow up on this absurdity.

Italy, 1944. General Anders, GOC Polish 2 Corps, part of the British Eighth Army, in conversation with Winston Churchill on Poland's future. Poland's future as a sovereign state was hardly superfluous to the Polish military. (PISM)

11 Harold Macmillan, *The Blast of War, 1939–1945*, Harper & Row, NY, 1968, p.416
12 Churchill, *Triumph and Tragedy*, pp.53–62.

Italy, 1944. Deputy Prime Minister Clement Attlee, leader of the British Labour Party in the British coalition government, also met with Anders. (PISM)

Italy, 1944. His Majesty King George VI visited the Polish 2 Corps in Italy and met with General Anders. (PISM)

Churchill also met with General Anders on August 26 and alluded to their meeting in Cairo in 1942. After courteous remarks about the success of the Polish 2 Corps, Churchill quoted Stalin's refusal to help as due to the Uprising being caused by "Sosnkowski's men". Churchill again repeated his Government's position that Polish boundaries were not part of the British guarantee, but had pledged a "free, independent, sovereign and great state free from any alien interference." Churchill also assured Anders – "You must trust us; we will keep our pledges." As the meeting came to an end Churchill stated, "we will not desert you".[13]

How did Churchill in his own mind reconcile his assurance to Anders about a Poland free of any alien interference, with his statements that the Soviets were entitled to expect a Polish Government friendly to the Soviets

During this time Churchill reacted to the ominous and pervasive silence of the British mass media about the Warsaw Uprising. He wrote to the British Minister of Information on 23 August 1944.

Is there any stop on the publicity for the fact about the agony of Warsaw, which seem, from the papers, to have been practically suppressed. There is no need to mention the strange and sinister behaviour of the Russians, but is there any reason why the consequences of such behaviour should not be made public?

It is far from clear whether this memorandum had any effect but the British Foreign Office had this internal memo in response to Churchill's memorandum:

Any intelligent reader of the British press would, I fear, draw the conclusion that Stalin could do almost anything he like with Mr. Mikołajczyk and the Poles without arousing any unfortunate reactions in this country. The Prime Minister's remarks about Poland in the debate on August 2nd in fact gave the press very much the line they have been following, that the Russians are reasonable people, that the National Committee and the Polish Government are to be regarded on the same level, that a fusion on the terms decided by Marshal Stalin is really our goal. This is not quite the position of His Majesty's Government but it is, I fear, the deduction drawn from the Prime Minister's statement.

---

13 Władysław Anders, *An Army in Exile*, Macmillan, London, 1981, pp.209–213. This meeting is not mentioned in Churchill's post-war memoirs, but the photo of the two is proof of the meeting. It should be also mentioned that Churchill does not mention the accident of General Sikorski, but the *London Illustrated News* photos of Churchill and Eden at the funeral mass in the Catholic Westminster Cathedral also more than prove his awareness of the significance of that event.

These minutes were reviewed by Sargent of the Foreign Office, who made this interesting comment:

I am sure nothing we can say to the press would persuade them to give direct support at the present juncture to the Polish Government. But I should have thought we might have pressed them to publicize the gallant fight which the Polish Army is putting up, especially in Warsaw. At present they are playing this down almost ostentatiously.[14]

This memorandum illustrates Churchill's paradox when it came to his own views and policies to the Soviets and the Poles. Well aware of the evil nature of communism and the malevolence of Stalin, he kept skirting around that issue. As the Foreign Office stated in reference to Stalin's insistence that the only Polish government was the Lublin-based communist committee, it was not the policy of His Majesty's Government that a "fusion on the terms decided by Marshal Stalin is really our goal", but that is exactly what happened in 1945. Yet, that is exactly what was intended by Churchill later in 1944 and what actually happened, a brokered shotgun marriage between a leader of the Peasant Party in London, not the Polish Government and the Lublin Committee.

After being insulted by Molotov about alleged British secret contacts with Romanian officials, Churchill demanded that the British ambassador communicate his displeasure. "This is not the way to get on with the Russians". Churchill's behavior to the Russians elicited this gossipy comment from Eden in the summer of 1944, "yet no one is more effusive to the Russians than the PM".[15]

It has been argued that already in 1943 the British hoped that the Soviets would be the balance of power in the world since in some Foreign Office quarters there was concern about American hegemony of all world affairs. This was analogous to the Foreign Office hope in 1938 that Germany would also be a responsible player on the European scene. Roosevelt again responded, stating that supplying Warsaw without permission from the Soviets to land on their territory was impossible. Churchill then urged that Allied aircraft should just land on Soviet bases that had been used in the shuttle bombing operation called Frantic regardless of permission.[16] Roosevelt again responded on August 26, 1944; "I do not consider it would prove advantageous to the long-range general war prospect for me to join with you in the proposed message to Stalin".

---

14   TNA FO 371/93408.
15   Llewellyn Woodward, *British Foreign Policy in the Second World War* Vol. III, HMSO, London, 1971, p.132.
16   Mark J. Conversino, *Fighting with the Soviets. The Failure of Operation Frantic, 1944–1945*, University of Kansas Press, Lawrence, 1997.

On 4 September Churchill again "begs" Roosevelt to fly supplies and land without permission. On September 5, 1944 Roosevelt sent this disingenuous message to Churchill. "I am informed by my Office of Military Intelligence that the fighting Poles have departed from Warsaw. And that the Germans are in full control." Was Roosevelt already so intellectually impaired that he actually believed that the "fighting Poles" could just move somewhere? This was similar to Stalin's lying answer in 1941 to Sikorski about missing Polish officers.

On September 10 Stalin suddenly changed tactics. Soviet artillery began to shell German positions. A couple of days later the Polish People's Division, part of the Soviet Front of Marshal Rokossowski, under the command of Berling, attempted to ford the river. The crossing under the command of a Soviet officer, Major Lotyshonka, was barely supported by artillery. The conscripted Polish soldiers, well meaning but raw, about a battalion in strength, ultimately shared the fate of the Polish Home Army. Berling was removed from his command.

At this time the Soviets also agreed to allow Americans to fly a supply mission.[17] Why this seeming change of policy? There can only be two possible answers, though both may be correct. Stalin may have decided on the basis of his ambassadorial reports that there was a growing anger at Soviet policy; or as many Poles, argue he wanted the uprising to continue to ensure that the Home Army was as catastrophically destroyed as possible.

AIR SUPPORT FOR THE WARSAW UPRISING

While Churchill, Roosevelt and Stalin were exchanging formal letters about the Polish Home Army and the Warsaw Uprising there was only one military option for aid to Warsaw, namely the Allied Special Duties units based in south Italy, near Brindisi. The gallant, tragic and controversial history of the attempts to aid Warsaw by air has many accounts, each with some special nuanced emphasis.[18]

The Polish Special Duties Flight 1586 based in Brindisi was dedicated to supplying the Polish Home Army by Polish London-based staff plans. This was not quite the way that the British Air Staff viewed the unit. The Polish crews, all veterans of a full tour of duty in bomber squadrons, were volunteers, and motivated by aiding their comrades in occupied Poland. RAF crews, however professional and brave, did not quite share this burning passion. The Polish Flight was administratively part

17   Thomas A. Julian, "The Role of the United States Army Air Forces In the Warsaw Uprising, Aug Sept, 1944", Air Power History, Vol. 4. 1995, pp.22–35.
18   Destiny Can Wait. The Polish Air Force in the Second World War, pp.216–228; K.A. Merrick, Flights of the Forgotten. Special Duties in World War Two, pp.207- 221; Jerzy Cynk, The Polish Air Force at War, 1943–1945, pp.468–484; Franciszek Kalinowski, Lotnictwo Polskie w Wielkiej Brytanii, 1940–1945, Instytut Literacki, Paris, 1969, pp.264–279; Kajetan Bieniecki, Lotnicze Wsparcie Armii Krajowej, Arcana, Kraków, 1994, pp.219–308.

of RAF 344 Wing and the British commanders saw it as much a part of the Allied Special Duties operations. Polish 1586 Flight was expected to fly to other countries, mostly Yugoslavia, and in turn RAF units were expected to fly to supply the Polish Home Army. From a practical and utilitarian view this made excellent sense. There were days when the weather just did not allow flights to Poland over the Carpathian Mountains. But in reality there was a sense among Polish crews that the burden was not quite equally shared and that the commitment of RAF commanders to much more dangerous flights to Poland was lacking.

In the United Kingdom, Polish fighter wings assigned to RAF Fighter Command, or later, 2nd Tactical Air Force, were an integral part of the Allied effort and flew wherever the highest echelons of the RAF deemed necessary. The Mediterranean Command viewed the Polish Special Duties flight in the same manner, but for Poles, Poland was different than for a Polish fighter pilot flying over France, Holland, Belgium or Germany where it was war against the German aggressor. Given how much effort was expected from Poles to fly to Yugoslavia, or Northern Italy, it was not surprising that once the Polish crews finished their tours of duty they did not wish to volunteer again!

Between January and May 1944 the Polish unit few a total of 317 sorties, of which 147 were to Poland. In June, because of the short nights, all flights to Poland ceased but the flight flew other missions for a total of 169 missions. In July flights to Poland resumed but of the 136 only 37 were to Poland, the rest to North Italy, Greece and Yugoslavia.[19]

When the Warsaw Uprising erupted, the Polish Flight had been at the end of a long spring and summer of intensive operations. A number of the crews were about to complete their tour of operations and were to be withdrawn and rested. The Polish base signaled London [VI Section] that the Polish Flight would be down to six crews by August 1 and down to four by the end of August. To make matters worse, one of the remaining Polish crews was shot down on a mission to Hungary.

The new Polish crews were all from 300 Squadron (Lancasters) and not familiar with either the Halifax or Liberator. They had all been trained in modern navigation, which was anything but the case when attempting at night to locate small obscure hamlets in rural Poland. These were all young crews, young men, not the pre-war professionals who knew their way around Poland.

The story of the ensuing missions to Warsaw makes for sad reading. On August 4 the whole of RAF 148 Squadron and all six Polish crews (two whose time was up volunteered to stay) were prepared to fly but Slessor rescinded the order to fly to Warsaw, although he did approve supply flights to other areas in Poland. The Polish flight commander, Major Eugeniusz Arciuszkiewicz, arranged for four Polish crews

---

19   Kalinowski, ibid. p.265.

to fly to Warsaw regardless. These were the first Allied planes to drop supplies, but many prominent historians attribute this as an RAF effort. Four of the RAF planes flying to other reception zones were shot down and one crashed on landing. This was a severe depletion of available planes in the first week of the Uprising. Slessor ordered a complete halt to all operations over Poland but under great pressure from the Polish C-in-C in London through the British Air Staff reluctantly agreed to Polish crews volunteering for flights to Warsaw. On August 9 he telegraphed the Chief of Air Staff:

> Three Poles went to Warsaw last night and dropped supplies on the city. A good many night fighters were seen and flak experienced at Warsaw, but they got away with it. A gallant show. They will send five more to-night. They are pressing me to send 148 Squadron also. But I intend to adhere to my original decision and not send any British Halifaxes till last quarter of moon, night of 11 or 12 of August. A few aircraft on a show like this will sometimes get away with it. Larger numbers will not.[20]

When Churchill was in Naples on August 11, he instructed that all possible aid be given the Polish insurgents and that bombers of 205 Group also fly supplies to Poland, if not actually to the city, overruling Air Marshal Sir John Slessor, who was placed in the most unenviable position of being tasked with a mission which was realistically impossible. Slessor's analysis, cold and realistic, was that the "an attempt to drop supplies from a low altitude into the middle of a great city would only result in heavy casualties with no prospect of sufficient arms reaching the Polish Home Army."[21] Between August 11 and 18 the Poles flew every night but one (the 13th), and were assisted by the RAF 148 and Royal South African Squadron. After four successful sorties, on the night of August 15 the Allies lost seven aircraft out of twenty-six.

Slessor summarized the operations to date in the following memorandum:

> Twelve successes, six failures, eight missing. In all cases the target was Warsaw. There were no other operations to Poland. Last night 26 dispatched, 11 successful, 8 missing, including 6 Liberators of 205 Group, one of 148 Squadron and one Pole. The two squadrons of 205 Group have lost 25% of their strength in two nights and it is obvious that we cannot go on at this rate of loss which fully justifies my misgivings about the whole operation.

Slessor asks the rhetorical question, "difficult to resist conviction that Russian failure to supply Warsaw is deliberate policy".

---

20   TNA AIR 8/1170/15969.
21   Hilary St. George John Saunders, *The Royal Air Force, 1939–1945 Vol. 3. The Fight is Won*, HMSO, London, 1993, pp.239–241.

On August 17 Slessor cabled:

> Eighteen aircraft dispatched, eight successful, six missing including four-Liberators of 20 Group and two Poles of 1586. This is a second occasion in three nights in which about 30% of aircraft has failed to return and our losses in 13 night operations to Poland have amounted to 21 lost, 3 destroyed on landing owing to flak damage, and many damaged. You will note that this rate of loss was not on Warsaw itself but on woods outside, of which value to the underground can only be rated as better than nothing. Have instructed a stop to all operations in Poland.

The Royal South African Squadrons suffered very heavy losses on missions which they barely understood.[22] At this point in time the Polish Flight only had six airworthy planes. RAF 148 only had three. Evill, the Royal Air Force Vice-Chief of

Italy 1944. A B–24 Liberator of the Polish Special Duties Flight 1586 in Italy in the summer of 1944. On the night of August 4, 1944 Captain Zbigniew Szostak, pictured with his crew, and other Polish fliers of the 1586 Flight, flew one of the first support missions to the Warsaw Uprising. On August 14, after repeated supply missions to the Polish Insurgents, this crew was lost over Poland. (PISM)

---

22   Neil Orpen, *Airlift to Warsaw: The Rising of 1944*, University of Oklahoma, Norman, 1984.

Staff, cabled back to Slessor that nine replacement Halifaxes were being flown to Italy and that the Poles in London had exerted pressure to resume supply flights to Poland. He also concluded that as soon as the moon and other conditions permit, "we hope you will again employ British crews."[23]

The British now introduced a barometric parachute, which allowed drops from a higher altitude with some assurance of accuracy. Slessor under pressure from London allowed Polish crews to volunteer for missions to Poland and was given an assurance that he would not be responsible for casualties and losses. But the situation regarding plane availability was catastrophic in both the Polish flight and RAF 148 Squadron.

On September 18 Stalin relented and gave permission for the Americans to make a shuttle run, dropping supplies over Warsaw and landing on Soviet bases. 107 B–17s of the American Army Air Force based in the UK, escorted part of the way by seventy P–51s, delivered over three hundred containers. The Americans lost two B–17s. It was too late for Warsaw, but proof of what could have been done if flown in early August when the insurgents controlled a much larger area of the city.

The American bombers returned back to the UK but the Soviets stopped all future shuttle missions.

DEMISE OF THE UPRISING

In September the Polish flight only managed 42 operations, of which 17 were to Warsaw, the rest to other countries. The last flight to Warsaw was on the night of September 20. Missions to Poland petered out, the final mission was flown on December 28.

During its existence the Polish flight lost 167 crew, with 18 missing and 49 taken prisoner of war. It delivered 292 tons of war material to Poland, and 1,284 to other countries. One of the last acts of the Polish Commander-in-Chief was to give the title of "Defenders of Warsaw" to the unit.

Warsaw finally capitulated on October 2 1944. That was the end of the Polish Home Army, though embers continued to smoulder on, and in December the British parachuted in their military mission – Freston – which was at least twelve months too late.

A debate took place on October 5 1944 in the House of Commons. Churchill announced that he had a statement to the House, "paying tribute to the heroic stand of the Polish Home Army and the Polish civilian population of Warsaw". He then made the following remark, and if one wishes for fatuous as ascribed to the Polish Government, then this was it, since Churchill added, "Despite all the efforts of the Soviet Army, the strength of the German positions on the Vistula could not be taken". Did anybody laugh in the House of Commons?[24]

---

23   TNA AIR 8/1170 15969.
24   Wacław Jędrzejewicz, *Poland in the British Parliament 1939–1945* Vol. III Summer 1944-Summer 1945, Jozef Piłsudski Institute of America, New York, 1962, pp.31–32.

11

POLAND AND THE
CONCLUSION OF THE WAR

Mikołajczyk flies to Moscow for a second time – Polish Government Crisis – Polish American Congress solicited for political help – Mikołajczyk resigns as Prime Minister – Polish Government still important for the British because of the allegiance of the Armed Forces in the West – British Military Mission to Poland – Yalta – House of Commons debate on Yalta – Polish Underground Leaders arrested by Soviets -Operation Unthinkable – Change in British Government – Incipient Cold War in Poland – Polish 2 Corps enters Bologna – Polish Armoured Division enters Wilhelmshaven – V-E Day.

The tragedy of the Warsaw Uprising and dismissal of General Sosnkowski was resented by the Polish Armed Forces. It was seen, in the way it was, as a cave in to the British, and ultimately to Stalin. The little esteem in which the Polish Prime Minister was held by the majority of the army cadre plummeted even further. The Poles in the West, the majority being in uniform, were firmly against appeasement and compromise. Possibly only in the Polish Air Force was there less sympathy for Sosnkowski, also some real question as to the necessity, or even advisability of a Commander-in-Chief position, given that Polish Forces were split and not of sufficient numbers to form a real army group. Sosnkowski's categorical orders to the Polish Special Duties Flight to aid Warsaw, were sensed as lacking understanding of the technical aspects of the air force and its actual capabilities. Comparing a RAF night bombing raid on Königsberg – a distance approximately the same as that to Warsaw- with attempting to fly and parachute supplies to insurgents, did not earn the Polish C-in-C respect from the blue service.

The decision to appoint the Home Army Commander, General Bór-Komorowski, to the vacated post only strengthened the perception of the redundancy of the position in the Polish situation. It also needs emphasizing that the appointment was greeted by the Lublin Committee with charges of criminality, threats of putting him on trial and disbelief that he had even been in Warsaw.

In late October 1944, with most of Poland under Soviet military control, and Churchill in Moscow, an invitation was extended – perhaps summons is a better word – to Mikołajczyk to attend. The Polish Prime Minister replied "I am ready to go to Moscow with some of my colleagues if the object is conversation between members of the Polish Government and Soviet Government while you are in Moscow". Mikołajczyk flew to Moscow and took part in a prolonged and clearly intimidating setting, in which he managed to hold his own with dignity. The main problem was not just the Soviet territorial claim, to which Mr. Mikołajczyk being from Western Poland had less of an emotional attachment, but the questions of Stalin's demands for changes in the Polish Constitution- back to 1921 – and changes in the Polish Government.

Churchill urged Mikołajczyk to go to Warsaw and become part of the Lublin Committee. It is far from clear that had Mikołajczyk acceded it would have been effected by the Soviets or that he would have become the prime minister as Churchill always implied. When Churchill wrote a proposed text about the Polish Government agreeing to the loss of Eastern Poland and taking premiership of the Lublin Committee, Stalin interjected, correcting this to "in accordance with agreement reached between the Polish Government in London and Polish Committee in Lublin". Stalin inevitably outsmarted and out-lawyered Churchill and Eden.[1] The Polish Government was now derided by its allies. Cadogan, the Permanent Foreign Office Secretary, called the Allied Polish Government "silly Poles", while Macmillan referred to them as "fatuous". It ill behoved the British statesmen to use such expressions about an ally whom they were about to sell out. But it made for a good feeling since how can one have much sympathy for fatuous and silly people?[2] While Warsaw had fought, and its citizens died, Polish Armed Forces in the West fought on land, air and sea. 2 Corps was fighting the bitter battles of Matrauro River and the German Gothic Line. The 1st Armoured Division had made a brilliant run from the Falaise triumph all the way through to Bruges and the Dutch border. Polish air wings and squadrons were engaged in maintaining air supremacy and destroying German ground targets. The small Polish Navy was also carrying out its arduous and seemingly dull tasks of convoying. The Polish forces were determined that their part in the

1   *Documents on Polish-Soviet Relations* Vol. II, 1943–1945, Heinemann, London, 1967, pp.405–422.
2   Anita Prażmowska, *Britain and Poland, 1939–1945: The Betrayed Ally,* Cambridge University Press, 1995. One of the best accounts of the issues is presented by Llewellyn Woodward, *British Foreign Policy in the Second World War.* Volume III, HMSO, London, 1971, pp.154–277, 490–558.

war against Germany would be unrelenting, and that they would uphold the Polish
-British Treaty of Mutual Assistance, even if the other partner wavered.

As the war continued and hundreds of thousands of American troops poured into
Europe the ratio of British and Canadian armies to the Americans shrunk. In late
1944, the British 21st Army Group had six corps of 22 divisions, while the Americans
in their two army groups had 16 corps of 64 divisions.

The Polish Army in the West was fielding a larger force than at any time after
being recreated in the West, although as a ratio to the overall forces they were beginning to be close to insignificant.

In this context the Polish Chief of Staff, General Stanisław Kopański, flew to
Belgium in late December 1944 to visit the Polish Armoured Division and also Field
Marshal Montgomery. Kopański, in his capacity as the Chief of Staff, requested
Montgomery's support to move the 4th Infantry Division and 16th Armoured
Brigade from Scotland, along with First Corps Headquarters, to join up the 1st Polish
Armoured Division and form a Polish Corps. This was part of the August 5 1940
Polish-British Military agreement that all Polish units would be centralized under
Polish command. Montgomery categorically rejected the idea since he did not want
any more corps headquarters in his Twenty First Army Group. Considering the
British shortages, this was undoubtedly a political decision, and not merely due to
Montgomery's xenophobic bias. Kopański states that he was disappointed since as an
ally the Poles were entitled to expect such an evolution. This was to come up again
when Anders met Alanbrooke in London in January 1945.[3]

THE POLISH AMERICAN CONGRESS

One of the last "political cards" played by the Poles was the Polish-American
Congress, which began to be very active in supporting the Polish cause. Created
on May 28 1944, it made a valiant attempt to protect Poland in American political
circles. Roosevelt now had to address his policy of accommodating Stalin with his
concern about winning the November elections.[4] Roosevelt continued to indulge in
his political games and after stalling the Polish-American Congress, finally concerned
about his November electoral college chances he invited them to the White House on
October 11 1944. Against a background of a map of Poland in its 1939 boundaries,
he warmly shook everybody's hand and assured them of his commitment to Poland.
Re-assured or possibly impotent, given that the Polish-American Community was

3   Stanisław Kopański, *Wspomnienia Wojenne*, 1939–1945, Veritas, London 1961, p.348.
4   Richard C. Lukas, *The Strange Allies. The United States and Poland. 1941–1945*, University of Ten-
      nessee Press, Knoxville, 1978.

"born" Democratic, they endorsed Roosevelt, rather than Dewey, who was already publicly speaking out against the Soviets.[5]

Following the disaster in Warsaw, Polish foreign policy had lost all of its options, which up to that time were meager at best. Even hope had begun to evaporate. The Polish coalition government now faced a major crisis as Churchill pressured the Poles to accommodate. After coming back to London from his second visit to Moscow, Mikołajczyk met with Churchill and Cadogan on November 2 1944. Churchill gave the Poles an ultimatum, agree to the Stalin demands, justified as reasonable by Churchill, or forget any further British involvement. Churchill did make one reasonable point, which by November 1944 was completely moot. He did state that he could understand the Polish concern about the future of a sovereign Poland, but had no sympathy whatsoever for Polish concerns about territorial losses to the Soviet Union.

This compromise was characterized by a British Member of Parliament opposed to Churchill's policy thus – give up 33% of the Polish population, 47% of your territory, agree to amalgamate with the Stalin-created Lublin Committee on a minority ratio of 25% to 75% and be friendly to the Soviet Union.

In fact the Polish Prime Minister was not even being guaranteed the position of Prime Minister in the proposed Soviet-sponsored government.[6]

It became a question not of the last political card, because all were held by Stalin, but of the last shot.

Mikołajczyk was unable to get support from his coalition government. This requires a segue – Poles were constantly being accused of lacking democratic principles, but Churchill wanted, expected and demanded that one man, the prime minister of a coalition government, overrule his cabinet and the consensus of the Clandestine State. It is more than obvious, except to critics of the Polish Government, that the questions was not boundaries, but Polish independence. Allowing the Lublin Committee any say in Poland was in all effect allowing the Soviets to rule Poland.

The Polish Government expressed dissatisfaction with the offered joint British-Soviet guarantee, and wanted a specific British and also an American guarantee of Polish independence.

After receiving a letter from President Roosevelt on October 26 1944 through the Polish ambassador in Washington, that American guarantees could not be offered Poland, the Polish coalition government refused to endorse the appeasement policy of the British ally and refused to support Mikołajczyk, who resigned as prime minister. All his Peasant Party coalition cabinet members also resigned. Tomasz Arciczewski, a socialist, was nominated as the new Prime Minister and was endorsed by the three

---

5   Donald Pienkos, *Polish American Efforts on Poland's Behalf, 1863–1991*, East European Monographs, Boulder, Colorado, 1991, p.116. A black and white photograph from that visit clearly shows the Polish map and is included in the book.

6   Krystyna Kersten, *The Establishment of Communist Rule in Poland, 1943–1948*, University of California Press, Berkeley, 1991.

political parties remaining in the coalition government. In all of this diplomatic and political confusion and actual Polish humiliation, three aspects require attention – the status of the Polish Government, the continued supply flights to the Polish Home Army, finally the despatch of the British military mission to the Polish Home Army Command.

The importance of the Polish Government was merely a reflection of the continued British need for the Polish Armed Forces. The forces may have proportionately shrunk in size to the Anglo-Saxon military, but the British were beginning to experience major manpower shortages. Montgomery was forced to cannibalize some of his units, while in Italy due to the major antagonism between the Americans and British over the decision to send troops to Greece, and as the Americans went to the south of France, shortages reached a critical point. Furthermore, the British were experiencing significant desertions amongst their units, which actually led to Field Marshal Alexander proposing military executions for offenders.

Apparently the British Prime Minister felt the need to explain to the Soviet dictator why the Polish Government was still being recognized. Llewellyn Woodward quotes Churchill's letter to Stalin of December 3rd 1944, that without Mikołajczyk as Prime Minister, the Polish Government would be treated coldly but correctly since "a change of Prime Ministers does not affect the formal relations between States". Churchill went on to point out that the Polish Government had control of the considerable Polish armed forces, over 80,000 excellent fighting men.[7]

A proposal for a British and American Military Mission to Poland came from the Polish government in February 1944. In February 1944 the British staff placed this on their agenda but the discussion was whether this was to be a strictly military mission in conjunction with *Overlord*; or semi-political to assess the strength, moral and intentions of the Secret Army. This was to partially address the continued Soviet allegations that the British knew nothing about the none-existent Polish clandestine forces loyal to the Polish Government, and to manifest a British interest in Polish independence!

After many months of obsessing and worrying about the impact on the Soviet sensibilities, finally it was decided to send a British military mission. Apparently the purpose was to convince Soviets and Poles that "a complete sell out of Poland to Russia is not the policy of His Majesty's Government".[8]

The question that springs to mind, what would be a partial sell out? Rettinger was flown in during April 1944, on what was undoubtedly a political exploration.

In July 1944 Churchill did decide to send in a military mission akin to those sent to Tito. He picked Colonel D.T. Hudson, who had already been on such a major mission

---

7   Llewellyn Woodward, *British Foreign Policy in the Second World War,* Volume III, pp.238–239; *Documents,* op.cit., p.485.
8   TNA HS 4/147 07181.

to Yugoslavia. After delays, the British requested Soviet concurrence for the mission, which was refused.

By the time the British Government decided to go ahead without seeking Soviet permission, in October 1944, Warsaw had capitulated, and General Bór-Komorowski was in a German prisoner of war camp. The British mission consisted of a total of five British service personnel and one Polish officer who was given a British cover as Captain Currie. The mission was once again delayed in Italy, pending a suitable weather forecast and then by political questions of whether to even go ahead after the Polish Prime Minister resigned.

Finally in December the mission got a green light and three attempts were made to fly the party to Poland, each aborted by local fog in the reception zone. Finally on December 26 the mission was parachuted and received by a unit of the Polish Home Army near Częstochowa.

The actual report of Colonel Hudson is secret but the SOE account transmitted to the Polish VI Bureau is probably near the truth.

- Observe and report on the activities of the Home Army.
- Report on the relationship of the Home Army and other clandestine groups and the Soviets.
- The mission is to contact and report to the Soviet Army as soon as Soviet forces are nearby.
- The mission is not to take part in combat operations unless its own safety is at stake.

The British military mission was received and protected by units of the Polish Home Army and had a good opportunity to meet with many locals and junior officers. Their meeting with General Okulicki, who had assumed command of the embers of the Home Army after the Warsaw Uprising failed, only took place on January 3 1945. Okulicki had been opposed to the whole mission and was perplexed, as are most historians, by the British decision to send a mission at this juncture. The Polish general outlined all the issues of Soviet perfidy to the Polish Home Army, such as arrests of their units, and lack of help to Warsaw.

Okulicki had only been inserted into Poland in early 1944 and had been on the staff of General Anders all the way back from the time when all were released – amnestied – by the Soviets in 1941. Unlike most Home Army senior officers, he was very much aware of the many currents of British policy to the Poles and did not trust them. He opposed the mission, because he was convinced that it would be a British attempt for him to establish contacts with the Soviets. Whether Okulicki was right is an open question, the events followed a different trajectory. In the meanwhile the British military mission was nearly captured by a German patrol and during the escape, which the Polish Home Unit protected, lost its wireless. From now on the British mission used Polish radios to communicate with the West. The original instructions were that the mission was to stay at the side of the Polish Home Army commander, but in fact he was reluctant to be encumbered by their presence. At this point, through the Polish radios, the mission received orders to contact the nearest approaching Soviet unit.

On January 16, already behind Soviet front lines, the Polish officer in command of the escort detail reported to Colonel Hudson that with the order issued by the President of Poland dissolving the Polish Home Army, and with the enmity of the Soviets to all Polish Home Army soldiers, he had to dissolve his unit.

The British officers once again put on their uniforms and rank distinctions and sent two of their group to find General Okulicki. On January 18 a Soviet truck, with the two officers, who had been sent to look for Okulicki, arrived and picked up the remaining members. Once in Soviet custody the interrogations began. Names, codes, contacts, names of superiors in London, mission target drop zone, etc. The mission was held incommunicado till February 12, 1945. They were then trucked to a military airfield and flown to Lublin before they boarded a train for Moscow, reached on February 17 1945. Only later was it clear to Hudson and his comrades that they were released on the last day of the Yalta Conference.

YALTA

Yalta in Polish historiography is the equivalent of treachery. It was at Yalta in the Soviet Crimea that two Western democracies completely acquiesced in every one of Stalin's disingenuous statements about Poland. The discussion on Poland was carried on without the presence of the Polish leadership. Prior to the meeting Cadogan asked the Polish Foreign Minister whether there was anything he wished to pass along before the meeting. The Poles answered "stick to the Atlantic Charter". The reply came back, "not very useful".

It would be outside the focus of this monograph to discuss and analyse all the agenda points dealing with Poland, but the general tenor was plain. Roosevelt was sick and only wished to have Stalin join in the Utopian United Nations plan. Roosevelt wanted Stalin's endorsement for a UN and the Polish question bored him, assuming he even understood the issues at the time. He told Stalin that coming from America, " he took a distant view of the Polish question." In his one on one meeting with Stalin he did his back stabbing nastily and complained about British greed and guile! Roosevelt made one reasonable suggestion that there should be a Polish Presidential Council. Stalin disputed this, arguing that the Poles (!) should make the provisional government. Roosevelt dropped the idea and asked that the Lublin Poles be invited to Yalta. Stalin stated that he could not find them. This preposterous lie was never challenged but illustrated the degree of disinterest and apathy on the part of Roosevelt, in particular, to the Polish question.

Roosevelt remarked on more than one occasion that the Polish question had been a problem for five hundred years. Undoubtedly it affected the Americans from colonial days! Yalta is still defended by some as a credible conference with sensible and progressive ideas but that the Soviets reneged. Everybody can judge for themselves.[9]

HOUSE OF COMMONS DEBATE ON YALTA

When Churchill presented the decisions reached at Yalta to the House of Commons and they became publicly known, albeit long suspected, the Poles were devastated, particularly the Polish 2 Corps in Italy, whose soldiers in overwhelming numbers were natives of the territories lost to Poland. The British were worried about the impact of the news on the Poles, and it could not have been a coincidence that all Polish warships were suddenly recalled to British ports for maintenance.[10]

On February 27 Churchill began to give an account of the Yalta Conference to the House of Parliament, which also had other items on the agenda in addition to the Polish issue.

Regarding Poland, Churchill admitted there were two problems, "Poland's frontiers and Freedom". In his memoirs Churchill admits that "Poland was the issue which disturbed the House". He spoke at length, primarily defending the British Government's acquiescence to Soviet claims to eastern Poland. It was the question of the Lublin Committee and the future Polish government as well as free elections that were challenged by some members of Parliament.

In the Commons report, Churchill once again indulged in a mixture of ahistoric logic and an emotional sympathy to the Polish military. Firstly, he presented the Yalta Conference as a great success for Poland's future, but blamed the Polish Government, implying that had it accepted his advice it would have been in Warsaw. If the Yalta decisions were so great then the past was moot. But Churchill conveniently forgot that Stalin never agreed to accept the Polish Government in Warsaw but only some selected members whose provenance was "friendly" to the Soviets.

On the second day, an amendment was raised objecting to the treatment of Poland at Yalta. One Parliamentarian made references to the Secret Protocol of the August 1939 Polish-British Treaty of Mutual Assistance. While the substance was acknowledged to deal with German aggression, the words of the secret protocol were cited.

---

9   Diana Shaver Clemens, *Yalta*, Oxford University Press, London, 1978; Fraser J. Harbutt, *Yalta 1945. Europe and America at the Cross Roads*, Cambridge University Press, Cambridge, 2010.
10   Jedrzejewicz, *Poland in the British Parliament, 1939–1945*, Volume III, Jozef Piłsudski Institute of America, New York, 1962, pp.334–593.

The undertakings mentioned in Article 6 of the Agreement, should they be entered into by one of the Contracting Parties with a third State, would of necessity be so framed that their execution should at no time prejudice either the sovereignty or territorial inviolability of the other contracting party.[11]

Eden first of all pleaded ignorance since he had not been in the Government in 1939 and then referred to "legal advisers". It is not clear what the legal advisers actually advised. Or what was the intent of both signatories? The debate showed considerable sympathy for the Poles, as well as some evidence of basic bias, not just coming from the sole communist member.

In the long and at time rancorous debate that followed Churchill's speech most voices were sympathetic to the Polish problem but in the finale, since it was a 'whipped' issue, the motion carried. Churchill writes that it was unqualified support for the attitude "we had taken at the Crimean [Yalta] Conference." Churchill had a clear majority from the British Parliament, but it was hardly 'unqualified", since twenty-five members of Parliament, mostly Conservative, voted against the motion, and eleven members of the Government abstained![12]

When it came to the Polish military Churchill said:

> In any event, His Majesty's Government will never forget the debt they owe to the Polish troops who served them so valiantly, and to all those who fought under our command. I earnestly hope it may be possible to offer them citizenship and freedom of the British Empire, if they so desire it.[13]

In late winter and spring of 1945, General Anders as acting Commander-in-Chief attempted to negotiate the centralization of all Polish land forces in North-West Europe. This was provided for by the August 1940 Agreement, Article 3, Number 2.

> In principle all the units of the Polish land forces will be used so as to form one operational formation in any one theatre of operations under the command of the Polish commander in that theatre or of a commander appointed by him.

Field Marshal Lord Alanbrooke in his diaries alluded to his meetings with General Anders, on January 24, and wrote,

---

11 Article 3 of the Secret Protocol. Also cited in full in *Destiny Can Wait. The Polish Air Force in the Second World War,* pp. 356–359. The Secret Protocol is not cited in the *British Blue Book*. I have my own opinion and a number of different historians have had completely contradictory opinions as to the relevance and meaning of that secret protocol article.
12 Churchill, op cit., p.352.
13 Jedrzejewicz, op. cit., pp.334–593.

Apparently they are anxious to start planning for the eventual assembly of Polish Forces in France to form them into an army with Anders at its head. They do not want to return from Italy to Poland via Vienna, as they consider this likely to lead to a clash with the Russians! They would sooner join up in France and swell their numbers with Poles from Germany, gradually returning through Germany and, if necessary, carrying out a period of occupation of Germany. I foresee that this may well lead to many complications politically and must discuss this matter with Anthony Eden.[14]

Most Polish generals fully expected, and many hoped, that it was a matter of months before hostilities would break out between the Soviets and the Western Powers. Given such circumstances the largest possible Polish military presence was of great importance. A base in France, with an occupying force in beaten Germany seemed a very advantageous location, rather than Italy. There were hundreds of thousands of Poles of military age, many liberated prisoners of war from 1939 and the Warsaw Uprising in Germany and the Polish forces could have been trebled in size by competent and in many cases experienced soldiers and officers.

The planning of the Polish generals was shortly also the thinking of Churchill when he asked his staffs for initial thoughts on "Operation Unthinkable". We all know how the political and international situation evolved in the immediate post-war years in Europe and the belief that a war between West and the Soviets was both imminent and inevitable was by no means far-fetched. It is a reasonable and very credible theory that were it not for the American atomic bomb option, Stalin may have taken a chance on pushing further west and used his Communist parties in France and Italy as excuses or as provocateurs.

The Yalta Conference communiqué on Poland was published on February 12 1945, and captioned "Declaration on Poland".[15]

As the news from Yalta of the final death knell of Poland's hopes for independence spread around the world, General Anders, back in Italy with his Corps, was shattered. He cabled the President and informed him that in the circumstances of the Yalta agreements he had formally requested that the Poles be pulled out of the front line. "I cannot in conscience demand at present any sacrifice of the soldiers' blood."

He made his case to the Eighth Army commander at the same time. The British were very concerned. The pro-Polish British general, Beaumont-Nesbitt, attempted to put a spin on this with a concluding statement, "they are facts which have to be faced and accepted. Their ultimate effect will be largely dependent on the attitude initially adopted by those most concerned". This was rather casuistic and delphian.[16]

---

14   Arthur Bryant, *Triumph in the West, 1943–1946. A history of the war years based on the dairies of Field –Marshal Lord Alanbrooke, Chief of the Imperial General Staff,* Doubleday, NY, 1959, p.295.
15   Documents, op.cit., p.520.
16   Anders, op.cit., pp.251–254.

Anders met with all the senior Allied commanders. General McCreery stated that there were insufficient Allied forces to fill the gap if the Poles were pulled out and appealed to the Polish "sense of duty". The overall Italian theater commander, the American General Mark Clark, assured him with the usual bombastic spin that President Roosevelt considered the four million Polish Americans who would have undoubtedly obtained guarantees for Poland.[17]

One of the archives emanating from the British War Office minces no words – "What happened at Yalta is a big injustice for Poland, but there must be some reason why men in whom we had faith signed something which is apparently contrary to everything what they promised us in words and writ. We still cannot know what it was, so let us wait until our superiors, who will be better informed, decide what we have to do."[18]

At the same time President Raczkiewicz summoned General Anders to London. Initially there were a number of excuses made for delaying his flight. Finally, after one more delay, Anders departed on February 20 1945 after a major meeting with generals Harding and Beaumont-Nesbitt.

On arrival in London Anders met with the President and then the delays became understandable, since he was invited to meet with Prime Minister Churchill and Sir Alexander Cadogan.

Anders writes that his aide and interpreter, Captain Łubienski, was not allowed in the room and the three men held their conversation in "French of a kind". I have been unable to find any British record of the substance of this meeting but Anders's account is credible given Churchill's cyclothymic personality and irritation with all Poles, who would not accept his benevolent handling of the Polish questions. It is important to remember that this was the third meeting of the British Prime Minister and the Polish 'Corps' commander. Churchill began the meeting with a statement that seemingly Anders was not satisfied with the Yalta conference. Anders gave a long response, "Our soldiers fought for Poland, for freedom, what can we, their commanders tell them?" Churchill put the blame on the Poles for not heeding his advice on the borders and told Anders that "we have enough troops. You can take away your divisions, we shall do without them".

The conversation ended by Churchill assuring Anders that the Warsaw-based Provisional Government, however composed, would only have the task of organizing free elections.[19] Immediately after that Anders met with Field Marshal Alanbrooke whose comment is a bland "very trying hour with general Anders".[20] Anders also obtained the Polish President's permission to visit the leader of the Peasant party, Mr.

---

17   Ibid.
18   TNA WO 204/5470.
19   Anders, op.cit., pp.256–257.
20   Bryant, op.cit., p.318.

Mikołajczyk. Anders writes that he made a strong attempt to dissuade Mikołajczyk from being Churchill's cover for the abandonment of Poland, but to no avail. Mikołajczyk argued that with British backing he would be able to prevail in the elections since his party had a clear and overwhelming majority in Poland. As they said goodbye – for the last time – Anders told his host, "within three months of the falsified elections you will be in prison, detained as a spy and traitor, perhaps even in my former cell at Lubianka."[21] Anders was only slightly off target. After the falsified election held in January 1947, as rigged trials and executions including many gallant Polish officers who had fought in the West became the rule, Mikołajczyk, aware of the danger to his person, escaped to the West in October 1947.

Anders once again met with the Polish President and members of the Polish Government in London, Anders was told that it was the policy of the Poles to continue to adhere to the Polish-British Treaty and to fight, and that the Polish armed forces were of the utmost importance in keeping the idea of a sovereign Poland. At this point the President also asked Anders to be acting Commander-in-Chief.

Anders writes bitterly that as the Presidential decree was promulgated, all of Anders' appointments with leading British figures were cancelled. "Such was the position of the Commander-in-Chief of the Polish forces on the eve of victory".

But the control of the Polish Forces, completely loyal to the Polish Government, presented the British Government with a dilemma. In March 1945 the British Foreign Office spelled out the contingent British policy. "Our aim should be to preserve the Polish Armed Forces as loyal and united formations for as long as their services are required in the war against Germany, and to ensure that as many Poles as possible should be able to return to Poland at the end of the German war."[22] This memorandum was not a mere hypothetical eventuality since the British high command in Italy warned London that rescission of diplomatic relations with the Poles would inevitably lead to a demand by the Polish Corps commander, General Władysław Anders, to be pulled out of the front line. The British generals warned that such a development would be militarily catastrophic since the Allies forces in Italy had already been depleted by the invasion of southern France and British intervention in Greece.

The Poles stayed true to their Mutual Treaty Obligation signed in August 1939. Harold Macmillan had expressed grave reservations after the Yalta conference about 2 Polish Corps, but admitted that "I had underestimated the marvelous dignity and devotion of Anders and his comrades. They fought with distinction in the front of the attack in the last battles of April. They had lost their country but kept their honour".[23]

---

21   Ibid., pp.256–260.
22   Memorandum. The Polish Armed Forces. TNA FO371/4766. N. 2724/123/55.
23   Harold Macmillan, *The Blast of War*, 1939–1945, Harper & Row, NY, 1968, p.573.

The Yalta honeymoon, if it was a honeymoon, did not last long. Churchill became aware of the various duplicities of Stalin and the persecution of the Poles who had been loyal to the Polish Government. These facts were well known in Britain, albeit down played, with the hope that something, passing for democracy, could still be salvaged. Furthermore, the Soviets were ignoring all the well-meaning caveats that had been introduced by Churchill and to some extent by Roosevelt at Yalta. Finally, on March 13 1945 Churchill turned to Roosevelt with a really plaintive letter.

> At Yalta we agreed to take the Russian view of the frontier line. Poland has lost her frontier. Is she now to lose her freedom? That is the question which will undoubtedly have to be fought out in Parliament and in public here. I do not wish to reveal a divergence between the British and the United States Governments, but it would certainly be necessary for me to make it clear that we are in presence of a great failure and utter breakdown of what was settled at Yalta, but that we British have not the necessary strength to carry the matter further and that the limits of our capacity have been reached.

The reply from Washington was in line with all of the recent American policies, of letting sleeping dogs lie, if one was not being bitten. An exchange between the two leaders followed. The Americans were seemingly satisfied, while Churchill noted that "all entry into Poland is barred to our representatives". "All liaison officers, British and American, who were to help in bringing back our rescued prisoners of war, had been requested to clear out." That is what Stalin managed, what the Poles predicted, and what the Western Leaders swallowed.[24]

It was during this time that the Soviets stuck their finger in the face of the Western leaders once again by arresting Polish Underground Leaders after inviting them to a meeting. With great encouragement from the West, the leadership of the Polish Clandestine State had received an invitation from General Ivanov to come out into the open and discuss the political aspects of the construction of the future Polish government. A written letter and guarantee of safety were given. In the negotiations, the Polish underground leaders requested permission from the Soviets to go to London to discuss matters with the Polish Government. This appears to have been a most naïve request, but it was granted. In March 1945 after arriving in Soviet headquarters they were told they were being flown to London, but arrived in Moscow. This information only came about many months later, after the Moscow trial which found three of the Poles innocent, who returned to Poland. But in March 1945, they simply disappeared. For many weeks the Soviets disclaimed all knowledge of their whereabouts. Suddenly on May 6 1945 at San Francisco at the inaugural session of the United Nations, Roosevelt's utopian dream, Molotov announced that they were

---

24   Churchill, *Triumph and Tragedy*, pp.367–385.

under arrest and being tried for anti-Soviet activities. In a Soviet court, deprived of any international support, thirteen of the Polish leaders were found guilty of subversion, terrorism and espionage. The last commanding officer of the Polish Home Army, Major General Leopold Okulicki, was sentenced to ten years and died in Soviet custody. There was a tragic symmetry of the fate of the Polish Home Army Commanders, parallel to that of Poland. The first, Major Stefan Rowecki, was captured by the Germans in 1943 and executed in 1944; the last Okulicki, died in Soviet captivity due to unknown causes. Churchill in his memoirs wrote:

> This was in fact the judicial liquidation of the leadership of the Polish Underground which had fought so heroically against Hitler. The Rank and file had already died in the ruins of Warsaw.[25]

But as these facts on the ground were developing Churchill, the ever-secretive statesman, asked his military chiefs to prepare contingency plans in event of a conflict with the Soviets.

At times it does seem that Churchill was driven by many different motives, always split between emotion and realism of the ever-increasing impotence of the British lion. In one of his comments he compared the British donkey –not lion – to being squeezed by the Russian bear and the American buffalo.

His charge to the British staff was simple and their response intriguing. The response by the Joint Planning Staff, dated May 22 1945, was for many years secret. The Staff made a very extensive study of the possibilities for an attack on the Soviets on July 1 1945. The following assumptions were cardinal:

- undertaking has full public support in both British Empire and the United States.
- Great Britain and the United States have full support from the Polish armed forces, and can count upon the use of German manpower.

The JPS spelled out the "object" as being imposing upon Russia the will of the United States and the British Empire.

The will was then defined as "no more than a square deal for Poland". The JPS discussed all the issues but again made one interesting comment, that the Western powers could count on the ten Polish People's Army divisions, called Berling, although in 1945 he was no longer in command, having been removed for his attempts to help the Warsaw insurgents in September 1944. After presenting their report, the JPS were also asked by Churchill to make plans for an eventual Soviet attack on Western Europe and even on Britain.[26]

---

25   Churchill, op.cit., p.435. Also, *Docs.*, pp.580–605; Woodward, op.cit., pp.540–545; Sir A. Clarks Kerr's [British ambassador in Moscow] report to Foreign Office, ibid., pp.556–558.
26   TNA CAB 120/691.

These background plans and concerns explain why the Polish Armed forces in the West continued to be trained, and the air force in particular continued to train new air crew. In March 1945 both the Secretary of State, Mr. Eden and the Minister for Air, Sir Archibald Sinclair, for reasons not quite obvious, joined forces in attempting to curtail Polish Aircrew Training. This was in line with a decision of 1944, that all Allied air crew training was to be phased down proportionately to merely make up the losses, which with victory imminent were moderating. All the air forces had reached their zenith, and the Poles were in an exceptional situation being allowed to increase their squadron number. The Poles appealed and it was rescinded for the Polish Air Force. The letter asked that the rescission be lifted since the training of the full quota of 125 Poles was interfering with RAF training and it was more than sufficient to maintain the 15 Polish squadrons and even to expand the Polish squadrons to 17 squadrons as accepted by the Chiefs of Staff.

The letter goes on to comment that the other allies might be perturbed, and that with Anders as Polish C-in-C, it might be difficult to justify "these entirely exceptional training facilities for the Polish Air Force" to the Soviets. The letter emphasized that this reduction would cover any post-German war wastage. This was not completely unreasonable since the RAF was still in the war against the Japanese, and any distraction from that had to be questioned.

Churchill replied on March 4, 1945:

> We shall see much more clearly on this field before the month of April is over. Meanwhile no change, but bring up then.[27]

The Polish Air Force was not the only branch of the Polish Armed Forces that was still recruiting and growing - 2 Corps in Italy on its way to the final battles of the river Po and capture of Bologna was enlarging; its two brigade infantry divisions swelled to three brigades, while its armored brigade became Poland's 2nd Armoured Division.

The gallant Polish 1st Armoured Division entered German territory and at war's end accepted the capitulation of Wilhelmshaven, beginning a two year stint of occupation of a small part of Germany. On its march through Belgium and Holland it had enjoyed the enthusiastic reception of any liberated cities. It did not have the opportunity to liberate any part of Poland, but it did enjoy and savor the moment when it freed a camp of Polish women prisoners at Oberlangen from the Warsaw Uprising.

'Operation Unthinkable' became shelved and secret for many decades. It is not at all clear from any available archives, either British or American, as to the real reason why it was not taken a step further. But one can assume that the Labour Partners in the British coalition Government were anything but in favour of this initiative and

---

27   TNA FO 371/47662.

undoubtedly the Americans, concerned about waging war against Japan and distrustful of British, perhaps more pertinently Churchillian imperialism, did not support it.

The British SOE archives for May 24 1945 document this interesting memorandum:

> While impolitic to consider the possibility of war with Russia, in such an eventuality Polish Forces could be useful and since the Poles will not go back to Russian-controlled Poland, then an option of placing them out of harm's way e.g. Italian East Africa, should be considered . The Poles themselves being mostly from the East [i.e. East Poland] and farmers would do well and would themselves like to be British Colony.[28]

CHANGE IN BRITISH GOVERNMENT

Shortly after the end of hostilities in Europe, the Labour Party partners in the British coalition government dropped out and asked for general elections. Churchill's request that this be delayed until the end of the war in the Pacific was not heeded. It is a matter of pure speculation but the question of "Operation Unthinkable" and other aspects of post-war foreign policy might have been as important as the sense of the inevitability of the economic and social pressures in the United Kingdom pushing for a major change of governance.

For a short time there was a British Conservative Government but in the general elections the Conservative Party lost and Clement Attlee became the new prime minister. Many Poles always believed that had Churchill won the elections and continued as prime minister the post-war fate of the Polish Forces would have been diametrically different.

INCIPIENT COLD WAR IN POLAND

Churchill had assured Stalin that the Polish Government would be treated coldly, but the British Government did much more than just that! The Polish Government was not even invited to the inaugural session of the United Nations. The first country to oppose German aggression was omitted. The country that started the war was present. It was also at that time that the Soviets finally admitted their final obscene and perfidious act, which was tolerated by the West.

On May 2, 1945, Anders once again flew to London. One again he met with the Polish Government. He was after not only the commanding officer of Poland's largest army formation , a cohesive, centralized and battle-hardened force, but also

---

28   TNA HS 4/ 291 31896.

the acting Commander–in–Chief. He also met with Field Marshal Alanbrooke. Since on a recent visit to London his scheduled visits had been canceled by the British Chief of Staff, one can only assume that this visit was arranged due to the innate courtesy of a British Field Marshal to an Allied general, or, possibly because the decision regarding "Operation Unthinkable" had not yet been closed. Perhaps, one might hope, both!

Alanbrooke for that date comments on his visitor. He noted that the Poles expressed a desire to take part in the occupation of Germany and moving the whole of 2 Corps to France and then Germany from Italy. Also given a chance and ability to recruit the hundreds of thousands of young Poles in Western Europe, slave labour, liberated prisoners of war from 1939 and Warsaw Uprising the troops could have a fighting chance to smash their way into Poland and of course be joined by the men of the Polish so-called People's Army. Alanbrooke commented that this "a pretty desperate problem the Polish Army is going to present us with".[29]

29   Arthur Bryant, *Triumph in the West*, p.345.

12

THE SIZE OF THE POLISH FORCES AT WAR'S END

Size of the Polish Forces at war's end – Polish war casualties- Polish Government "disavowed" by the British and Americans – Polish Forces in limbo – Polish Forces demobilized – Polish Resettlement Corps- Victory Parade – British and Polish financial accounting – Fraudulent elections in Soviet occupied Poland.

At war's end the Polish Armed Forces in the West numbered 194,460 officers and men, of whom 171,220 were in the ground forces, 19,400 in the Air Force and 3,840 in the Navy. This included 6,700 Polish women who served in all the three branches. These forces were distributed in a number of different locations.

During military operations in the West, the Polish forces suffered the following casualties – in combat operations in exile (i.e. after the September Campaign) the Poles suffered 7,698 officers and men killed and 10,605 wounded.

The Land Forces were administratively divided into two Army Corps: First Army Corps, (General Officer Commanding, Lieutenant General Stanisław Maczek), consisted of the 1st Armoured Division (part of the British Army of the Rhine), and the 4th Grenadier Division and 16th Armoured Brigade, both in Scotland; while 2 Army Corps, (General Officer Commanding, Lieutenant General Władysław Anders) was in Italy and consisted of the 3rd Carpathian, 5th Kresowa infantry divisions and 2nd Warsaw Armoured Division. There were many logistical, training and liaison units, mostly in the United Kingdom but also in Egypt.

During the war the Polish VI Bureau expedited a total of 600 tons of mostly military material to the Polish Home Army. Much of it was German arms, captured in Italy, that was useful in the Polish situation where German ammunition could be

Post-war Germany, 1945. Sherman tanks of the Polish 1st Armoured Division on final parade. (PISM)

obtained, by various means, captured, and at times even purchased from the less than reliable soldiers of so called German allies.

A total of 34,82,163 dollars, paper and gold was inserted as well as one thousand plus British sterling gold coins, nineteen million German marks, and forty million of the German occupation zloty currency, to support the clandestine effort, and as a form of salary for those close to 65,000 people who were full time in the Home army. 300 Polish military were inserted and 28 political couriers, representing the parties in the Polish coalition cabinet. Of this number, 100 were killed, captured and executed.

This was one of the major problems confronting the British Government when on July 5 1945 , after victory over Germany, the two Western powers rescinded recognition of the Polish Government and granted and established diplomatic relations with the Provisional Government of National Unity in Warsaw, essentially a Soviet puppet clique.1 This step was preceded by Stalin agreeing at Churchill's great insistence to have Mikołajczyk join the Communist group in Warsaw. Mikołajczyk was not a member of the Polish coalition government at this time, but he was the head of the Polish Peasant Party, arguably the largest political party in Poland. This allowed Churchill and the American governments to recognize the Warsaw Regime as a Provisional Government of National Unity since on the surface it was consistent with the Yalta Agreements regarding the Polish provisional government and free elections. Churchill described this as a "disavowal", while the Poles saw it as a sellout,

---

1   Winston Churchill, *Triumph and Tragedy*, Cassell, London, 1954, p.564.

or Munich 2, but whatever term reflects the flavor of the day, the day was foreseen by all the Poles. One of the hints of this was the increasing use of the word émigré to describe the Polish constitutional government in London. By little increments in the use of this term, the public had been subtly influenced to accept the Warsaw-based communist committee, or Lublin provisional government as the government of Poland and the London Constitutional Government as émigré!

This decision was anything but a surprise for the Polish Government, bitter as it was. Many Polish archives had already been transferred to the Polish consulate in Dublin, since the Irish Free State continued to have formal diplomatic relations with the London Poles.

The decision to establish diplomatic relations with the Warsaw regime presented the British Government with a dilemma as to how to deal with the Polish forces in the West. Nobody in the chain of command of the three services was in any way about to accept the authority of the Warsaw communists or acknowledge the Provisional Government of so-called National Unity as having any legitimate authority. This was no small matter.

The British were understandably concerned. Having just experienced a mutiny of a Greek brigade and even a mutiny of some of their troops in Italy, the mere thought of the Poles resorting to armed resistance was anathema. 2 Polish Corps was nearly an autonomous state of its own around Ancona, while the 4th Infantry and 16th Armoured Brigades in Scotland could easily control British ports and logistical depots. There were hardly any British units in Scotland.

The British had to proceed carefully. Their first step was to assure the Polish Chief of Staff, the two Service Chiefs (Navy and Air Force)] and Anders in Italy that nothing was going to change except that the chain of command would now lead to the British Chiefs of Staff and not to the Polish C-in-C or Polish Government. The British also informed the Polish generals that their command structure would be exercised through the Polish Chief of Staff in London, General Kopański.

Churchill writes in his memoirs that he was pressed by Stalin at Potsdam to turn over the command of the Polish army to the Lublin Poles, likewise all the Polish gold and Polish merchant marine. Churchill was undoubtedly being rather careful but his description of the Polish 2 Corps is probably close to the truth – "a Polish Corps of three divisions in Italy in a highly excited state of mind and grave moral distress."[2]

In turn the Polish generals advised the British that they accepted the unfortunate development but that President Raczkiewicz was their legitimate and constitutional head and they expected him to be treated in a courteous manner. The President in turn finessed the political debacle by making Kopański Chief of the General Staff and granting him all the privileges of the constitutional C-in- C. This back and forth

---

2   Churchill, op.cit., p.564.

*Post-war II Corps Victory Parade, Italy 1945. Sherman tanks of the Polish
2nd Armoured Division of the Polish 2 Corps in Italy. (PISM)*

went on, with the British expressing their own perception that surely the Polish military owed allegiance to Poland, not the President. The Poles responded that until free
elections in Poland, the situation was as it was.

The British having formally recognized the Warsaw-based and Communist-
dominated Provisional Government of National Unity, then logic would seem to
suggest that the top of the chain of command should have been in Warsaw. For
a number of months the Warsaw regime acted that way and attempted to impose
their command by creating a staff of the Army of West and as its head placed Karol
Swierczewski, a Soviet communist agent. His political officer was a Colonel Wiktor
Gross, actually Izaak Medres, a journalist for the pre-war Polish communist paper
– *Robotnik.*

The British Government was attempting to induce as many Poles as possible to go
back to Poland, and this gauche move on the part of Warsaw was unacceptable. The
British realized that this was going to really foment unrest if allowed to take place. It is
still a historic enigma how some of these decisions were being made in Warsaw. Were
the communist Poles so encouraged by Stalin's successes in dealing with the West that
they assumed 'anything goes'? Or, was it a calculated move to ensure that over 200,000
military personnel, openly hostile to the Soviets and communism, would not be transported to Poland and possibly strengthen Mikołajczyk's Peasant party?

Some Polish soldiers from the western regions were being demobilized and electing to go home. A number of senior officers also opted for repatriation, the most prominent being General Izydor Modelski. But the small numbers of men who left were filled by the thousands of Poles who hoped to join the Polish forces, and only British restrictions on enlarging the forces stood in the way. The British rather reluctantly and somewhat discreetly allowed the Polish land forces to keep up their established strength. In the case of the air force only Polish personnel who had been taken prisoner of war while operating out of British bases were automatically returned to duty. This was very unfair to air personnel taken prisoner of war in the September Campaign, 1939.

Finally, on February 14 1946, the Warsaw regime communicated to the British that the Polish forces in the West were no longer part of the Polish People's Army and each soldier, airman and sailor would have to make his own application to obtain a visa to return, if he met the conditions, i.e. not a fascist or unfriendly to the Polish People's Republic. The British strongly protested this; it appears it was somewhat loosely applied by the communists.

There was also another group involved in the painful dispute. British Labour Unions, mindful of the economic blight after the First World War and its ensuing catastrophic unemployment, were agitating for the Poles to be repatriated by force if necessary. Again the spin was that these men were reactionary feudal fascists, unwilling to contribute to Poland's reconstruction. One of the illogical arguments was that the Poles were lazy and at the same time they would take work away from the British worker.

Palestine, 1943. General Władysław Anders shown visiting a camp for Polish children. Many orphans were saved from the Soviet gulags by Anders. He was seen by the overwhelming numbers of Poles in the Middle East, military and civilian, as the man who brought them out of the Soviet Union and its gulags. (PISM)

Churchill, now in opposition since the Conservatives had lost general elections in 1945, proposed that the Poles be placed on occupation duties in Germany to allow British troops to be demobilized. This did not find any support in the Labour Government, but a number of other exotic suggestions were also touted. One which found great favour amongst the Poles was to place the military, civilians, orphanages in Tripolitania. But the proposal foundered due to vehement opposition from the Soviets who had their own sights on the Italian colony, also to no avail.

THE DEMOBILIZATION OR DISSOLUTION OF THE POLISH ARMED FORCES IN THE WEST

Finally the issue came to a head with the final steps for the Italian peace treaty. The Italian Government, which actually had good relations with General Anders and 2 Polish Corps, demanded that all foreign troops leave its territory.

Prime Minister Clement Attlee called a meeting of the Polish Chief of General Staff and all the service chiefs, but most importantly with General Anders from Italy. Again it is noteworthy how important Anders was in all of these negotiations. The British understood that regardless of Anders being a source of unending irritation to them, he was the senior Polish general and had unquestioned loyalty in the Polish 2 Corps. The other Polish generals were held in high esteem and professional respect by their services, but Anders was the man who delivered "his people" from the Soviet

UK, 1946. Avro Lancasters of the Polish 300 Bomber Squadron make their final flight before giving up their planes. The squadron was the last remaining Polish formation in Bomber Command. It had the distinction of having flown more sorties and suffered more casualties than any other squadron in RAF Bomber Command. (PISM)

gulags. He was obviously the man to talk to since he represented a Corps of well over a 100,000 men, all fully armed.

All the Polish generals met with the British Secretary of State, Bevin, but Attlee met one on one with Anders. The British confronted the Poles with their decision to demobilize the Polish forces. Apart from many political aspects, including constant aggravation with the Soviets, the British also faced an economic problem.

The Poles urged that nothing be done until there were free elections in Poland, but the British Government stated that their decision was final.

The process of demobilization began in mid-1946 but continued till early 1947, when finally the Polish Armoured Division, on occupation duties in Germany as part of the BAOR, was transported back to the United Kingdom.

The Polish 2 Corps left its equipment in Italy. The Polish Air Force gave up its planes. There was a near glitch when it came to the Polish Destroyers, *Burza* and *Błyskawica*. Both were pre-war Polish warships and Polish sovereign territory. The Polish admiral refused to hand the ship over to the communists, but stated in the case of *force majeure* he would issue orders for the ships to be handed over to the British Admiralty. This was done and eventually in 1947 the two ships arrived in Polish waters. A number of naval officers had urged that the two warships be scuttled. Admiral Swirski issued specific orders forbidding this gesture.[3]

BRITISH VICTORY PARADE OF 1946

In 1946 the British organized a victory parade in London. Polish forces in the West were not invited, instead the invite was sent to Warsaw, and was ignored. Ten Polish generals in the West were invited by the British Chief of Staff to the reviewing stand. In the circumstances the Polish generals refused to attend. The Poles staged their own small victory ceremony and retired their regimental colours to the Polish Historical-Sikorski Museum.

THE POLISH RESETTLEMENT CORPS

The British Government and many senior British generals endorsed the statement that the Poles who refused to go back to a Soviet-dominated Poland should be given the option of British citizenship. The British Government decided that a

---

3   Michael Hope, *The Abandoned Legion. A Study of the Background and process of the Post-War dissolution of Polish Forces in the West*, Veritas, London, 2005.This short and excellent book is the only English language study of this topic. However, the use of the term "legion" is incongruous since the Poles were never called that and never called themselves a "legion". For the Polish language reader, see the extensive monograph by Mieczysław Nurek, *Gorycz Zwycięstwa*, Wydawnictwo Uniwersytetu Gdańskiego, 2009.

pre-condition of this would be enrollment in a newly-created organization, the Polish Resettlement Corps. This was a voluntary institution which was to be neither a Polish Army nor quite a British one. The men and women who enrolled would have the right to be in the United Kingdom and be eligible for applying for British citizenship. During the maximum stint of two years, the enrollees would have an opportunity to acquire civilian skills. This included professional education, training and for most who had not been based in the United Kingdom, English language education. While the maximum time in the Corps was two years, any enrollee could opt out at any time to pursue civilian employment in the United Kingdom, assuming he or she could find a job, or emigrate or go to Poland. A committee called the Committee for Education of Poles in Great Britain was formed and facilitated the education and future of thousands of Poles. While the Royal Navy and British Army did not accept any Polish citizens, the Royal Air Force opened its doors to many hundreds of Polish airmen. The Royal Navy refused to have anything to do with this arrangement and Polish naval personnel were given the option of enrolling in the Army branch. So Polish personnel were given army ranks, commensurate with their naval rank. This has led to much confusion in the descendants of naval personnel who settled in Britain, since they assumed that the Polish navy had army ranks!

In the Resettlement Corps all enrollees, while disarmed, were to be in British uniform and subject to British military discipline. However, the basic Polish military structure was to be maintained. Polish officers were in charge of the Polish soldiers though at the level of what might have been a brigade the British held command.

At this point nearly 100,000 Poles decided to go home! The question might well be asked – why now, when the news from Poland were becoming progressively more discouraging?

There is no definitive answer, but as long as they were in Polish uniform, with some semblance of expectation that their service might be important to Poland, they stayed in exile. When it was obvious that all was lost, then homesickness and for many social adjustment problems in a country that had become hostile became primary motivations. Except for the Polish Naval and Air Force personnel who had served alongside their British comrades and where English was the operational language, land army cadre had served in all-Polish units with Polish language as the default. The percentage of returnees from the Navy and Air Force was well less than a quarter.

FINANCIAL ACCOUNTING OF THE POLISH DEBT TO THE UNITED KINGDOM

While the British were trying to persuade as many Poles to go home to Poland to do their "patriotic duty", financial discussions began on the matter of the Polish military debt to Britain and the return of the gold of the Polish Central Bank.[4]

These negotiations were carried on in relatively civilized manner, and attempted to close the account. The Polish, British Treasury and other British agency figures for the debt are all different. Churchill in meeting with Stalin at Potsdam stated that the British had paid (loaned surely?), £120,000,000.[5] A British Foreign Office figure states that £98 million was advanced for military credits and £23 million for the Polish civilian budget. One could say that this is close enough for government budgeting.[6]

At the beginning of the financial discussions the Warsaw regime, with a modicum of logic, stated that any expenses incurred by the British after July 5, 1945 was not their affair, but they wanted the Polish gold back to rebuild the country. The British presented the Warsaw representative with a statement for £122 million, of which £75 million was deleted due to Lend-Lease arrangements. But £47 million was for salaries and they expected to be reimbursed. The Warsaw side adamantly refused to pay for salaries, using the bizarre precedent, which even more absurdly the British accepted, that the Soviets did not expect to be reimbursed for salaries of the Berling divisions. The Warsaw side did agree to pay for all Polish Government civilian expenses.

An agreement was signed and presented to the House of Commons as Treaty Series no. 44 (1947).[7]

FRAUDULENT ELECTIONS IN SOVIET OCCUPIED POLAND

In January 1947 the Communists staged their Potemkin charade of elections. Izydor Modelski once again changed sides and chose "freedom" in Washington, as did Kot.

Mikołajczyk, afraid for his life fled Poland, with the aid of the American ambassador, leaving his followers to their fate. His escape was probably tacitly condoned by the Communist clique, since it gave them a great deal of propaganda. A Polish Peasant Party leader, being helped by Western Capitalists, while others suffered!

Those who stayed behind were at the very best victimized, deprived of their jobs, and too frequently arrested and again, at best, spent years in communist prisons until there was a significant thaw in Communist Poland in 1956.

---

4   Wojciech Rojek, *Odyseja Skarbu Rzeczypospolitej. Losy złota Banku Polskiego, 1939–1950*, Wydawnictwo Literackie, Kraków, 2000.
5   Churchill, op.cit., p. 564.
6   TNA FO 371/ 47700.
7   TNA T 160/1399. HMSO, London.

Polish officers, many heroes of the war, were arrested and executed.

I particularly wish to mention Colonel Szczepan Ścibior, since his personal tragedy was typical of many! A family friend, a great comrade of my father, both attended the Polish Air Force Staff Academy in Warsaw. In the United Kingdom he commanded Flight B of 305 Polish Bomber squadron. He was shot down over Belgium in 1941 and taken prisoner of war. Liberated in 1945, he decided to return to Poland in March 1946 after the Polish forces were demobilized. One may assume that his primary motivation was his family, a wife and two daughters. He was inducted back into military service, and promoted to a colonelcy in the Polish People's Air Force, and shortly thereafter assumed the post of commandant of the Polish Air Force Academy in Dęblin in August 1947.

There were few real Polish air force officers in the People's Air Force and there was an initial attempt by some so-called nationalist communists, like Rola–Zymierski, to have Poles in the People's Armed Forces. The Stalinist repressions reached their height in that period, Poland was forced into the Warsaw Pact, made to refuse American Marshal Aid, and a Soviet Marshal, Rokossowski, was appointed to be the Supreme Commander of the satellite army. It was at this time that Colonel Ścibior was arrested in August 1951 and executed on August 7 1952.

On April 26 1956, Colonel Ścibior was declared innocent of any alleged charges against him, and rehabilitated. But that was the fate of hundreds of Poland's war-time heroes.[8]

---

8   Józef Zieliński, *Szczepan Ścibior*, Zespól Wydawniczy Sił Powietrznych, Warsaw, Poland. 2007. Written with the assistance of Mrs. Barbara Sopyłło, the Colonel's daughter.

FINAL COMMENTS

In about five years Poland will be celebrating the hundredth anniversary of regaining its freedom and national sovereignty in 1918, lost for well over a hundred years. November 11 became one of the two major State Holidays, the other being May 3, Polish Constitution Day. These two dates bracketed well over a hundred years of foreign rule.

Like all of us who achieve a certain age, and look back on life and its accomplishments and failings, rather than looking forward to new challenges, questions begin to be asked, what ifs? For an academic historian the "what if" is taboo.

Historians dislike any such intellectual and purely theoretical exercise, but it is not unreasonable to at least identify certain points in time, where choices were possibly present, and which if pursued differently might have led to a different outcome. But there is no answer to the "what if?" There are no double blind studies in the lives of nations.

Polish 20th Century history has a number of dates, and foreign policy challenges, where the Polish Government faced such "what ifs", and while there is no answer to the consequences of alternative choice, assuming they really existed, critics of the Polish Government and foreign policy are quite vocal in second guessing the policy followed.

For academic historians, the parameters of acceptable history are the archives. It is also well accepted by most that we understand more than we know. It is this intuitive sense that leads us to the pursuit of archives, and if absent, or not found, or still held under some protective seventy year rule, the resulting disappointment should not lead to the abandonment of the original theses. Negatives cannot be proven and negatives are not proof. The fact that we do not possess an archival proof does not mean these hypotheses were absurd.

The major "what ifs" in Polish foreign and strategic policy decisions have to begin with Polish-Czech disunion.

There was a mutual failure by both Prague and Warsaw to embrace each other and be part of the French alliance. The Poles just could not get over the Czech behavior over Cieszyn (Teschen) and the Czechs were unwilling to be tied to a country like Poland which had territorial disputes with Germany, since until early 1938 the Czechs had no disputes with Germany. When the situation tilted, and the Czechs were confronted over the Sudetenland, the Poles in turn were no longer interested.

That was human, but petty, and had the Poles managed this in a different manner, who knows?

The most striking what if was the decision of the Polish Government in early 1938 to oppose Hitler's Germany and base its future on two Western allies, one of which, France, was already judged to be less than reliable.

Taking this anti-German stance, and opposing any territorial concessions,

Józef Beck was not just guided by his own diplomatic sophistry but what is often not appreciated, unanimously supported by the Polish nation. Poland was not going to be pushed off the Baltic! Having taken such a posture, the events unfolded in a manner in which the Polish Government had ever decreasing room to maneuver.

There was another warning sign in midsummer 1939, when Polish negotiations in London for military credits went nowhere, and when in the staff discussions in Warsaw absolutely nothing tangible was offered by the West. But the option here was to cave in to Hitler's megalomaniac drive for expansion in the east.

Critics of Polish foreign policy will point at the absolute unwillingness of the Poles to enter into any formal military discussions with the Soviets, as urged by the French, and to a lesser degree by the British.

Here Polish history played a role. The Poles had on many occasions in the late 18th Century seen and experienced major Russian military incursions which inevitably led to semi-permanent occupations and major meddling in Polish internal politics. That was as unacceptable to the Polish nation as giving up access to the Baltic.

The final result in 1945 was exactly what the Poles feared and it is not at all unreasonable to assume that an invited presence in 1939 would have led to a different result, except perhaps for far fewer casualties and material damage.

In the months after September 1939 the what ifs begin to be less and less obvious. Certainly in 1940 in London, Raczkiewicz, could have remained steadfast in his decision to dismiss Sikorski from the post of Prime Minister. This Polish crisis forced Sikorski into the willing embrace and patronage of Churchill.

Another possible point strongly argued by communist sympathizers was the Sikorski visit to Moscow in December, 1941. Allegedly Stalin made an offer to Sikorski, which would have required his concessions to territorial losses. However if we look at what happened to Beneš and the Czechs, then that line of reasoning begins to be thin.

The Polish Government could have actually ordered the Polish Home Army not to undertake the Warsaw Uprising. But nobody could have foreseen the lack of response on the part of the Western Allies, and the machiavellian evil genius of Stalin. Of all the what ifs that is the most plausible. Even if they had staged a so-called communist uprising and the city was occupied by Soviet armies, Warsaw would have been a major center of Polish independence.

Many during the years preceding the war and during the war itself discretely advised the Poles that they had no choice but to be in the German or Soviet camp. The fact that the Poles wished for neither was not conceived as a viable option.

Those Poles who are under twenty will have a choice and be witnesses of whether the current geopolitical situation of Poland, seemingly anchored in a German-led Europe, and an international military alliance – NATO – will be able to face the many crises that are always on the horizon.

Appendix A
Chronology of Events

December 11, 1918	Poland regains independence after more than a hundred years of being partitioned by Germany and Russia. Piłsudski and Sosnkowski released from German prison and arrive in Warsaw. The German-created Regency Council appoint Piłsudski Head of State.
March 3, 1919	Outbreak of Polish–Soviet War.
August 18, 1920	Poles win Battle of Warsaw.
October 18, 1920	Conclusion of Hostilities between Poland and Russia.
February, 21, 1921	Polish-French political and military agreement signed in Paris by Piłsudski and Sosnkowski. Both sides agree to collaborate in event of German aggression against either party. Poland agrees to keep a standing army of 30 infantry divisions in event of war with Germany, while France agrees to keep sea lanes open in event of Polish-Soviet war.
March 3, 1921	Polish-Romanian Treaty of Mutual Assistance in event of threat from the Soviet Union.
March, 18, 1921	Treaty of Riga signed between Poland and the Soviet Union finalizes the armistice and borders.
March, 1921	The "1921" Polish Constitution enacted by the Polish *Sejm*. Modeled on the French Constitution it gave proportional representation to all political parties, which were numerous. This led to frequent changes of party alliances and changes in the Government.
April, 16, 1922	Rapallo Treaty between Germany and the Soviet Union.
January 11, 1923	French and Belgian troops occupy the Ruhr. French Marshal Foch visits Warsaw.
April, 26, 1925	Polish Prime Minister Władysław Sikorski visits Paris and signs a protocol to the Polish-French Treaty of 1921 and obtains significant loans for Polish economic development and the Polish military.

October 16, 1925	Locarno Treaty. Weimar Germany accepts the Western borders with France as final, but merely agrees that it will not use military force to change the Polish-German border.
May, 12, 1926	Piłsudski's *coup d'état*.
June 12, 1932	Polish-Soviet Non-aggression Treaty signed in Moscow.
January 30, 1933.	Adolf Hitler becomes chancellor of Germany.
January 26,1934.	Polish-German Declaration of Non-Aggression.
April 23, 1935.	New Polish Constitution enacted, which gives the elected President considerable power.
May 11, 1935.	Piłsudski dies.
March 7,1936.	Germans march into Rhineland, breaking the Versailles Treaty
September 6, 1936.	Marshal Edward Smigły-Rydz, Inspector General of the Polish Armed Forces, visits France, and signs a major military loan agreement for modernizing the Polish military at Rambouillet.
March, 1938.	Germany annexes Austria.
September 29, 1938.	Munich Conference. Sacrifices Czecho-Slovak Territory.
March 15, 1939.	German troops enter Prague, and assume total control over the Czech Republic, naming renaming it the Protectorate of Bohemia.
March 31, 1939.	Britain guarantees Polish Sovereignty.
April, 28, 1939.	Germany renounces the Non-Aggression declaration with Poland.
August 23, 1939.	Molotov-Ribbentrop Pact.
August 25, 1939.	Polish-United Kingdom Treaty of Mutual Assistance.
August 25, 1939.	Polish Air Force (Military Aviation) placed on secret mobilization and begins dispersal. Polish Merchant Marine instructed to stay out of the Baltic or to leave Baltic ports immediately.
August 31, 1939.	Polish Destroyer Division sails for the United Kingdom.
September 1, 1939.	Germany invades Poland.

September 3, 1939.	Great Britain and France declare war on Germany after an ultimatum for the Germans to withdraw from Poland.
September 17, 1939.	The Soviet Union breaks its non-aggression treaty with Poland and invades Eastern Poland.
September 18, 1939.	Polish Government crosses into Romania, hoping to be able to travel to allied France, but all members are interned.
September 27, 1939.	Warsaw receives orders flown in by a courier from the interned Marshal Smigły-Rydz to capitulate and form a clandestine military organization.
September 30, 1939.	The Interned Polish President – Ignacy Mośćiski – under the emergency provisions, Article 13, of the 1935 Constitution appoints Władysław Raczkiewicz already in Paris to be the next President of Poland.
September 30, 1939.	President Raczkiewicz appoints Władysław Sikorski to the post of Prime Minister, Minister of Defence and Commander-in-Chief.
November 18, 1939.	Sikorski visits Great Britain and signs the Polish-British Naval agreement.
January 4, 1940.	Polish-French Military Agreement.
June 17, 1940.	France seeks an armistice with Germany.
June 18, 1940.	Polish troops and airmen begin to evacuate from France to Great Britain.
June 22, 1940.	France capitulates.
August 5, 1940.	Polish-British Military agreement. Regulates the legal and financial aspects of the Polish Forces based in the United Kingdom and its possessions.
February 15, 1941.	First attempt by a RAF crew to fly couriers to occupied Poland. Codenamed Adolphus, the mission on an old bomber, a Whitley, became lost and the couriers were dropped over Germany. The couriers made their way to Polish territory, but all monies were lost.
April 3, 1941.	Sikorski makes first trip to the USA.
June 21, 1941.	Germany attacks the Soviet Union.

August 30, 1941.	Sikorski and Soviet ambassador in London, Maisky, sign an agreement establishing diplomatic relations between the two countries and allowing the Poles to form a Polish Army in the Soviet Union.
November 7, 1941.	A Polish crew flying a Halifax, delivered to the Polish Special Duties Flight, makes the first successful supply flight to Poland. Codename Ructon.
December 7, 1941.	Japanese attack Pearl Harbor, which brings the USA into the war with Japan. Germany then declares war on the United States.
December 30, 1941.	Sikorski visits the Soviet Union and inspects the Polish Army being formed. On way to the Soviet Union he stops off at the beleaguered fortress of Tobruk, North Africa, and inspects the Polish Carpathian Brigade.
February 15, 1942.	Singapore falls to the Japanese. This leads to the Australians pulling back troops to defend their territory. In turn this leaves the British with a significant shortage of troops in the Middle East.
March 20, 1942.	Sikorski's second visit to the USA.
April 1, 1942.	Sikorski hosts a conference in London of all senior Polish generals regarding the specific dispositions of the Polish forces.
July 4, 1942.	By agreements between Churchill and Stalin, all Polish Forces moved from the Soviet Union to the British controlled Middle East to buttress the British Forces.
November 29, 1942.	Sikorski's third and last visit to the United States.
April 13, 1943.	Radio Berlin announces the discovery of mass graves of Polish officers near Katyn, in German occupied Soviet Union.
April 25, 1943.	After the Polish Government's request for an impartial International Red Cross investigation of the Katyn Graves, the Soviet Union breaks off relations with the Polish Government.
May 25, 1943.	Sikorski begins his visit to the Polish Army in the Middle East.

July 4, 1943.	Sikorski dies in a plane accident on taking off from Gibraltar on the way back to London. The President appoints Mikołajczyk to be the Prime Minister and Sosnkowski to the post of Commander-in-Chief.
November 1943.	Sosnkowski makes first visit to the Polish Army in the Middle East, which is about to enter operations in Italy.
March, 1944.	Sosnkowski makes second visit to the Polish Corps in Italy.
April 15, 1944.	First successful Wildhorn flight to Poland.
May 6, 1944.	Mikołajczyk visits the United States.
June 6, 1944.	D-Day. Western allies invade Normandy.
July, 1944.	Stalin recognizes the Communist-controlled and dominated Committee in Lublin as the Polish Government.
August 1, 1944.	The Polish Home Army stages an Uprising in Warsaw.
October 2, 1944.	Warsaw capitulates.
November 25, 1944.	Mikołajczyk resigns as Prime Minister of the Polish coalition Government.
January 1, 1945.	The Polish President dissolves the Polish Home Army.
February, 1945.	Yalta Conference.
March 31, 1945.	Polish Underground leadership accepts an invitation to meet with Soviet representatives and are arrested and flown to Moscow to stand trial. General Leopold Okulicki, the last General Officer Commanding the Polish Home Army, dies in Soviet captivity in Moscow.
May 8, 1945.	Victory in Europe.
July 5, 1945.	Britain rescinds recognition of the Polish Government and establishes diplomatic relations with the enlarged Lublin Committee, called the Provisional Government of National Unity. Polish Armed Forces in the West begin to be demobilized.

January, 1947.	Communists stage an election in Poland and win overwhelming majority. Rewrite Polish Constitution.
December 19, 1990.	First free elections in Poland.
December 22, 1990.	Ryszard Kaczarowski, the last of the line of Constitutional Presidents in Exile, flies to Warsaw and invests the first freely-elected President, Lech Walesa, with the Presidential insignia.

APPENDIX B
THE CONTROVERSY OVER
GENERAL SIKORSKI'S
ACCIDENT

In late June 1943, flying back from the Middle East to the United Kingdom the plane carrying General Sikorski and his party stopped off at Gibraltar. On the evening of July 4 1943 they once again boarded their plane, an American-built B–24 Liberator, # AL523, on the establishment of the RAF Squadron 511 whose task was to fly VIPs. Taking off in the dusk, the four-engined modified bomber hit the sea within minutes at an angle estimated between 15 and 20 degrees, and estimated speed of 165 mph. The point of impact was about 1,200 yards from the shore. The wreck at the bottom of the sea was given between five to six fathoms. The crash was observed from the shore and the sea rescue boat, always on-call, motored to the crash scene. All aboard were killed except for the pilot, a Czech, Edward Prchal, in the RAF who was contused, confused and had suffered multiple lacerations.

Accompanying General Sikorski, and all killed, were Major General Tadeusz Klimecki (Chief of Polish Staff), Colonel Andrzej Marecki (Chief of Operations of the Polish Army), Mrs Zofia Leśniowska, the general's daughter and his personal secretary, Lt. Józef Ponikiewski, an officer in the Polish Navy and the general's adjutant. Also aboard and killed was Major Victor Cazalet, MP, the British liaison officer to Sikorski. There were also a number of British officials.

A number of bodies were recovered, including that of General Sikorski.

An aerial photograph taken in the morning showed the B–24 upside down.

The Polish destroyer O.P.P. *Orkan* was immediately ordered to Gibraltar to bring the body the Polish Commander-in Chief to the United Kingdom. The formal religious ceremony took place at the Catholic Cathedral of Westminster, in London. Representatives of the three Polish services and a battalion of the Coldstream Guards provided the military guard of honour. The mass was attended by the Polish

President and all the members of the Polish Government and military staffs, while Prime Minister Churchill, Anthony Eden and many other prominent British leaders were also present. Following the mass, General Sikorski was laid to rest at the Polish military cemetery in Newark, England, amongst the more than 400 Polish airmen who either died in accidents or whose planes coming back from operations failed them when nearly home.

RAF COURT OF INQUIRY

Consistent with normal RAF procedure a Court of Inquiry was convened on July 7 1943 by the order of Air Marshal Sir John C. Slessor, and chaired by Group Captain J.G. Elton. Major Stanisław Dudziński, a Polish Air Force engineer, was invited to observe the proceedings but without any right to ask questions. The court interviewed about 30 people who had been on duty in Gibraltar's airfield and vicinity.[1] This addressed the general protection of the air base, since it is very close to the Spanish border, as well as the protection of the VIP aircraft. The Court interviewed the pilot who had sustained major contusions and lacerations and a broken ankle.

The complete wreck was never recovered, merely some parts of it.

The Court accepted the pilot's assertion that he took off in his typical manner, but when he went to the next step of increasing height he found the elevators jammed. Not being able to increase altitude, with his plane on a down trajectory he throttled down before hitting water. Flaps were at half and undercarriage was retracted.

The Court of Inquiry made a number of administrative suggestions and closed on July 24 1943 with the statement that the accident was due to jamming of the elevators, cause unknown.

Air Marshal Slessor was not satisfied and reconvened the Inquiry, which met on August 3 through August 7 at RAF Coastal Command H.Q.

Mr. Irving, asking for a new look, pointed out all the inconsistencies in the original and final report. In his summary of the request for reopening, Mr. Irving interviewed many of the individuals who had been witnesses to the accident and had testified, but he also found a couple who had not been interviewed by the Court. One strongly asserted that the Liberator was on level flight and made a perfect 'belly landing' and stayed afloat for about ten minutes. This was confirmed by a second eyewitness. Both British military personnel were based on the Rock.

The Court now concentrated on the issue of the pilot's statement that his elevators had jammed. Experts from the Royal Aircraft Establishment, Farnborough, as well as from the Accident Branch of the Air Ministry were interviewed and testified

---

1   Keith Sword, ed., *Sikorski : Soldier and Statesman,* Orbis Books, London, 1990. The book has a complete facsimile of 7 July 1943 Court of Inquiry, pp.167–209.

that after examining those parts of the plane recovered, there was no evidence of jamming, but that a Liberator could take off with the elevator controls locked.

The final conclusion was that "the elevators controls were jammed by some means other than the flying controls' locking mechanism."[2]

At this point rumors of sabotage and assassination of Sikorski were rife and worldwide. Even before the final report came out from the Court of Inquiry, fingers were being pointed at potential agents. Goebbels jumped on this as he had with breaking news about Katyn and blamed the British. Stalin soon warned a senior Yugoslav not to visit Britain since they were known to murder foreign leaders. Coming from Stalin this was a bizarre warning and was probably not taken seriously even by a dedicated communist. The British even hinted that the group responsible was probably the Polish Military Intelligence Services. It was a fact the core of the Polish Second Bureau [dwójka] intensely disliked Sikorski, and were completely opposed to his British-influenced and pro-Soviet policies. They were in the Sosnkowski camp. But the very idea that Polish army officers had any access to the British fortress of Gibraltar is quite preposterous.

The official Polish position in London was nonplussed. It was far from clear whether this was an accident or possibly sabotage. If sabotage, the Poles looked to Moscow as the perpetrators. But the Polish diplomatic silence was challenged by the British official report presented to the Poles for approval.

This came from the British Foreign Office to the Polish ambassador:

> I have the honour to submit to your excellency the draft of the Air Ministry Press Communiqué which the Air Ministry is anxious to issue immediately on the approval of the Polish authority.

The official report, after all the usual preliminaries, came down to the following:

> After the most careful examination of all available evidence, including that of the pilot, it has not been possible to determine how the jamming occurred, But is has been established that there was no sabotage. It is also clear that the captain of the aircraft, who is a pilot of great experience and exceptional ability, was in no way to blame.[3]

This began to raise questions in the Polish Government. The report was inherently illogical and the Poles refused to endorse it, but it was released anyway.

The Polish Government asked the Polish Ministry of the Interior to analyse the formal British report and this was done by Mr Ullman, an engineer. He formally questioned the Air Ministry report. The Polish Air Force also appointed a commission

2   TNA AIR 2/9234.
3   *The Times*, September 21, 1943.

and again its only evidence was the Court of Inquiry plus the verbal report of Major Dudziński, who had observed the proceedings.

The Polish Air Force commission stated that the pilot's version of elevator jamming could not be substantiated because all parts of the plane had not been recovered. The Polish Air Force Commission stated that the conclusion that sabotage was ruled out could not be borne out by the facts. But as often happens with plane accidents the cause of the accident could not be determined.

Finally the Polish Minister of Justice empanelled a three-man commission chaired by the State prosecutor, Tadeusz Cyprian.

The Polish Commission formally stated that the available evidence did not allow any conclusion as to the cause of the accident, and that it shared the opinion and conclusion of the Polish Air Force Commission.

So the Polish authorities were confronted by a dilemma. Coming within months of the bombshell of Katyn, and the reluctance of the British to accept openly the reality of the tragedy, the Poles were between the anvil and the hammer of pushing an investigation based on little except British lack of logic. But those Poles who actually believed the accident to have been sabotage were firmly convinced that it was Stalin's work.

The conspiracy theories multiplied as the years went on. David Irving wrote his book, argued that it was sabotage and seemed to imply the British were behind it.[4] A German playwright, Hochhuth, wrote a most controversial play in which he clearly implicated Churchill as the person who ordered the assassination.

Then it became evident that the Soviet spy, Kim Philby, was in Gibraltar at about that time, and by his own admission had been implicated in assassination attempts against Franco supporters during the Civil War.[5] Spanish agents could have possibly managed to infiltrate Gibraltar.

Most conspiracy proponents accepted or assumed that Sikorski was the target. But if indeed this was not an accident, there was another man killed who presented a greater threat to the British policies of the time than did Sikorski, policies accommodating to Stalin.

That man was Colonel Victor Cazalet, M.P. A very conservative member of the lower British Houses of Parliament, the House of Commons, who was the British liaison officer to Sikorski. Cazalet was a member of the Imperial Defence Group, which included many prominent members of the Conservative Party, in the House of Commons as well as in the House of Lords and also in the back corridors of British political power. It included Lord Selborne and the Chief Whip. The secretary of this group was Kenneth de Courcy, himself a close friend of Menzies.

---

4   David Irving, *Accident. The Death of General Sikorski*, London, 1968.

5   Genrikh Borovik, *The Philby Files*, Little, Brown and Company, Boston, 1994. Borovik interviewed Philby in Moscow after his defection.

This group had never been enamored with Churchill, had actually favored Lord Halifax in 1940 to replace Chamberlain and had worked hard to abort the 1942 British-Soviet negotiations for a Twenty Year treaty which would have included British acquiescence in the Soviet takeover of the three Baltic Republics.[6]

Furthermore Cazalet had accompanied Sikorski to Russia in 1941 and wrote a short private edition booklet – *With Sikorski to Russia*, Curwen, London, 1942. Highly critical of the Soviets, the book and Cazalet's other political activities strongly irritated Churchill.

It is unlikely that in our lifetime, we will ever know for sure whether it was an accident or sabotage. The fact that Churchill omits any mention of the accident or of his very visible presence at this funeral mass or the very emotional speech he gave and which was published in the *Daily Telegraph*, July 15, 1943, seems to hint at something that was best unsaid.[7]

In Poland, the controversy suddenly erupted following the overthrow of communism. One of the proponents of this sabotage theory even based his opinion on various computer programs and came to the conclusion that the whole accident was simulated, that a bomb had been placed and that its location was under the seat occupied by Victor Cazalet! However, Kisielewicz strongly believed the target was Sikorski.[8] But as a result of intense pressure, the body of General Sikorski was exhumed from its resting place in the Royal Cathedral on Wawel Hill in Cracow and subjected to a forensic pathological examination. This failed to reveal any evidence of an explosion but showed evidence of major trauma consistent with a crash at close to 160 mph.

In Britain, David Irving, author of a book *The Accident*, and reasonably accused of self-serving publicity, in 1967 asked the British Government to reopen the Inquiry. His argument was based on a number of alleged distortions and even of some level of perjury by some witnesses. After reviewing the points raised by Mr. Irving, the request was denied.[9]

---

6   Oliver Harvey, *The War Diaries of Oliver Harvey, 1941–1945,* London, 1987, p.118; Miner, Steven Merritt, *Between Churchill and Stalin. The Soviet Union, Great Britain and the Origins of the Grand Alliance,* University of North Carolina Press, Chapel Hill, 1988, p.230.
7   Draft of Churchill's obituary, TNA FO 371/7863.
8   Tadeusz A. Kisielewski, *Zamach. Tropem Zabójców Generała Sikorskiego,* Dom Wydawniczy Rebis, Poznań, 2006.
9   TNA PREM 13/2644.

APPENDIX C
BIOGRAPHICAL SKETCHES

Anders, General Władysław. In 1939 commanded a cavalry brigade. Taken prisoner by the Soviets, released and amnestied by Soviets. Appointed Commanding General of the Polish army in the Soviet Union by Sikorski. His army was relocated by an agreement reached by Churchill and Stalin to the Middle East. Anders assumed command of all the Polish Forces in the Middle East but personally led Polish 2 Corps through the Italian Campaign. Decorated with the Virtuti Militari II class (Commnder's Cross), the Virtuti Militari III Class, the Commander of the Order of Polonia Restituta, the Honorary companion of the Order of the Bath. Military Division, French Commander of the Legion d'Honneur and Croix de Guerre avec Palme, American Legion of Merit. For a short time was acting Polish Commander-in-Chief. Stayed in exile in the United Kingdom and was buried with his soldiers at the Polish cemetery in Monte Cassino in 1970.

Arciszewski, Tomasz. Socialist politician. Member of the Polish Parliament from 1931 to 1939 and a member of the Clandestine Leadership. Extracted out of Poland in 1944 by a Wildhorn III Mission. In November 1944 became Prime Minister of the Polish coalition Government.

Beck, Józef. Minister of Foreign affairs from 1932 to 1939. Interned by the Romanians where he died in 1944.

Berling, Lt. Colonel Zygmunt. Taken prisoner by Soviets in 1939 he became progressively influenced by his perception and political convictions that Poland's future lay with the Soviets and not the Western Powers. Amnestied in 1941 and for a time in the Polish Army under General Anders. In 1942 he made a decision to stay in the Soviet Union when the Polish Army was being transported to the British Middle East to replace the departing Australian forces. Berling was one of a very small number of Polish officers left in the Soviet Union, and was made a general by Stalin to command the 'Berling' division. In September 1944 his forces made an attempt to cross the Vistula to aid the Warsaw insurgents. Berling was removed from his command by the Soviets.

Bór-Komorowski, General Tadeusz. Awarded the Virtuti Militari 2nd Class. In September 1939 commanded the 39th Reserve Infantry Division. Stayed in occupied Poland joining the Polish Home Army. In 1944 appointed its Commanding General. Taken prisoner by Germans when the Uprising had to capitulate. Liberated by Americans and flown to London. Stayed in exile.

Cadogan, Sir Alexander. British senior civil servant in the Foreign Office. Permanent Secretary of State during the war.

Cazalet, Major Victor MP. British liaison to General Sikorski, and killed with him on July 4, 1943.

Ciechanowski, Jan. Member of the Polish Diplomatic Service. Polish ambassador to the United States during the Second World War.

Dalton, Hugh. British statesman. Member of the Labour Party. First Minister of Economic Warfare responsible for the Special Operation Executive.

Iżycki, Major General Mateusz. Commanding officer of the Polish Air Force, 1943–1945. Awarded the honorary Knight Commander of the Order of the Bath, Military Division (KCB). Stayed in exile.

Karasiewicz-Tokarzewski, General Michael. In September General Officer Commanding an operational group (i.e. corps) of the Pomorze Army. The first organizer of the Polish Home Army as early as September 26 1939. In late 1939 ordered by Sikorski to go to Lwów to organize the clandestine forces under Soviet occupation, he was arrested by the Soviets but not identified as an officer. He survived and was released by Soviets in 1941, initially became the commanding officer of the 6th Infantry Division and then GOC of the 3rd Polish Corps in the Middle East. Awarded the Virtuti Militari 2nd and 5th Class, Polish Order of Merit, British Honorary Companion of the Order of the Bath, Military Division. Stayed in exile.

Kopański, Lt. General Stanisław. In September, 1939 chief of operations of the Polish Staff. Seconded to the Middle East to assume command of the Polish Carpathian Brigade, which was to be the core of the Polish Forces in event of a Balkan operation. Commanded his brigade in the protracted siege of Tobruk. Appointed to the position of Chief of Staff of the Polish forces in 1943. Awarded the Virtuti Militari4th and 5th Class. The Order of Polonia Restituta. The British DSO, and Honorary Companion of the Order of the Bath. Military Division. Stayed in Exile.

Klimecki, Major General Tadeusz. Awarded the Virtuti Militari for gallantry in the Polish–Soviet war. Polish Chief of Staff. Killed with Sikorski on July 4, 1943.

Kossakowski, Lt. General Tadeusz. Engineer and commander of the engineering (sapper) section of the Polish Armed Forces in 1939. Assumed command of Polish military engineers in the Polish First Corps in Scotland and responsible for fortifying the Polish sector of the Scottish coast. His engineers also developed the Polish land mine detector, which was used by the British Eighth Army at El Alamein. Inserted into Poland in May 1944 on a Wildhorne II flight. He was tasked with developing clandestine arms production since the quantity of material being flown in was insufficient for the arming of the Polish Home Army. Taken prisoner at the conclusion of the Warsaw Uprising in October 1944, liberated by Allies in 1945.

In December 1945 returned to Poland. Awarded the Virtuti Militari 5th Class, the Polish Order of Merit and British Honorary Companion of the Order of the Bath, Military Division. Stayed in exile.

Kot,Stanisław. A prominent member of the Polish Peasant Party. First Polish ambassador to Moscow in 1941. One of the first Polish politicians to go back to communist Poland, espousing many communist slogans including slanderous remarks about Anders. Served as Communist ambassador to Rome and defected to the West in 1947.

Kowalski, Lt. Colonel Jan. Polish cryptologist responsible for breaking Soviet codes and ciphers during the Polish-Soviet War of 1920 contributing to the success of the Battle of Warsaw. In the interwar period he held intelligence-related positions of military attaché in Moscow and Budapest. During the war based in Lisbon and responsible for negotiations with Italy, Hungary and Romania attempting to get them to change sides. This was part of the Polish Balkan strategy.

Stayed in exile.

Kukiel, Lt. General Marian. Initially commanding officers of the First Polish Corps in Scotland and then became Minister of War in the Polish Government. Awarded the honorary Knight Commander of the Order of the Bath, Military Division (KCB). Remained in exile.

Lerski, Jerzy. Political courier between Polish Clandestine Government – Delegatura – and the Polish government in London.

Marecki, Colonel Andrzej. Director of III Operational Section of the Polish Staff. Killed with Sikorski on July 4, 1943.

Mościski, Ignacy. Polish President from 1925 to his abdication in 1939. Interned in Romania, due to primarily American influence he was released and moved to Switzerland where he died in 1946. The first freely elected president of Poland after the war, Lech Walesa, had his body moved to the crypts of the Arch-cathedral of Saint John in Warsaw.

Maczek, Lt. General Stanisław. In 1939 commanded the 10th Motorized Cavalry Brigade, the famous 'Black Brigade'. In 1940 in Scotland, he organized the Polish 1st Armoured Division which he commanded throughout most of the fighting in North-West Europe. In 1945 promoted to Lt. General and appointed to the command of the Polish First Corps. Received numerous Polish, British, French and other foreign orders. Specifically, the Virtuti Militari Commander's Cross (3rd Class), the British

DSO, the Honorary Companion of the Order of the Bath, Military Division, the French Legion d'Honneur, Commander. Stayed in exile, and lived to see Poland free!

Mikołajczyk, Stanisław. Senior leader of the Polish Peasant Party in the Polish Coalition Government. Prime Minister from July 1943 to November 1944. Persuaded by Churchill to join the Communist provisional Government in Warsaw in 1945 as Deputy Prime Minister. After the fraudulent elections in January 1947 he allegedly escaped with American help to the West. All evidence is that his escape was evident to the Communists who achieved their goal of getting rid of a potential political martyr and embarrassing his party in the general population.

Nowak, Jan. Polish political courier between German-occupied Poland and the West.

Okulicki, Major General Leopold. Awarded the Virtuti Militari 4th and 5th Class. Joined the Polish Home Army, sent to the Soviet Zone of occupation and captured in January 1941 by Soviets, after the murder of Polish officers in places like Katyn which took place in April 1940. Released in 1941 he became chief of staff to General Anders and was then commanding general of the 7th Infantry Division. He volunteered to be parachuted into occupied Poland in May 1944 and became assistant chief of staff to the Commanding General of the Home Army, General Bór-Komorowski. Took part in the Warsaw Uprising but was ordered to evade being taken prisoner of war and assumed command of the Home Army in late 1944. Arrested by the Soviets with other civilian leaders of the Polish Clandestine State, he was taken to Moscow, found guilty of anti-Soviet activities, in other words, being a Polish patriot, and sentenced to ten years in prison. Died in Soviet captivity in December 1946.

O'Malley, Sir Owen. British Ambassador to the Polish Government 1943–1945.

Paszkiewicz, Major General Gustaw. Polish Army. Returned to Poland.

Piłsudski, Józef. Interim Head of State in 1918–1921. Led the Polish armies in the war against the Soviets in 1919–1920. Elevated to the rank of Marshal of Poland by the Polish Parliament. In 1926 staged a coup against the Parliament. Then assumed the position of Inspector of the Polish Forces till his death in 1935. Awarded the Virtuti Militari 1st Class, Order of the White Eagle.

Raczkiewicz, Władysław. President of the Polish Senate, 1930–1935, President of the World Association of Poles Abroad, 1934–1939, President of Poland, 1939–1947. Buried at the Polish military cemetery in Newark, England.

Rettinger, Józef Hieronim. Born in Poland. Lived most of his life in the United Kingdom. A socialist by ideology. Friend of many prominent people, including Sikorski. A major, but discreet and confidential contact between the Polish Government and British leaders. A man who knew everybody worth knowing.

Romer, Tadeusz. Polish diplomat. Polish Minister to Portugal 1937–1941, Ambassador to Japan, 1941–1943, Ambassador to Soviet Union 1943–1944, Polish

Foreign Minister, 1944. Following the war settled in Canada and became Lecturer at McGill University.

Sikorski, General Władysław. A distinguished statesman and successful commander in the Polish war against the Soviets. His campaign in the battle of the river Wkra and then later his motorized raid against a Soviet rail junction were highly successful and earned him the accolade of the second best general, in Piłsudski's opinion. Ultimately became a member of the opposition following Piłsudski's *coup d'état* in 1926. He became a very active member of the strong Francophile Front Morges. Appointed Commander–in-Chief of the Polish Forces by Raczkiewicz in 1939; nominated to be Prime Minister of the multi-party Polish coalition government in 1943. Killed in a plane accident in July 1943. Awarded the British Honorary Knight Grand Cross in the Military Division of the Order of the British Empire.

Smigły-Rydz, Edward. Marshal of Poland. In the Polish-Soviet War brilliantly commanded the Polish armies that defeated the Soviets in the Battle of the Niemen. Piłsudski rated him the best Polish general. Inspector General of the Polish Armed Forces, 1936–1939. Commander-in-Chief of the Polish Forces in the September Campaign. Order of the White Eagle and Virtuti Militari 2nd Class.

Sosnkowski, General Kazimierz. Very close associate of Piłsudski. Vice Minister of War during the Polish-Soviet War. Minister of War, Minister of War, 1927–1939, Commander-in Chief of the Home Army (while based in Paris)] 1939–1941, Minister without portfolio, 1940–1941, Commander-in-Chief, 1943–1944. Awarded the British Honorary Knight Commander of the Military Division of the Order of the British Empire (KBE).

Selborne, Lord. Member of the Imperial Defence Group, Minister of Economic Warfare after Hugh Dalton. Responsible for the activities of SOE.

Sinclair, Sir Archibald. Member of the Churchill coalition government representing the Liberal Party. British Minister for Air.

Sosabowski, Major General Stanisław Franciszek. Commanding general of the Polish Parachute Brigade. Remained in exile.

Swierczewski, Karol. Probably Polish-born Soviet agent who made a name for himself in the Spanish Civil War as a prominent leader of the Communist forces.

Made a general in the Polish People's Army by Stalin, he was assassinated by Ukrainian nationalists in 1947.

Swirski, Vice-Admiral Jerzy. Commandant of the Polish Navy from 1929 through the war. Awarded the Honorary Knight Commander of the Order of the Bath, Military Division. Stayed in exile.

Tatar, Major General Stanisław. Gunner. Awarded the Virtuti Militari 4th Class and 5th Class. In 1939 commanded the divisional artillery of the 3rd Infantry

Division. Taken prisoner of war by the Germans but quickly escaped and joined the Polish Home Army, becoming the head of its organization department. Extracted by a Wildhorn flight, arrived in London and became the Assistant Chief of Staff for Home Affairs. For a short time head of I Corps artillery. Returned to Poland in 1947. Arrested, tried and sentenced to ten years for alleged anti-Polish activities. He was assumed to be a confidante of Mikołajczyk, who escaped in 1947 from Poland to the West. In 1956 rehabilitated and released. Honorary Companion of the Order of the Bath, Military Division .

Ujejski, Major General Stanisław. In 1939 head of the air force section of the Polish Staff. Awarded the honorary Knight Commander of the Order of the Bath, Military Division.

Zając, General Józef Ludwik. Polish Army General, who was appointed inspector general of the Polish anti-aircraft defenses in late 1938. His analysis of the situation led to a concerted effort to build up the fighter squadrons. Also to a contract with France for 100 Morane-Saulnier fighter planes which never arrived. General Zając was in effect Commanding Officer of the Polish Military Aviation in the September Campaign and continued in this role in France. He was partially responsible for the June 1940 Polish-British Air Agreement. In September 1941 appointed deputy commander of the Polish First Corps in Scotland, then in September 1941 GOC of the Polish Forces in the Middle East. Promoted to Lt. General, brought back to the United Kingdom to assume a staff position in Polish headquarters. Stayed in exile.

Zaleski, August. Polish diplomat. Between 1918 and 1926 Polish minister to Athens and Rome. In 1926 appointed Poland's Foreign Minister. Dismissed by Piłsudski in 1932 because of perception that his pro-French policy was not serving Poland well. Again, because of this French orientation, he was appointed Foreign Minister in the Sikorski coalition government formed in Paris. Resigned because of disagreements with Sikorski over the Sikorski-Maisky Pact of 1941.

A close confidante of Raczkiewicz, succeeded him as President in exile in 1947.

BIBLIOGRAPHY

Since this book is primarily addressed to the English-language reader the bibliography, while not limited to English language historical literature, does give it primacy. Polish historical literature is cited when there is no credible English source, e.g. the memoirs of some prominent Polish generals and senior officers.

The seminal Polish language works that are important are the six volumes of the Polish Armed Forces in World War Two, *Polskie Siły Zbrojne w Drugiej Wojnie Światowej*. This work, published by the Polish Institute and General Sikorski Museum in London, over a number of years, 1950 through 1975, was written and edited by the Historical Commission of the Polish General Staff that had been established by the last Chief of the Polish General Staff, General Stanisław Kopański in December 1946. The three chairmen of the Historical Commission were General Tadeusz Kutrzeba, General Marian Kukiel and specifically for the Polish Home Army, General Tadeusz Pełczyński.

Separately from the above, the Polish Home Army Trust in London, after the war, published a five volume work, *Armia Krajowa w Dokumentach 1939–1945*, edited by a Committee, General Tadeusz Pełczyński (chair), Halina Czarnocka, Józef Garliński, Kazmierz Iranek-Osmecki and Włodzimierz Otocki.

The primary archives consulted and cited are the British National Archives in Kew (TNA) and the Polish Institute and General Sikorski Museum Archives in London (PISM).

Alexander, Harold R.L.G., *The Memoirs of Field Marshal Earl Alexander of Tunis, 1940–1945,* Cassell, London, 1962.

Anglo-Polish Historical Committee, Tessa Stirling, Daria Nałecz, Tadeusz Dubicki, *Intelligence Co-operation between Poland and Great Britain during World War II – The Report of the Anglo-Polish Historical Committee.* Vol. 1. London, Vallentine Mitchell, 2005. Vol. 2. *Polsko-Brytyjska współpraca*

wywiadowcza podczas II wojny Światowej. Wybór Dokumentów. Intelligence Co-Operation between Poland and Great Britain during World War II. Vol. 2 Documents. Warsaw, Naczelna Dyrekcja Archiwów Panstwowych, Warsaw, 2005.

Anders, Władysław. 1981. *An Army in Exile.* Macmillan, London, 1949.

Aster, Sidney, *1939. The Making of the Second World War*, Simon and Schuster, New York, 1973.

Atkinson, Rick, *The Day of the Battle. The War in Sicily and Italy, 1943–1944*, Henry Holt & Company, New York, 2007.

Baldwin, Hanson W., *The Crucial Years, 1939–1941.* Harper & Row, New York, 1976.

Baldwin, Hanson W., *Battles Lost and Won*, Harper & Row, New York, 1966.

Beale, Peter, *The Great Mistake. The Battle for Antwerp and Beveland Peninsula, September 1944*, Sutton Publishing, Stroud, 2004.

Beaumont, Joan, *British Aid to Russia, 1941–1945. Comrades in Arms*, Davis-Poynter, London, 1980.

Beck, Józef. *Final Report*, Speller, New York, 1957.

Bekker, Cajus, *The Luftwaffe War Diaries*, Ballantine, New York, 1969.

Bell, P.M.H. (Philip Michael Hitt), *John Bull and the Bear. British Public Opinion, Foreign Policy and the Soviet Union, 1941–1945*, Edward Arnold, , London, 1990.

Bethel, Nicholas, *The War Hitler Won. The Fall of Poland, September, 1939*, Holt, Rinehart & Winston, New York, 1972.

Bieniecki, Kajetan, *Lotnicze Wsparcie Armii Krajowej*, Dom Wydawniczy Bellona, Warsaw, 2005.

Blackwell, Ian, *Cassino*, Pen and Sword, Barnsley, 2005.

Bor-Komorowski, Tadeusz, *The Secret Army*, Victor Gollancz, London, 1950.

Borodziej, Włodzimierz, *The Warsaw Uprising of 1944*, University of Wisconsin Press, Madison, 2005.

Borowiec Andrew , *Destroy Warsaw! Hitler's Punishment. Stalin's Revenge, ,* London, Praeger, 2001

Borzecki, Jerzy, *The Soviet-Polish Peace of 1921 and the Creation of Interwar Europe,* Yale University Press, New Haven, 2008.

Brereton, Lewis H., *The Brereton Diaries*, William Morrow & Company, New York, 1946.

British War Blue Book. Documents concerning German- Polish Relations and the outbreak of hostilities between Great Britain and Germany on September 3,1939, His Majesty's Stationary Office, London, 1939.

Bryant, Arthur, *The Turn of the Tide, 1939–1943*, Doubleday & Company, New York, 1957.

Bryant, Arthur, *Triumph in the West, 1943–1946*, Doubleday and Company, Garden City, New York, 1959.

Buckingham, William, F., *Arnhem, 1944*, Tempus Publishing, Stroud, 2002.

Budurowycz, Bohdan B., *Polish-Soviet Relations. 1932–1939*, Columbia University Press, New York, 1963.

Cannistraro, Philip V., Wynot, Edward D. Jr., and Kovaleff, Theodore P. *Poland and the Coming of the Second World War. The Diplomatic Papers of A.J. Drexel Biddle Jr., United States Ambassador to Poland, 1937–1939*. Ohio State University Press, Columbus, 1976.

Ciechanowski, Jan, *Defeat in Victory*, Victor Gollancz, London, 1948.

Ciechanowski, Jan M., *The Warsaw Rising of 1944*, Cambridge University Press, Cambridge, 1974.

Cienciala, Anna M. and Tytus Komarnicki, *From Versailles to Locarno. Keys to Polish Foreign Policy, 1919–1925,* University Press of Kansas, Lawrence, 1984.

Cienciala, Anna M, *Poland and the Western Powers. A Study in the Interdependence of Eastern and Western Europe*, University of Toronto Press, Toronto, 1968.

Clark, Lloyd, *Arnhem. Operation Market Garden, September 1944*, Sutton Publishing, Stroud, 2002.

Cholewczynski, George E., *Poles Apart. The Polish Airborne at the Battle of Arnhem*, Sarpendon, New York, 1993.

Churchill, Winston S., *The Second World War*, Cassell, London, 1948.

Conversino, Mark J., *Fighting with the Soviets: The Failure of Operation Frantic, 1944–1945*, University of Kansas Press, Lawrence, 1997.

Coutouvidis, John and Reynolds, Jaime, *Poland, 1939–1947*, Holmes and Meier, New York, 1986.

Craven, Wesley Frank and Cate, James Lea (edited and prepared by), *The Army Air Forces in World War II*. Office of Air History, Washington DC, 1983. 7 volumes.

Cynk, Jerzy B., *The Polish Air Force at War,* Schiffer Publishing, Atglen, 1998. 2 volumes.

Danchev, Alex and Todman, Daniel, eds., *War Diaries, 1939–1945. Field Marshal Lord Alanbrooke*, University of California Press, Berkeley, 2001.

Destiny Can Wait. The History of the Polish Air Force in Great Britain, London, William Heinemann, 1949. Reprinted by Battery Press of Nashville, 1988.

Dilks, David, ed., *The Diaries of Sir Alexander Cadogan*, G.P. Putnam's Sons, London, 1972.

Documents on Polish-Soviet Relations 1939–1945. Edited by the Sikorski Institute, Heinemann, London, 1961 and 1967.

Denniston, Robin, *Churchill's Secret War. Diplomatic decrypts, the Foreign Office and Turkey, 1942–1944.* Sutton Publishing, Stroud, 1997.

Dziewanowski, Marian Kamil, *Joseph Piłsudski. A European Federalist, 1918–1922,* Hoover Institute, Stanford, 1969.

Dziewanowski, Marian Kamil, *War at any Price. World War II in Europe, 1939–1945,* Prentice-Hall, Englewood Cliffs, 1987.

Eden, Anthony, *The Memoirs of Anthony Eden, Earl of Avon: the Reckoning,* Houghton Mifflin, Boston, 1965.

Englert, Juliusz and Krzysztof Barbarski, Krzysztof, *General Anders,* Polish Institute and Sikorski Museum, London, 1989.

Estreicher, Karol, Jr., *Dziennik Wypadków,* Tom 1 1939–1945, Pałac Sztuki, Kraków, 2001.

Eubank, Keith. *Summit at Tehran. The Untold Story.* William Morrow & Company, New York, 1985.

Feis, Herbert, *Between War and Peace. The Potsdam Conference,* Princeton University Press, Princeton, 1960.

Foot, M.R.D., *SOE. The Special Operations Executive, 1940–1946,* University Publications of America, Lanham, 1984.

Forty, George, *Battle for Cassino,* Ian Allen, Hersham, 2004.

Ford, Ken, *Cassino 1944, Breaking the Gustav Line,* Osprey Publishing, Oxford, 2004.

Franks, Norman, *Battle of the Airfields. Operation Bodenplatte, 1 January, 1945,* Grub Street, London, 1994.

Franks, Norman, *The Greatest Air Battle. Dieppe. 19th August, 1942,* Grub Street, London, 1992.

Gaddis, John Lewis, *United States and the Origins of the Cold War, 1941–1947,* Columbia University Press, New York, 1972.

Gates, Eleanor M., *End of the Affair. The Collapse of the Anglo-French Alliance, 1939–1940,* University of California Press, Berkeley, 1981.

Garliński, Józef, *Poland, SOE and the Allies,* George Allen & Unwin, London, 1969.

Garliński, Józef, *Intercept. Secrets of the Enigma War,* J.M. Dent & Sons, London, 1979.

Garliński, Józef, *Hitler's Last Weapons. The Underground War Against the V1 and V2,* Times Books, London, 1978.

Garliński, Józef, *Poland in the Second World War,* London, The Macmillan Press, 1985.

Gilbert, Martin. *The Second World War. A Complete History*. Henry Holt and Company, New York, 1989.

Glantz, David M. and House, Jonathan M. *When Titans Clashed. How the Red Army Stopped Hitler,* University of Kansas Press, Lawrence, 2003

Gooderson, Ian, *Cassino 1944*, Brassey's, London, 2003.

Gretzyngier, Robert and Matusiak, Wojtek, *Polish Aces of World War 2,* Osprey, London, 1998.

Gretzyngier, Robert , *Poles in Defence of Britain. A Day-by-Day Chronology of Polish Day and Night Fighter Pilot Operations: June 1940-July 1941,* Grub Street, London, 2001.

Gross, Jan T. *Polish Society Under German Occupation: The Generalgouvernment, 1939–1944,* Princeton University Press, Princeton, 1979.

Gross, Jan T., *Revolution from Abroad: The Soviet Conquest of Poland's Western Ukraine and Western Belorussia*, Princeton University Press, Princeton, 1988.

Hargreaves, Richard, *Blitzkrieg Unleashed. The German Invasion of Poland, 1939.* Pen and Sword, Barnsley, 2008.

Harbutt, Fraser J., *Yalta 1945. Europe and America at the Crossroads*, Cambridge University Press, Cambridge, 2010.

Harbutt, Fraser J., *The Iron Curtain. Churchill, America and Origins of the Cold War,* Oxford University Press, Oxford, 1986.

Hastings, Sir Max, *Bomber Command. The Myths and Reality of the Bombing Offensive, 1939–1945*, The Dial Press/James Wade, New York, 1979.

Hastings, Sir Max, *Overlord: D-Day and the Battle for Normandy*, Pan Books, London, 1985.

Hastings Sir Max, *Armaggedon. The Battle for Germany, 1944–1945*, Alfred A. Knopf, New York, 2004.

Hastings, Sir Max, *Winston's War. Churchill 1940–1945,* Alfred A. Knopf, New York, 2010.

Harvey, A.D., *Arnhem,* Cassell, London, 2001.

Hehn, Paul N., *A Low Dishonest Decade. The Great Powers, Eastern Europe, and the Economic Origins of World War II, 1930–1941,* Continuum International Publishing, New York, 2002.

Hinsley, F. Harry and Stripp Alan, *Code Breakers: The Inside Story of Bletchley Park.* Oxford University Press, Oxford, 1994.

Hope, Michael, *The Abandoned Legion*, Veritas Foundation Publishing Center, London, 2005.

Howard, Michael. *The Mediterranean Strategy in the Second World War.* Greenhill Books, London, 1993.

Imlay, Talbot C., *Facing the Second World War. Strategy, Politics and Economics in Britain and France, 1938–1939*, Oxford University Press, Oxford, 2003.

Iranek-Osmecki, George, ed., *The Unseen and Silent. Adventures of Paratroopers of the Polish Home Army,* Sheed and Ward, London, 1954.

Jedrzejewicz, Wacław, ed., *Józef Lipski: Diplomat in Berlin, 1933–1939*, Columbia University Press, New York, 1968.

Jedrzejewicz, Wacław. Ed. *Julian Łukasiewicz: Diplomat in Paris*, Columbia University Press, New York, 1970.

Jedrzejewicz, Wacław. *Poland in the British Parliament, 1939–1945*, Józef Piłsudski Institute of America, New York, 1962.

Jedrzejewicz, Wacław. *Piłsudski. A Life for Poland*, Hippocrene Books, New York, 1982.

Kacewicz, George, *Great Britain, The Soviet Union and the Polish Government in Exile (1939–1945)*, Martinus Nijhoff Publishers, The Hague, 1979.

Karski, Jan, *The Great Powers and Poland. 1919–1945. From Versailles to Yalta*, University Press of America, New York, 1985.

Karski, Jan, *Story of a Secret State.* Houghton Mifflin Company, Boston, 1985.

Keegan, John, *Six Armies in Normandy*, The Viking Press, New York, 1982.

Kennedy, Robert M., *The German Campaign in Poland (1939),* Dept. of the Army (USA) Pamphlet, No. 20–255, Washington DC, 1956.

Kemp, Peter, *No Colours or Crest*, Cassell, London, 1958.

Kersten, Krystyna , *The Establishment of Communist Rule in Poland, 1943–1948,* University of California Press, Berkeley, 1991.

Kimball Warren F. ed., *Churchill and Roosevelt: The Complete Correspondence*, Princeton University Press, Princeton, 1984. 3 volumes.

Kitchen, Martin, *British Policy Towards the Soviet Union during the Second World War*, St. Martin's Press, New York, 1986.

Kochanski, Halik, *The Eagle Unbowed. Poland and the Poles in the Second World War,* Allen Lane, London, 2012.

Korbel, Józef, *Poland Between East and West: Soviet and German Diplomacy toward Poland, 1918–1933.* Princeton University Press, Princeton, 1963.

Kot, Stanisław, *Conversations with the Kremlin*, Oxford University Press, Oxford, 1963.

Kozaczuk, Władysław (translated by Christopher Kasparek), *Enigma, How the German machine cipher was broken, and how it was read by the Allies in World War Two*, University Publications of America, Lanham, 1984.

Lane, Bliss A., *I Saw Poland Betrayed: An American Ambassador Reports to the American People*, Bobbs-Merrill, Indianapolis, 1948.

Laquer, Walter, *The Terrible Secret. Suppression of the Truth About Hitler's Final Solution.* Little, Brown and Company, Boston, 1980.

Leasor, James, *War at the Top. Experiences of General Sir Leslie Hollis KCB KBE*, Michael Joseph, London, 1959.

Lewin, Ronald, *Ultra Goes to War. First Account of World's War II's Greatest Secret Based on Official Documents,* Hutchinson, London, 1978.

Lewis, Julian, *Changing Directions. British Military Planning for Post-War Strategic Defence, 1942–1947*, Sherwood Press, London, 2003.

Lind, Lew, *Battle of the Wine Dark Sea. The Aegean Campaign, 1940–1945*, Kangaroo Press, Kenthurst, Australia, 1994.

Lucas, James and Barker, James, *The Battle of Normandy. The Falaise Gap*, Holmes and Meier Publishers,New York, 1978.

Lukas, Richard C., *The Strange Allies. United States and Poland, 1941–1945*, University of Tennessee Press, Knoxville, 1978.

Lukas, Richard C., *Forgotten Holocaust. The Poles under German Occupation, 1939–1944*, University Press of Kentucky, Lexington, 1986.

Mackenzie, William, *The Secret History of SOE. The Special Operations Executive 1940–1945*, St. Ermin's Press, London, 2000.

Majdalany, Fred, *The Battle of Cassino*, Houghton Mifflin Co., Boston, 1957.

Mason, Francis K., *Battle over Britain*, Doubleday & Company, New York, 1969.

Matloff, Maurice & Edwin M. Snell, *Strategic Planning for Coalition Warfare, 1941–1942*, Office of the Chief of Military History, Dept. of the Army, Washington, DC. 1953.

May, Ernest R., *Strange Victory. Hitler's Conquest of France*, Hill and Wang, New York, 2000.

McLeod, R. and Denis Kelly, *Time Unguarded, The Ironside Diaries 1937–1940*, David McKay Company, New York, 1962,

Merrick, K.A., *Flights of the Forgotten. Special Operations in World War Two*, New York, Sterling Publishing Co., New York, 1989.

Middlebrook, Martin, *Arnhem, 1944. The Airborne Battle*, Westview Press, Boulder, Colorado, 1994.

Miner, Steven Merritt, *Between Churchill and Stalin. The Soviet Union, Great Britain and the Origins of the Grand Alliance,* University of North Carolina Press, Chapel Hill, 1988.

Moulton, J.L., *Battle for Antwerp. The Liberation of the City and the Opening of the Scheldt, 1944,* Hippocrene Books, New York, 1978.

Murray, Williamson and Millett, Allan R. *A War to be Won. Fighting the Second World War.* Belknap Press of Harvard University, Cambridge, MA, 2000.

Neillands, Robin, *The Bomber War,* The Overlook Press, Woodstock and New York, 2001.

Neillands, Robin, *The Battle for the Rhine. The Battle of the Bulge and the Ardennes Campaign, 1944,* The Overlook Press, Woodstock and New York, 2001.

Nekrich, Aleksandr M, *Pariahs, Partners, Predators. German-Soviet Relations, 1922–1941,* Columbia University Press, New York, 1997.

Newman, Simon. *March 1939: The British Guarantee to Poland,* Oxford University Press, London, 1976.

Neugebauer, Norwid M., *The Defense of Poland, September, 1939,* M.I. Kolin, London, 1942.

Nowak, Jan, *Courier from Warsaw,* Wayne State University Press, Detroit, 1982.

Offer, Dalia, *Escaping the Holocaust. Illegal Immigration to the Land of Israel, 1939–1945.* Oxford University Press, Oxford, 1990.

O'Malley, Sir Owen, *The Phantom Caravan,* Murray, London, 1954.

Orpen, Neil, *Airlift to Warsaw: The Rising of 1944,* University of Oklahoma, Norman, 1984.

Osborn, Patrick R., *Operation Pike. Britain Versus the Soviet Union, 1939–1941.*

Greenwood Press, Westport, 2000.

Paczkowski, Andrzej. *Stanisław Mikołajczyk. Czyli Klęska Realisty* [Stanisław Mikołajczyk, the defeat of a realist], Omnipress, Warsaw, 1991.

Parker, Mathew, *Monte Cassino, The Hardest Fought Battle of World War II,* Doubleday, New York, 2003.

Pestkowska, Maria, *Kazimierz Sosnkowski,* Zakład Narowody im. Ossolińskich, Warszawa, 1995.

Pestkowka, Maria, *Za Kulisami Rzadu Polskiego na Emigracji* [Behind the Scenes of the Polish Government in Exile], Oficyna Wydawnicza Rytm, Warszawa, 2000.

Peszke, Michael Alfred, *Poland's Navy, 1918–1945,* Hippocrene Books, New York, 1999.

Piekałkiewicz, Janusz, *Cassino. Anatomy of the Battle*, Orbis Publishing, London, 1980.

Piekałkiewicz, Janusz, *Arnhem, 1944*, Charles Scribner's Sons, New York, 1976.

Pienkos, Donald, *For Your Freedom Through Ours: Polish American Efforts on Poland's Behalf, 1863–1991*, East European Monographs, Boulder, 1991.

Antony Polonsky, *The Great Powers and the Polish Question, 1941–1945*, London School of Economics and Political Science, London, 1976.

Antony Polonsky, *Politics in Independent Poland. 1921–1939*, Oxford University Press, London, 1972.

Ponting, Clive, *1940. Myth and Reality*, Ivan R. Dee, Chicago, 1991.

Prażmowska, Anita, *Britain, Poland and the Eastern Front, 1939*, Cambridge University Press, Cambridge, 1987.

Prażmowska, Anita, *Britain and Poland, 1939–1945: The Betrayed Ally*, Cambridge University Press, Cambridge, 1995.

Raczyński, Edward, *In Allied London*, Weidenfeld and Nicolson, London, 1962.

Rees, Laurence, *WWII Behind Closed Doors, Stalin, the Nazis and the West*, Pantheon Books, New York, 2008.

Richards, Denis, *Royal Air Force, 1939–1945, Volume 1. The Fight at Odds*, HMSO, London, 1993.

Riekhoff, Harald von, *German –Polish Relations, 1918–1933*, Johns Hopkins Press, Baltimore, 1971.

Roberts, Geoffrey, *The Unholy Alliance. Stalin's Pact with Hitler*, Indiana University Press, Bloomington, 1989.

Roos, Hans, *A History of Modern Poland*, Alfred A. Knopf, New York, 1966.

Rossino, Alexander B. *Hitler Strikes Poland. Bliztkrieg, Ideology and Atrocity*. University Press of Kansas, Lawrence, 2003.

Ross, Graham (ed.), *The Foreign Office and the Kremlin. British documents on Anglo-Soviet relations, 1941–1945*. Cambridge University Press, London, 1984.

Rothschild, Joseph, *Piłsudski's Coup d'Etat*, Columbia University Press, New York, 1966.

Rothschild, Joseph and Wingfield, Nancy M., *Return to Diversity. A Political History of East Central Europe Since World War II*, Oxford University Press, Oxford, 2000.

Sanford, George, *Katyn and the Soviet Massacre of 1940, Truth, Justice and Memory*, Routledge, Taylor & Francis Group, New York, 2009.

Siemaszko, Zbigniew. *Łączność i Polityka* [Signals and Politics], Polish Cultural Foundation, London, 1992.

Smith, Colin, *England's Last War Against France. Fighting Vichy 1940–1942*, Weidenfeld & Nicolson, London, 2009.

Smith, E.D., *The Battles for Cassino*, Charles Scribner's Sons, New York, 1975.

Snyder, Timothy, *Bloodlands. Europe Between Hitler and Stalin*, Basic Books, New York, 2010.

Stafford, David, *Britain and Resistance, 1940–1945. A Survey of the Special Operations Executive with Documents*, University of Toronto Press, Toronto, 1980.

Sword, Keith, ed., *Sikorski; Soldier and Statesman*, Orbis Books, London, 1990.

Sword, Keith, *Deportation and Exile. Poles in the Soviet Union, 1939–1948*, Macmillan, London, 1996.

Taylor, Telford, *The March of Conquest: The German Victories in Western Europe, 1940*, Simon and Schuster, New York, 1958.

Terraine, John, *A Time for Courage. The Royal Air Force in the European War, 1939–1945*, Macmillan Publishing Company, New York, 1985.

Terry, Sarah Meiklejohn. *Poland's Place in Europe*. Princeton University Press, Princeton, 1983.

Turnbull, Elizabeth and Suchcitz, Andrzej, eds., *Edward Roland Sword. The Diary and Despatches of a Military Attaché in Warsaw, 1938–1939*. Polish Cultural Foundation, London, 2001.

Umiastowski, Roman, *Poland, Russia and Great Britain, 1941–1945*, Hollis & Carter, London, 1946.

Urquhart, R.E. *Arnhem*, W.W. Norton & Company, New York, 1958.

Valentine, Ian, *Station 43. Audley End House and SOE's Polish Section*, Sutton Publishing, Stroud, 2004.

Walker, Jonathan, *Poland Alone. Britain, SOE and the Collapse of Polish Resistance, 1944*, The History Press, Stroud, 2008.

Wandycz, Piotr S., *The United States and Poland*, Harvard University Press, Cambridge, 1980.

Wandycz, Piotr S., *Czechoslovak-Polish Confederation and the Great Powers, 1940–1943*, Indiana University Press, Bloomington, 1956.

Wandycz, Piotr S., *Lands of Partitioned Poland, 1795–1921*, Harvard University Press, Cambridge, 1969.

Wandycz, Piotr S., *France and her Eastern Allies, 1919–1925*, Minnesota University Press, Minneapolis, 1961.

Wandycz, Piotr S., *Twilight of French Eastern Alliance, 1926–1936*, Princeton University Press, Princeton, 1988.

Wandycz, Piotr S., *Polish Diplomacy. Aims and Achievements 1919–1945*, Published for the School of Slavonic and East European Studies by Orbis Books, London, 1988.

Watt, Richard M., *Bitter Glory. Poland and its Fate, 1918–1939*, Simon and Schuster, New York, 1979.

Weinberg, Gerhard L, *The Foreign Policy of Hitler's Germany. Starting World War II, 1937–1939.* University of Chicago Press, Chicago, 1980.

Whitaker, Denis and Whitaker, Shelagh, *Tug of War. The Allied Victory that Opened Antwerp,* Stoddart, Toronto, 2000.

Williamson, David G., *Poland Betrayed. The Nazi-Soviet Invasions of 1939.*

Pen and Sword, Barnsley, 2009.

Williamson, David G., *The Polish Underground 1939–1947*, Pen and Sword, Barnsley, 2012.

Wilkinson, Peter and Astley, Joan Bright, *Gubbins and SOE.* Leo Cooper, London, 1993.

Wood, E. Thomas, *Karski. How One Man Tried to Stop the Holocaust.* John Wiley & Sons, New York, 1944.

Woodward, Llewellyn, *British Foreign Policy in the Second World War.* HMSO, London, 1970–71. 3 volumes.

Woytak, Richard A., *On the Border of War and Peace. Polish Intelligence and Diplomacy in 1937–1939 and the origins of the Ultra Secret*, East European Monographs, Boulder, 1979.

Young, Robert J., *In Command of France. French Foreign Policy and Military Planning, 1933–1940.* Harvard University Press, Cambridge, 1978.

Zagórski, Wacław, *Seventy Days: A Diary of the Warsaw Insurrection 1944,* Muller, London, 1957.

Zaloga, Steven J., *Poland 1939. The Birth of Blitzkrieg*, Osprey, London, 2002.

Zaloga, Steven, *The Polish Army, 1939–1945*, Osprey, London, 1982.

Zamoyski, Adam, *Warsaw 1920. Lenin's Failed Conquest of Europe*, Harper Press, London, 2007.

Zawodny, Janusz K., *Nothing but Honor, The Story of the Warsaw Uprising, 1944,* Hoover Institution Press, Stanford, 1978.

Zawodny, Janusz K., *Death in the Forest: The Story of the Katyn Forest Massacre,* University of Notre Dame Press, South Bend, 1962.

Zaron, Piotr, *Kierunek Wschodni w strategii wojskowo-politycznej gen. Władysława Sikorskiego, 1940–1943* [The Eastern vision of the military-political strategy of General Władysław Sikorski], Państwowe Wydawnictwo Naukowe, Warsaw, 1988.

INDEX

INDEX OF PEOPLE

INDEX OF PLACES

INDEX OF MILITARY UNITS

N.b. formations listed in alphabetical then numeric order.

BRITISH MILITARY UNITS

ARMY

ROYAL AIR FORCE

ROYAL NAVY

POLISH MILITARY UNITS

INDEX OF MISCELLANEOUS TERMS

HELION STUDIES IN MILITARY HISTORY

Lightning Source UK Ltd.
Milton Keynes UK
UKOW03f1152061013

218550UK00001B/8/P